GARDENING
ESSENTIALS

COMPLETE GARDENER'S LIBRARY™

GARDENING
ESSENTIALS

Barbara Pleasant

NATIONAL HOME
GARDENING CLUB

National Home Gardening Club
Minnetonka, Minnesota

ABOUT THE AUTHOR

When Barbara Pleasant is not tending to her gardening projects, she is writing about her experiences. Barbara is a NHGC member who has written numerous books for both the NHGC and other publishers, covering topics that include vegetables, cutting gardens, garden insects, weeds, container gardens, lawns, and flower beds and borders.

Barbara works her gardening magic on the 13 acres of land surrounding her home near the Alabama-Tennessee state line. She has every type of garden on her property, giving her plenty of hands-in-the-dirt experience. She has transferred her knowledge of gardening skills and projects to *Gardening Essentials*.

Her hope is that this book helps you in your quest to make gardening simple and pleasurable, and tells you what you need to know—the essentials—so you can succeed in all your gardening adventures.

Gardening Essentials

Copyright © 1999 National Home Gardening Club

Tom Carpenter
Director of Book Development

Julie Cisler
Book Design & Production

Michele Teigen
Senior Book Development Coordinator

Gina Germ
Photo Editor

Natalia Hamill
Maggie Oster
Contributing Writers

Dr. Stephen Garton
Horticultural Consultant

Nancy Wirsig McClure, Hand to Mouse Arts
Illustration

5 6 7 8 9 / 05 04 03 02
ISBN 1-58159-019-9

National Home Gardening Club
12301 Whitewater Drive
Minnetonka, Minnesota 55343
www.gardeningclub.com

HOW TO USE THIS BOOK   2

◀ CHAPTER 1 ▶
HOW TO GARDEN:
BREAK THE RULES, KEEP IT SIMPLE, HAVE FUN   4
Finding Yourself in the Garden   8

◀ CHAPTER 2 ▶
DESIGN:
WORKING YOUR SITE   10
Water and Drainage   12
Planning Your Landscape   14
Creating a Garden Room   16
Expanding Small Spaces   18
Taming a Slope   20
Grow a Shade Garden   22

◀ CHAPTER 3 ▶
SOIL:
CREATING A SOLID FOUNDATION   24
Learning Your Soil Type   26
Improving Your Soil   28
Choosing and Using Fertilizers   30
Creative Composting   32
Foliar Feeding   34
Great Ways to Water   36
Marvelous Mulches   38

◀ CHAPTER 4 ▶
LAWNS:
GROWING GRASSES AND GROUNDCOVERS   40
Cultivating Your Landscape's Floor   42
Choosing Grasses for Your Lawn   44
Improving an Existing Lawn   46
Framing a Small Lawn   48
Using Groundcovers   50

CONTENTS

◀ CHAPTER 5 ▶
WALKWAYS:
PAVING YOUR WAY WITH MULCH, CONCRETE, STONE AND BRICK   52

Materials for Walkways   54
Improve Your Entryway   56
Natural Pathways and Play Areas   58
Working with Concrete   60
Walkways of Brick and Stone   64

◀ CHAPTER 6 ▶
BOUNDARIES:
FENCES, SCREENS AND WALLS   66

Materials for Boundaries   68
Plant a Living Fence   70
Build a Wood Fence   72
Charm Your Chain Link Fence   74
Enrich a Woodland Edge   76
Create a Stone Wall Garden   78

◀ CHAPTER 7 ▶
FLOWERS:
GROWING ANNUALS, PERENNIALS AND BULBS   80

Develop a Style   82
Containers and Window Boxes   84
Plant a Bouquet Garden   86
Bird and Butterfly Gardens   88
Bulbs on Parade   90
Paint Your Garden with Wildflowers   92
Plant an American Border   96

◀ CHAPTER 8 ▶
FRAGRANCE:
GROWING SCENTED PLANTS   100

Maximizing Fragrance   102
Landscaping for Fragrance   104
Fragrance in Containers   106
Marrying Roses and Herbs   108
A Scented Evening Garden   110

◀ CHAPTER 9 ▶
FLAVOR:
GROWING VEGETABLES, HERBS AND FRUITS   112

Seasons in the Edible Garden   114
Plant an Edible Landscape   116
Grow a Salad Garden   118
Terrific Tomatoes   122
Growing Gourmet Herbs   124
A Garden for Kids   126
Bright and Bountiful Berries   128

◀ CHAPTER 10 ▶
SPECIAL FEATURES:
ACCENTING YOUR LANDSCAPE   130

Locating Special Features   132
Creating Raised Beds   134
Build an Easy Water Garden   136
Plants for a Natural Pond   138
Lighting Your Garden   140

◀ CHAPTER 11 ▶
WINTER CARE:
PROTECTING AND MAINTAINING PLANTS   142

Preventing Winter Damage   144
Working Winter Under Cover   146
Use a Winter Tunnel   148
Natural Pruning: Trees   150
Pruning Shrubs and Vines   152

◀ CHAPTER 12 ▶
PROPAGATION:
SEEDS, DIVISIONS AND CUTTINGS   154

Reproduction and Propagation   156
Starting Seeds Indoors   158
Saving Your Own Seeds   160
Dividing Perennials   162
Dividing Bulbs, Corms and Tubers   164
Rooting Stem Cuttings   166

◀ CHAPTER 13 ▶
PESTS:
CONTROLLING DISEASES, INSECTS AND WEEDS   168

Preventing & Identifying Problems   170
Waste Your Weeds   172
A Haven for Beneficial Bugs   174
Managing Garden Pests   176
Ways to Use Rowcovers   178
Pest Controls from Your Kitchen   180

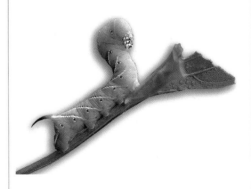

Resources   182
Index of Plants   183
General Index   187

WELCOME TO *GARDENING ESSENTIALS*!

A garden is a very personal place. For many of us, it's an escape from life's rapid pace—somewhere we can slow down and get the hands working to create something beautiful, fragrant, even delicious. For others, a garden is a way of life—a facet of our existence that defines who we are and how we see ourselves.

Each of us also has special preferences and talents in the garden. For some, a perennial garden is where it's at. Or maybe it's wildflowers and a natural-looking, woodland landscape that makes the heart beat with a little more joy. For others, bulbs in formal beds may add true excitement to garden strategies. Vegetables bring rewards in the kitchen as well as the backyard. Children need gardening space of their own. A showcase yard needs careful planning, and then good landscaping work, to follow through on the dream.

No matter what kind of gardening you love the most, or where you garden, or even why you garden, there's always a thirst for more …

- **More ideas**, to expand your gardening horizons.

- **More knowledge**, to better understand the intricate relationships that make things "work."

- **More lists**, to help you select the specific components that will help quench that never-ending gardening thirst.

- **More instructions**, to show you how to master new skills.

- **More project ideas**, to bring specific solutions to gardening challenges.

These are the reasons we created *Gardening Essentials*—to give you the essential ideas, knowledge, lists, instructions and projects you need to make better gardening decisions and meet your own personal gardening goals, be they big or small or somewhere in between.

Consider this your "must-have" gardening reference book—the one that covers the topics you're interested in, or could be pursuing in the future. The one that is easy-to-use, beautiful to look at, and filled with things you need to make gardening an even more rewarding pastime … or way of life.

How to Use This Book

Tip boxes describe all kinds of ideas, projects, skills, tactics and tips.

Clear, concise text spells out ideas, instructions and important gardening lore in a straightforward manner.

Beautiful photos present gardening ideas and rewards in full, vibrant color.

Plant lists give you real ideas of what to plant, for what purpose.

78

Gardening Essentials

CREATE A STONE WALL GARDEN

When the boundary for your garden ends in an upward slope, a stone wall will stop erosion while enriching the scene with a look of rugged permanence. Best of all, your wall doubles as a rock garden as you fill crevices with plants that delight in wrapping their roots around rocks.

Tools & Materials

- ✓ Shovel
- ✓ Wheelbarrow
- ✓ Heavy work gloves
- ✓ Soil amendments
- ✓ Sand
- ✓ Stones

Beds and passageways within this elevated garden are held in place with stone. Cascading plants help soften craggy edges.

Building a stone wall garden is not difficult, but it's not a project to speed through quickly. Handling stones is heavy work, and stacking them is an artful process that deserves slow and careful scrutiny.

Building the Wall

1 Dig a foundation for the wall. To help the wall withstand the slope's natural pressure, angle the foundation slightly so the back edge is 2 inches deeper than the front. Place your largest, flattest stones in the foundation to form the first layer. Fill large crevices with a mixture of soil and sand.

2 Set the second tier of stones in an offset pattern so they are centered over the crevices in the previous layer. The wall will tilt slightly into the slope if you set each tier so the front edge is ¼ to ½ inch behind the edge of the tier below it. Use small rocks as wedges to help hold wobbly rocks in place. Stand back and take a look at your work. Rearrange any rocks that appear awkward.

3 Begin planting crevices and backfilling behind the wall as soon as the rocks are in place. Place soil behind the wall and use a broom handle to poke soil into pockets and crevices. Backfill soil a few inches at a time. Stop often to water the loose soil to settle it. Set aside some large, flat rocks and use these for your wall's top tier. Although you may not plan to sit or walk on the wall, any child left to their own devices certainly will.

WALL BUILDING TOOLS

You will need a shovel, wheelbarrow and at least two pairs of heavy work gloves. To protect your toes from accidents, always wear sturdy shoes or steel-toed boots when handling heavy stones. Place a piece of plywood over nearby areas of lawn and park your stones on the plywood until you get them stacked. As your wall nears completion and you start filling pockets and crevices with plants, you will also need soil amendments including compost, peat moss and sand.

Heavy gloves are required equipment for building a stone wall.

SLOPING WALLS

A stone wall built into a slope will get plenty of support from the soil behind it, so there is no need to use mortar. The slope will also exert constant pressure on the wall. Low walls (less than 2 feet high) can withstand this pressure, but higher walls may crumble or pop loose after heavy rains. If this is your first time working with stone, stick with a low wall about 18 inches high and 12 to 14 inches deep.

79

Boundaries: Fences, Screens and Walls

Planting Your Wall

Setting a plant in a stone wall involves stuffing a suitable soil mixture into the planting crevices, then laying in the plant with its roots spread as wide as possible. Top the roots and adjoining rocks with ½ to 1 inch of the soil mixture. Then water thoroughly and go on to the next tier of rocks.

Three levels of low stone walls give this garden plenty of depth, and allow for the use of lawn, formal plantings of 'Autumn Joy' sedum, and an informal garden where plants can be grown just for the fun of it.

- **For ferns** set near the base of the wall, use a mixture of 2 parts soil, 2 parts peat moss and 1 part each sand and composted manure.

- **For fibrous-rooted plants** such as basket-of-gold (*Aurinia saxatile*) and moss pink (*Phlox subulata*), mix equal parts of soil, composted manure and sand.

- **For succulents** such as sedums and sempervivums, mix equal parts of soil, leaf mold, sand and composted manure.

BUYING STACKING STONE

Limestone, sandstone and other types of stratified rock naturally break into flat-sided blocks, so they are easy to stack into a stable wall without the help of mortar. Stone is customarily sold by the ton. Most suppliers will deliver large orders. You will need one ton of stone to build a wall 18 inches high and 20 feet long. Buy extra stone if you can. When building gets underway, it's great to have a big pile to pick through when you're looking for just the right rock.

When you shop for stone, judge with your hands and your eyes. Very large pieces may be too heavy for one person to handle.

PERENNIALS FOR A STONE WALL GARDEN

Small plants such as these allow your stone wall's beauty and texture to show through their flowers and foliage. Although these and other rock garden plants do not need constant water, do keep them lightly moist for the first two months after planting. When you water the wall, sufficient water should seep through the crevices to the plants' roots.

Name	Botanical Name	Description	Adaptability
Basket-of-gold	Aurinia saxatilis	Cascading green stems covered with gold flowers in spring.	Sun or partial shade in Zones 5 to 10.
Hen-and-chickens, houseleek	Sempervivum spp.	Hardy succulents with gray or green leaves.	Full sun to partial shade in Zones 4 to 9.
Moss pink	Phlox subulata	Narrow green leaves; spring flowers in pink, white or lavender.	Sun or partial shade in Zones 3 to 9.
Rock cress	Arabis spp.	Gray-green leaves; fragrant white or pink flowers in spring.	Sun and gritty soil in Zones 3 to 9.
Stonecrop	Sedum spp.	Green leaves, mostly yellow flowers in late spring.	Sun or partial shade in Zones 4 to 9.

Basket-of-gold (Aurinia saxatilis) is an evergreen with colorful late spring flowers. It grows to 8 inches high and spreads to 20 inches wide.

Hen-and-chickens will cover wall areas with new flocks of delightful rosettes.

Moss pink.

Stonecrop.

Ideas fill every page, making sure you're never short of ways to improve your garden, or solutions to gardening problems.

Helpful charts, big and small, offer essential background information, warnings and suggestions.

Step-by-step instructions, utilizing photos or illustrations and concise text in plain English, take away any guesswork when it's time to dig in and start working.

◄ CHAPTER 1 ►

HOW TO GARDEN:
BREAK THE RULES,
KEEP IT SIMPLE, HAVE FUN

Imagination, persistence and a willingness to be amazed: These are the three characteristics you must have to be a successful gardener.

This chapter has an ambitious title, but it is far from ridiculous. Most of this book is about specific gardening skills and projects you can use to improve your garden. But there are larger truths about gardening that also must be explained.

Because these are the kinds of things most often learned the hard way—from experience—it makes sense to share them as true stories. In the three tales that follow, names have been changed to protect the innocent.

When gardeners apply a little care and know-how, their plants will thrive like this magnificent lilac.

Breaking the Rules

Plants don't read books. "They don't read seed packets, either," says Harold Moss, who is willing to follow most of the rules of good gardening—up to a point. He never digs in his hard clay soil when it's wet, and is careful not to plant the same vegetable in the same place two years in a row. But Harold is also a renegade gardener of sorts. If a garden situation seems to justify

extreme measures, that is exactly what Harold will do.

"My wife cried when I took the chain saw to an old lilac," he says. "But I was tired of looking at all that mildew and thought maybe if the roots got a second chance there was still hope for the old girl." The beheaded bush grew back into a marvelous specimen, Harold's wife forgave him and it seemed that the story would have a happy ending.

Then Harold got interested in wallflowers, specifically the fragrant ones grown in English gardens since the time of Chaucer, which are believed to be *Cheiranthus cheiri*. He grew some seedlings and set them in his garden. Despite his attentive care and a string of beautiful spring days, they sulked. Frustrated, he dug up a few and put them in pots filled with potting soil that would please any plant. Still no progress. Now on the verge of real anger, he remembered that he had once heard that English gardeners used a lot of lime. Harold prepared new pots and cast a big fistful of lime into the bottom of each, hardly bothering to mix it in.

"Any other plant would have burned to a crisp in that soil, but the wallflowers loved it," he says, not being boastful, for he will forever be amazed that his radical remedy worked. The moral of this story is that sometimes you need to break some rules. "People think you have to always do things an exact way or you're doomed. That's just not true," Harold advises.

Imagination, ideas and a little work make wonderful gardens. A few years ago, this was just another backyard.

The right plant in the right place: These English wallflowers (Cheiranthus cheiri) *dance with color—and fragrance—atop a wall in springtime.*

Gardens aren't static creations. They provide us with an ever-changing seasonal display—here, a nice bed of mums glows with its bright colors set off by a traditional white picket fence.

Gardens are for nature to enjoy, too. Here, a song sparrow rests on a pink azalea.

Don't Make It Brain Surgery . . . then Enjoy the View

Jennifer knows that she is, by nature, a fastidious person who tends to become preoccupied with details. So when she took up gardening, she often visited Happy Valley Greenhouse and Nursery. She looked at the plants and compared them to hers. She made lists of Latin names to look up in heavy books. But most of all, she presented the owner, Meg, with so many questions that Meg's brain felt bruised by the time Jennifer's car pulled out onto the highway.

On a slow Saturday afternoon, after she saw Jennifer's anxious face amidst a sea of pink petunias, Meg decided to take action. "Instead of you coming to my garden, why don't I come to yours?" she asked, causing Jennifer to become pale with alarm. "It's not ready," she protested. "I have so much more to do!" But Meg insisted, and a short time later they entered Jennifer's backyard together.

A crisp white picket fence surrounded a symmetrical border of neatly trimmed annuals and Meg saw nothing that she would call a problem, much less an embarrassment. "I haven't deadheaded the snapdragons in days," Jennifer wailed. "I'm sure I planted the nasturtium seeds too deep. And exactly what is the proper spacing for these marigolds?" The tedious questions continued and Meg looked around for a place to sit. There was none. Apparently all Jennifer did in her garden was work, worry and wish she knew all the answers.

"You do have a problem but it's not what you think," Meg said. She strode through the garden taking big steps, circled it three times and stopped by a bed of pansies. "You need to take these out and put a comfortable chair here instead. Then you have to sit in it quietly for a half hour every day. That's the one thing you must start doing differently."

Meg did not see Jennifer for several weeks afterward. Then one day Jennifer appeared carrying a white handkerchief tied to a long stick. "I fought it at first, but then gave in to your advice," she said. "I was taking something really easy and making it hard, but I couldn't see that because I was so excited."

Don't let this happen to you. Gardening is not brain surgery, it's supposed to be fun.

Gardens are places to live in, especially if you think of them as outdoor rooms. Wouldn't you rather sit outside if you had a haven like this?

Gardens are extensions of the home. A floor of pebbles, a table with an umbrella, and a roof of blue sky make this a simple-to-create outdoor living room.

Agony and Ecstasy . . . and Don't Give Up

On the speaker evaluation forms turned in at the end of the Master Gardener course, Jeff Clark's name was always at the top of the list as one of the students' favorite speakers. Jeff did not have professional credentials, and his talk bore the simple title of "Local Gardening." The county agent, Myra Glover, never knew exactly what Jeff would have to say, but it was always worth hearing. In addition to his comments, Jeff brought beans dug from his garden to show students the nitrogen nodules on their roots, passed around bits of fragrant herbs and once even made the students put on blindfolds to taste an assortment of odd tomatoes.

Because of his hands-in-the-dirt approach, Myra was not surprised when he showed up at a February session in a truck carrying trees, pots of dormant perennials and a half dozen weather-worn digging tools. "Today I want to talk about all the things you are going to plant and then watch them die," he began. He pulled out a little whip of a cherry

Potting benches are little laboratories of creation. They're darned handy, too, because you've got all of your tools and equipment within arm's reach.

tree, discussed the best way to plant it and grow it to maturity. Then he announced that in two years borers would get into the trunk and the tree would die.

"That's when you will have a new opportunity. You went to all that trouble to dig that planting hole and you probably made plans for how your yard would look with that cherry tree growing there," he said. "It's bad news, but it's good news, too. Now maybe you can plant a sturdy oak, or maybe a nice little apple tree."

By the time the session ended, Jeff had convinced the group that blackened petunias, speckled rose leaves, and withered rosemary were actually assets in the garden. "Fantastic gardeners like me? We lose plants all the time. That just gives you more chances to enjoy the thrill of the hunt as you look for better plants and better ways to grow them."

Gardening is not an exact science. Rather, it is a constantly changing place in which unpredictable things happen. In the garden, every challenge can lead to a surprising reward.

"Work" becomes enjoyable when you can do it in fine weather. This potting bench is the result of simple design work, some lumber and stain, and a few hours of construction.

A brick patio, a stone walkway and wooden furniture are an unbeatable combination, especially when they lead you to where the perennial border's flowery fragrance abides.

FINDING YOURSELF IN THE GARDEN

An important part of gardening's language is knowing your zone. The zones on this hardiness zone map, based on average minimum winter temperatures, are widely used in seed catalogs and gardening books, including this one. Sometimes you will also hear gardeners talking about being in "Zone 7a" or "Zone 5b." An "a" after the zone number indicates a climate within the zone where cold is especially predominant or prolonged. A "b" indicates a warmer area than is typical elsewhere in the zone. We've also included a rainfall map, to help you gauge precipitation where you live. Armed with the information from these maps, you've found yourself in the big garden picture and are ready to start identifying gardening strategies and projects, and selecting plants.

USDA Plant Hardiness Zone Map

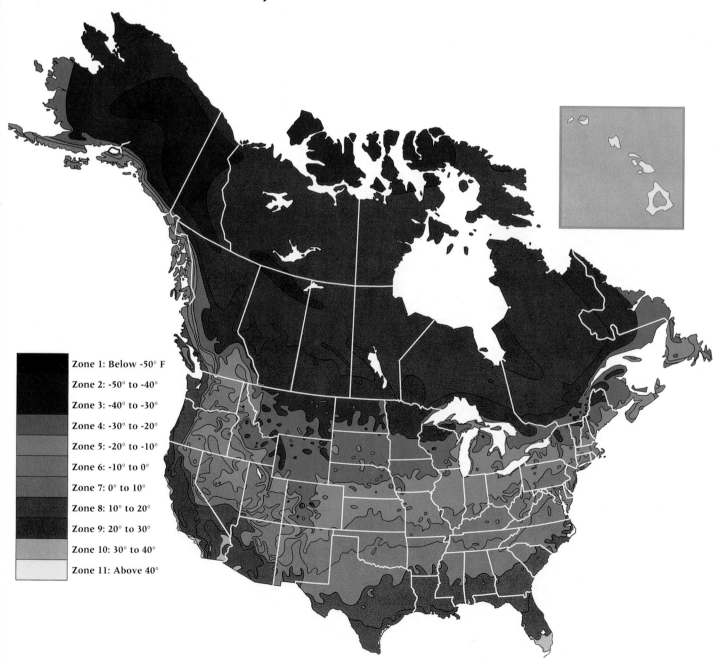

Zone 1: Below -50° F
Zone 2: -50° to -40°
Zone 3: -40° to -30°
Zone 4: -30° to -20°
Zone 5: -20° to -10°
Zone 6: -10° to 0°
Zone 7: 0° to 10°
Zone 8: 10° to 20°
Zone 9: 20° to 30°
Zone 10: 30° to 40°
Zone 11: Above 40°

Zones reflect average minimum temperatures. When you know your zone, selecting the right plants is much easier.

Rainfall Map

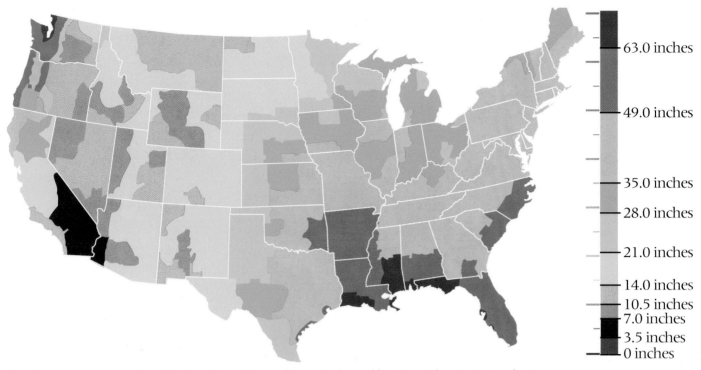

—	63.0 inches
—	49.0 inches
—	35.0 inches
—	28.0 inches
—	21.0 inches
—	14.0 inches
—	10.5 inches
—	7.0 inches
—	3.5 inches
—	0 inches

Knowing your average annual precipitation patterns helps you figure out when and how to provide water to your plants.

FROST DATES FOR SOME AMERICAN CITIES

Zone 3

Great Falls, MT	S-May 9	F-September 25
Grand Forks, ND	S-May 24	F-September 13

Zone 4

Albany, NY	S-May 18	F-September 24
Minneapolis, MN	S-May 17	F-September 22
Casper, WY	S-June 8	F-September 10

Zone 5

Boston, MA	S-May 7	F-October 2
Chicago, IL	S-May 17	F-September 30
St. Louis, MO	S-April 21	F-October 17
Denver, CO	S-May 18	F-September 29
Spokane, WA	S-May 23	F-September 21

Zone 6

New York, NY	S-April 14	F-October 30
Lexington, KY	S-April 29	F-October 14
Salt Lake City, UT	S-May 20	F-September 27
Las Alamos, NM	S-May 23	F-October 2
Walla Walla, WA	S-April 22	F-October 29

Zone 7

Raleigh, NC	S-April 1	F-November 6
Birmingham, AL	S-April 10	F-October 25
Oklahoma City, OK	S-April 21	F-October 14
Lubbock, TX	S-April 1	F-November 9
Chico, CA	S-March 30	F-November 16

Zone 8

Charleston, SC	S-March 28	F-November 9
Jackson, MS	S-April 17	F-October 10
Dallas, TX	S-March 18	F-November 17
Phoenix, AZ	S-March 1	F-November 30
Seattle, WA	S-April 22	F-October 29

Zone 9

Tampa, FL	S-February 9	F-December 8
New Orleans, LA	S-February 20	F-December 9
Corpus Christi, TX	S-March 9	F-November 23
Tucson, AZ	S-March 19	F-November 19
Sacramento, CA	S-March 25	F-November 17

S—*Average last spring frost*   **F**—*Average first fall frost*

Note – *Frost dates will vary widely from year to year. These dates are long-term averages.*

CHAPTER 2

DESIGN:
WORKING YOUR SITE

Pleasing gardens result from careful thought regarding the arrangement of garden space and the plants used. This process is called design.

Designing a garden is an endeavor both scientific and creative.

The scientific gardener evaluates a site's potential by considering existing plants, soil type and drainage, available sunlight and shade, wind exposure and other environmental factors.

The creative gardener selects and arranges plants based on pleasing color, form and texture combinations ... while never losing sight of the garden's purpose, which might be to create beauty, produce food or perhaps serve as scenery

From agave to sedums, succulents large and small fill an arid garden with multiple shades of green. Scant supplemental water is needed to satisfy plants that are native to dry climates. Consider native plants when planning your garden's design.

for outdoor living. As your garden's design evolves over time, constantly be aware of changes or improvements that can make your landscape fit your lifestyle.

Garden design is a series of choices. If we understand fundamental site analysis (what you have to work with) and the basic intention of the garden (what purpose the garden serves or what feeling it invokes) we can make better choices as we go about planning our own little piece of paradise.

Site Analysis Checklist

☑ Existing features

Note specific plants or groups of plants you want to keep or eliminate. The lovely sugar maple will probably be a keeper while the overgrown spiraea hedge might be replaced. Also note unattractive areas that need to be hidden and areas that need sprucing up.

☑ Exposure

Exposure is the site orientation in relation to sun and wind—the direction your garden faces. Exposure affects soil and air temperature, soil moisture and the amount of sunlight a garden receives.

☑ Wind

Windburn and scorching result when sustained wind dries out plants and soil so persistently that plants simply cannot keep up with the water loss. A screen of shrubs or an open fence will break up and filter large gusts and cuts the wind significantly.

☑ Slope

A hilltop is windier and drier than the bottom of a hill. Low spots also trap cold air as it moves downhill and settles in frost pockets. Don't lament the challenges of these spots. Rather, plan your design accordingly.

Filtered shade cools down this dry-climate garden. The contrasting textures of prickly pear cactus and flowing clumps of fountain grass create year-round drama.

☑ Moisture

In addition to soil type (see pages 26-27), soil moisture is affected by slope, large plants such as trees and of course, weather. Dry shade often exists near walls and large trees while moist areas often occur at the bottom of a slope. To improve the moisture-holding capacity of chronically dry soil, add organic matter. Find ways to overcome poor drainage on pages 12-13.

Shade is always a factor in determining the best garden site. Early-season bulbs bask in the dappled springtime shade of an old fruit tree, which will shade the area more densely in the summer.

WATER AND DRAINAGE

You cannot read a seed catalog, gardening magazine or book about plants without encountering the subject of drainage. It is always a critical element that affects how a plant adjusts to the place where it is grown. Simply put, drainage is the movement of water through the soil. Water moving quickly through the soil, drainage is said to be good or fast, and the soil is referred to as well drained.

This shady glen and garden pond need a drainage ditch to carry away excess water. Blue phlox and pink primrose, stabilized with large stones, accent the scene beautifully.

When water moves very slow, drainage is poor.

You can make a garden in poorly drained soil but your plant choices will be limited to species that are accustomed to wet soil conditions. And there are ways to improve drainage (see below). Fast-draining sandy soil in arid desert regions also can support a variety of plants, but you must choose plants that adapt to the low levels of soil moisture.

Improving Poor Drainage

Poorly drained soil doesn't mean you can't grow a good garden. It only means that you have to pay special attention to drainage and select appropriate plants as you plan your garden. There are many options for working with soil that is persistently or periodically wet.

- **Level out low-lying areas:** Fill them in with good quality topsoil. Fill small areas by hand or rent a skid steer loader, such as a Bobcat, to fill and grade larger areas.

- **Amend tight clay soil:** Spread a 4- to 6-inch layer of organic matter and rototill or dig it in 12 inches deep.

Raised beds improve soil drainage while making plants accessible in all types of weather. These beds are packed with cabbage, fragrant signet marigolds, gray artemisia, 'Purple Wave' petunias and ornamental kale.

- **Use raised beds** to grow plants that need more soil depth than your site provides. See page 134 for information on building a raised bed.

- **Contour the site** with berms and swales. A berm is a low, rolling hill that sits above the surrounding soil level and channels water's flow. A swale is an open grassy drainage ditch, with sloping sides, that carries away excess water. Use berms and swales together in areas where standing water is a frequent problem. Building berms and swales requires the use of a skid steer loader, backhoe or bulldozer.

A gently-sloping berm planted with thyme (Thymus praecox) helps channel rainwater while slowing its rate of flow.

- **Create a dry creek bed** lined with rock. A dry creek bed functions like a swale, carrying away excess water. Ornamental grasses, ferns and other plants with well-defined textures look smashing when massed along a dry creek bed.

This dry creek bed floods following heavy deluges. But even in dry weather, it suggests the cooling presence of water.

A mossy water run lined with smooth stones provides a moist but well-drained environment for the roots of Vinca minor, white forget-me-nots and hardy ferns.

- **Make a bog garden** in an area that stays permanently damp. In addition to accommodating interesting plants such as willows (*Salix* spp.), sedge (*Carex* spp.) and Japanese iris (*Iris ensata*), bog gardens attract aquatic-loving wildlife such as dragonflies, frogs and turtles.

- **Install a French drain.** This is an underground drainage system made of 4-inch wide perforated pipe which is laid in a bed of gravel 2 feet below the surface. Because water flows downhill, you will need an outlet area such as a drainage ditch that is lower than the area that needs to be drained. A 4-inch-wide pipe will drain 25 square feet of area on either side of it.

EFFECTS OF POOR DRAINAGE

- Soil stays cold and wet in the spring, which delays planting and reduces seed germination.
- Plants drown due to lack of oxygen in the soil.
- Plants develop shallow roots.
- Roots and crowns rot during the winter.

TIP   Testing for Drainage

Run a simple test to see how your soil drains. Dig a hole 18 to 24 inches across and 18 to 24 inches deep. Fill the hole with water. If water disappears from the hole in 10 minutes or less you have sandy soil with fast drainage. If the water takes one hour or more to drain away you have clay soil or a hardpan (an impermeable layer of compacted soil beneath the soil surface) and the soil is poorly drained. There are many acceptable variations between these two extremes.

PLANTS FOR DIFFICULT PLACES

Drought-Tolerant Shrubs

Many herbs tolerate drought well, including thyme and rosemary.

Apache plume (*Fallugia paradoxa*)
Blue mist spiraea (*Caryopteris* x *clandonensis*)
Cinquefoil (*Potentilla fruticosa*)
Fragrant sumac (*Rhus aromatica*)

Blue mist spiraea.

Drought-Tolerant Perennials

Golden flax (*Linum flavum*)
Gray santolina (*Santolina chamaecyparissus*)
Hyssop (*Agastache* spp.)
Jupiter's beard (*Centranthus ruber*)

Russian sage.

Lavender (*Lavandula* spp.)
Mexican hat (*Ratibida columnifera*)
Penstemon (*Penstemon* spp.)
Russian sage (*Perovskia atriplicifolia*)
Salvia (*Salvia* spp.)
Snow daisy (*Tanacetum niveum*)
Soapwort (*Saponaria* spp.)
Sulphur flower (*Eriogonum umbellatum*)
Wormwood (*Artemisia* spp.)
Yarrow (*Achillea* spp.)

Drought-Tolerant Groundcovers

Lamb's-ear (*Stachys byzantina*)
Mat daisy (*Anacylus depressus*)
Poppy mallow (*Callirhoë involucrata*)
Snow-in-summer (*Cerastium tomentosum*)
Speedwell (*Veronica cinerea*)
Thyme (*Thymus* spp.)

Thyme.

Moisture-Loving Shrubs

Chokeberry (*Aronia* spp.)
Common winterberry (*Ilex verticillata*)
Inkberry (*Ilex glabra*)
Summersweet (*Clethra alnifolia*)
Swamp azalea (*Rhododendron viscosum*)
Virginia sweetspire (*Itea virginica*)
Willow (*Salix* spp.)

Moisture-Loving Perennials

Bee balm (*Monarda* spp.)
Bergenia (*Bergenia cordifolia*)
Cardinal flower (*Lobelia cardinalis*)
Daylily (*Hemerocallis* spp.)
Globeflower (*Trollius* spp.)
Hardy hibiscus (*Hibiscus* spp.)
Japanese iris (*Iris ensata*)
Joe Pye weed (*Eupatorium* spp.)
Meadowsweet (*Filipendula* spp.)
Primrose (*Primula* spp.)
Rodgersia (*Rodgersia* spp.)
Siberian iris (*Iris sibirica*)
Spiderwort (*Tradescantia* spp.)

Bee balm.

Moisture-Loving Groundcovers

Ferns (various species)
Marsh marigold (*Ranunculus repens*)
Moneywort (*Lysimachia nummularia*)
Ribbon grass (*Phalaris arundinacea* var. *picta*)

Ostrich fern.

Large stones hold the roots of spring-blooming primroses just above water level. The roots of Siberian iris tolerate damp conditions too, and are ready to show off their blooms just as the primroses begin to fade.

PLANNING YOUR LANDSCAPE

Planning a garden is fun. You get to make a wish list of all the things you want in your garden such as cut flowers, vegetables, a perennial border or perhaps a tranquil reflecting pool. But before you start digging and planting or daydreaming about garden parties, you must think about how your landscape can best fit your lifestyle. You also must look carefully at your resources in terms of time, money and physical energy. The strategies outlined here, as well as the questions below, can help you make many early planning decisions.

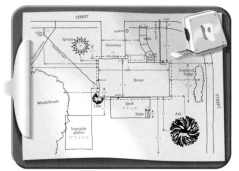

A base map gives you parameters and a detailed overview of your property.

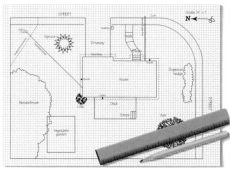

On graph paper, transfer the outlines of physical features to get a scaled–down picture of your layout. Make several copies.

Develop a Priority List

Simply enough, rank your gardening priorities—what you want to do most in your garden.

Develop a Base Map

Once you know what you want in your garden it's time to create a base map. Get out your property survey (sometimes called a land plat) to find your property boundaries, as well as easements and right-of-ways that might affect your use of the boundaries. If you don't have a plat for your property, check with the company that holds your mortgage.

Using a pencil and ruler, transfer your property lines and the location of your house and driveway onto a piece of 18 by 24-inch graph paper with a grid pattern of 4 squares to the inch. Each square represents one foot, so your scale will be ¼ inch = 1 foot.

Draw in your house. Record orientation with a north-south arrow. Also note outdoor faucets, electric outlets, overhead or buried power lines, your septic tank if you have one, and important trees. At this point, make at least five photocopies so you will not have to redraw your base map over and over.

PLANNING:
TEN CRUCIAL QUESTIONS

1. How many people are in your family and how does each person use the yard?
2. How does your family go in and out of the house?
3. Is the entry safe, functional and inviting?
4. Do you have enough privacy both indoors and out?
5. Do you need a play area for children?
6. Is there a pet to consider now or in the future?
7. What kinds of plants do you want to grow?
8. Do you watch birds or other wildlife?
9. How much time do you have to devote to garden maintenance?
10. How much physical strength do you have for garden tasks?

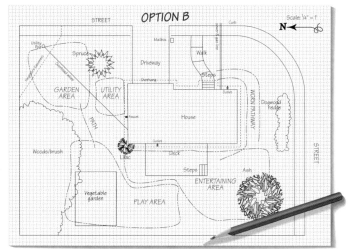

Pencil in rough layouts or "bubbles" of your activity areas. Here's where you experiment and let your imagination run free!

Bubble Diagrams

Use circles or other approximately shaped "bubbles" to roughly lay out major use areas such as a children's play area, a utility space for compost bins, trash barrels or tool shed, an entertaining area, garden areas and frequently used walkways. Refer to your priority list as you develop the use areas, and pay attention to your site analysis as you place different features.

Use the extra copies of your base map to try at least three different designs. You might find that your property is not large enough to accommodate all the features you want to include. If that is the case, review your priorities and whittle away until you get a bubble diagram that fits together.

Now take all three concepts and give the bubbles their actual shapes and dimensions. Use a ruler or an architect's scale to draw the true size of the new garden shed, deck, walkways, garden spaces and other features. Don't worry about using fancy shapes—simple lines and gentle curves generally work best in the landscape.

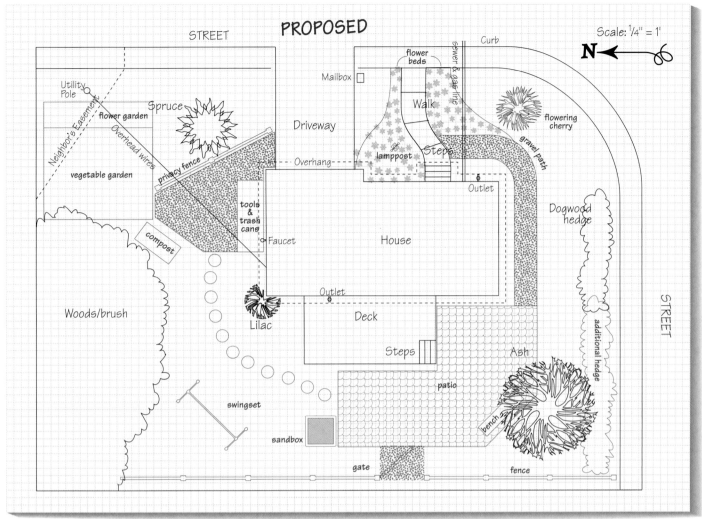

Finally, walk around outside and see if your plan makes sense visually. Make any final adjustments and voilà *—you've got a plan.*

Finalize Your Design

Assess the three drawings and highlight the features you really like. Using a new base map, transfer the best features from each of the previous three drawings onto the final plan. Once everything is positioned, take your plan outdoors, walk the property and try the design on for size and practicality. For example, you'll want to make sure you place roses where they will get plenty of sun, and keep herbs out of boggy areas.

Once you have the final design, develop a budget and a timeline. For big projects, call several contractors to get bids. Check the prices of materials and large plants you will need for do-it-yourself projects. Prioritize your wish list and add new features as you can afford them.

Develop native mosses, which grow in shady spots, into a soft groundcover: Pull out weeds and grasses, and rake off fallen leaves.

KEEP A GARDEN JOURNAL

One way to help yourself plan a garden is to keep a garden scrapbook, notebook, file or journal that you can refer to when you need inspiration or when you just want to find a particular plant's name so you can order more. You can use a garden journal to collect magazine articles, pictures and ideas for improving your garden. This is also a great way to keep notes about plants that you already have, including planting dates, bloom times and plant performance.

Many gardeners take pictures of their gardens every few weeks and use the pictures as part of their record-keeping system. Also set aside a box or drawer for other useful items such as plant tags and care information that come with new plants, seed company packing lists and an inexpensive calendar for recording planting dates and to-do reminders. Sort through this information every few weeks and put some notes together. A large 3-ring binder with pockets serves as a practical garden journal.

CREATING A GARDEN ROOM

Garden rooms provide great impact in both large and small spaces. You can divide large spaces into smaller "rooms" with different themes and different seasonal appeal. For example, a vegetable garden, a shade garden *and* a flower garden could surround a water feature. If your property is small, use the room concept to make your garden more private and beautiful.

A garden room has the same structural elements as you would have in any room in your house—walls, a floor and a ceiling. Then add amenities that make a room welcoming, such as seating and other attractive furnishings.

Sketching out a garden room is like moving your living room furniture around, only a little more fun: All you lift here is your pencil—and your imagination.

Your simple plans will become an outdoor living area that you'll enjoy for years and years.

Floors and Paths

Lawn is the carpeting of choice in many American gardens and it can be very effective in garden rooms if it is well maintained. But many other options such as groundcovers, flagstone, brick, pea gravel or wood are available. Most garden room floors use a combination of lawn and hard paving surface. The paving material is used for paths and seating areas, while the lawn is a refreshing foil for the plants that grow above it.

When working in a small space, shape your lawn to make the room look deeper. Have the lawn gradually narrow as it moves back to the property line. This creates an optical illusion of a longer distance.

Pebble mulch paves the floor of a woodland garden room. The pebble mulch enriches the site with a new texture while providing all-weather access for people.

Despite its small size, a neat lawn edged in brick creates a garden room that feels open and spacious.

Walls

Walls enclose the garden space, provide privacy, screen external views and soften the garden's edges. Use any number of materials including hedges, layered shrubs and trees, wood fences, stone or brick walls or even the sides of adjacent buildings. A combination of materials is often successful. For example, walls made of hard materials such as brick or stone might be dressed with narrow, upright evergreens and a few flowering shrubs, with small annuals, perennials or vines planted at their feet.

One of the most enchanting things about garden rooms is that you can design them so that the entire garden is not visible at one glance. Instead, a wall or hedge may offer a narrow opening that draws us from one garden room into another. Another way to screen an area: Place a group of evergreen shrubs so that a path curves around them into a second hidden room. It is delightful indeed to find a secret sitting area, a treasured statue or a water feature at the end of a path.

Spikes of foxglove accent the vertical lines of a white wooden fence. Planted around the base of the tree, ranunculus serve as the centerpiece in this courtyard garden.

Ceilings

A ceiling of clear sky is but one option for a garden room. If you need shade, build a small pergola or attach a lattice panel to posts. Carefully prune tree limbs to make a gracious living ceiling for a garden room.

An arbor covered with fast-growing vines can provide shade, color and fragrance; you can use low-maintenance native plants such as Virginia creeper, also called woodbine (*Parthenocissus quinquefolia*). Virginia creeper will grow 6 to 10 feet in a single season; this perennial, deciduous vine clings to any sturdy surface with adhesive-tipped tendrils. Several good fragrant vines are discussed on page 110.

To make your room as private as possible, place the arbor near a fence or wall so you can "borrow" the existing surface as a backdrop. Alternatively, consider partially enclosing your arbor with an informal hedge of shrubs.

Furnishings and Accents

As in all rooms, you need a spot to sit and read a book or enjoy a cup of coffee. You may also want to entertain. Benches, chairs and tables placed on top of a stone terrace or wood deck should act as an invitation to pause in the garden and rest. As you locate resting areas in your garden, consider the view from sitting level and place accents of interest nearby.

Some outdoor rooms have such strong architectural elements that they don't need much decoration. Most rooms benefit from the addition of judiciously selected pots, vases, statues, fountains or sculpture. As you consider possibilities, keep in mind that the object should blend harmoniously in terms of scale and material so that it does not overpower surrounding plants. To provide focus within an otherwise confusing tumble of plants, introduce an interesting stone that marks a path, a bird bath or a moss-covered architectural fragment.

A lattice-backed pergola transforms a narrow sun-baked patio into a warm nook for reading and relaxing. The filtered shade also creates a new niche for flowers.

Gardens need sun, but people need cool places in the shade. A small open area between this arbor and stucco wall prevents dampness and promotes good air circulation.

TIP Mirror Magic

With proper placement, a mirror can visually extend a small garden area. Frame the mirror with a climbing evergreen vine such as English ivy (*Hedera helix*) or use upright evergreen shrubs to soften the edges. Use tempered mirror glass in the garden instead of a regular indoor mirror. Coat the silvered back with varnish (test a small area first to be sure the varnish doesn't harm the mirror). Mount the mirror on a solid surface with rubber grommets to prevent the mirror from cracking. Clean the mirror often so the effect is not ruined by mud, dust or plant debris.

EXPANDING SMALL SPACES

To make a small garden appear large and lush, you can use special design tricks that work in all types of climates. One factor to keep in mind is mystery. We are naturally inclined to explore and discover a garden, but if the entire garden is easily seen in a glance there is no reason to go any farther. A well-designed small garden provides a sense of direction and a motive for moving. This draws you into the garden and compels you to move from one enriched area to another.

The first step in making a small garden seem larger is to frame it with a boundary to focus attention on what is inside the boundary rather than what is beyond. Besides improving privacy, a boundary isolates the garden from urban and other distractions, and unwanted views. If you happen to have a small garden space with a wonderful view such as a mountain range, a body of water or a majestic church steeple, leave an opening in your wall or fence; or use low-growing plants so your line of sight clears the boundary.

Defining Different Spaces

Small gardens benefit from being divided into rooms, even if the division is as subtle as a single shrub used to define a special feature or a change in grade to signal a change in garden theme. If the natural grade change is steep, use a low stone retaining wall with steps to announce the transition from one room to another. Within a relatively flat site, a wooden beam flanked with shrubs on each side invites the viewer through the opening to see what is beyond. To further emphasize change, you might devote the upper level to an herb or butterfly garden and use the lower level for a small water garden.

Separated by a broad stone walkway, richly colored impatiens turn a plain entryway into a party.

What was once a plain backyard is now two very different gardens. Pruned hedges frame the formal area of roses, while the informal area is a more relaxed collection of cut flowers, vegetables and herbs.

Surfacing and Paths

If grade changes are not possible, consider using different surfacing materials to subtly indicate changes of scene. You might pave the area nearest the house with brick or stone, while the area farther away is paved with grass; either option lends a spacious feeling to a small garden. Locate a small lawn area where it will not be subjected to heavy foot traffic; otherwise it will never look like a healthy, verdant carpet of green.

Separated by level landings, concrete steps make this garden built on a slope more convenient to enjoy and maintain.

Layers of Plants

To make more room for plants, you might just forget about lawn and use your limited space to make deep planting beds divided by broad paths (at least 5 feet wide). This approach leaves some open space or breathing room, while maximizing every square inch of plantable soil.

Gardens of all sizes benefit from layered plantings, but this is an essential strategy in a small garden. Layering means arranging plants so that they are at least three deep.

- **Trees**, large upright shrubs or vines trained onto vertical trellises typically occupy the back layer. Climbing roses, annual vines and tall columnar junipers take up little space and make strong vertical accents.

- **Use small shrubs** and large perennials for the middle section, particularly species that are attractive in and out of season.
- **Small annuals**, perennials, bulbs and groundcovers fill the front space.

When composing layers, take advantage of differences in the shape, color and texture of foliage. For example, iris bloom only in spring, but their pointed, strappy leaves persist as useful textural elements that are unlike any other plants. Plants with red or gray foliage provide welcome relief in gardens planted mostly with green-leafed plants.

This small garden celebrates every square inch of available planting space by making use of graduated layers: tall trees, large shrubs, compact perennials and a unifying swath of vibrant green lawn.

Selecting Plants

This is the design element that causes small garden owners the most grief. What gardener doesn't want to grow at least one of every pretty plant they discover? In this regard, discipline and a knowledge of plants goes a long way in creating a pleasing small garden.

In this mostly green garden, the brightly colored chair and table are both ornamental and practical.

Use a Limited Range of Plants

To make a small garden seem larger, use a small collection of plant species. This makes the garden seem restful rather than jumbled. So instead of planting a sunny garden with one daylily, one peony, one coreopsis and one salvia, you would plant lush drifts of fewer species ... such as five daylilies and three peonies.

Select the Very Best Plants

Because your plant palette is limited, be sure to choose plants that will grow heartily in your garden soil and microclimate. Among trees and shrubs, carefully consider the plants' sculptural characteristic and leaf texture. Choose all plants with year-round interest in mind.

A butterfly bush forms a backdrop for a cozy hideaway at the garden's edge.

Garden walls need not be plain. Here lattice panels, painted green and mounted on the brick surface, support vines and provide color in the courtyard during the winter months.

Keep Your Plants in Prime Health

Sickly plants easily stand out in a small garden because everything is open to such close scrutiny. Remove plants that fail to thrive and replace them with something better suited to the site.

Keep Up with Pruning and Grooming

Prune trees high to keep light coming into the garden and to make space for layers of shrubs and perennials. Keep all woody plants pruned to the scale of your yard. Remove old flowers from blooming perennials and roses, to keep new flowers coming.

TAMING A SLOPE

Most of us have some kind of slope in our landscape. If you're lucky, you have a gentle slope that rolls away from your house. A less fortunate site has something like the side of a mountain sliding down the side yard. Whatever the case, the key to taming a slope is to stabilize it and then find a way to integrate it into your landscape.

One of the biggest challenges to taming a slope is controlling erosion. Erosion occurs when vegetation and topsoil are lost from sloping ground due to rainfall, wind and freezing and thawing. Established plants help control erosion, as do heavy mulches, rocks and special fabrics made to help stabilize sloping ground.

Gentle Slopes

Plant gentle slopes (20 degrees or less) with groundcovers to protect bare soil and stop erosion. Because slopes are difficult to weed and water, consider long-lived shrubby groundcovers such as spreading junipers or cotoneaster. Vigorous perennials such as English ivy and the other groundcovers described on pages 50-51 also work well. The best groundcovers for a slope are evergreens because they protect the soil all year long.

When planting on a slope, place plants in staggered rows. Offset each row of plants from the row before it. Your planting will fill in evenly this way.

Because the staggered plants break the flow of water, this planting arrangement prevents gullies from forming when it rains. Another technique for stopping water and soil runoff in new groundcover plantings is to create a small basin or berm around each plant's downhill side, to collect water.

As soon as you are finished planting groundcover plants, snake a soaker hose through the planting and then cover all open spaces with mulch. If you try to water a slope with a hose or sprinkler, much of the water will run down the incline instead of soaking into the soil. Soaker hoses or drip irrigation pipes work much better.

Sloped gardens are naturally dramatic. Combinations that partner stone with spreading plants such as thymes, armeria and hardy ferns limit erosion while making the most of changes in elevation.

Moderate Slopes

When thoughtfully shaped and planted, sloping gardens are often powerfully dramatic as they rise or fall away from the viewer. Tame moderate slopes (between 20 and 30 degrees) with a short stone retaining wall (see page 78), groups of large stones that form planting pockets and hold the soil, or a series of terraces held in place with landscape timbers. If the slope is expansive or inaccessible, simply covering it with spill rock may be a good option.

Degrees of Slope

0° slope

10° slope

20° slope (gentle)

30° slope (moderate)

Slopes are measured in degrees, which you find by estimating the angle of the slope. Level land has a 0 degree slope, while gentle slopes range from 10 to 20 degrees. Moderate slopes measure around 30 degrees and they require some type of reinforcement to stabilize them. More severe slopes (a sheer dropoff is 90 degrees) call for professional help. Building retaining walls strong enough to withstand pressure from earth and water is not a practical project to handle yourself.

Lilies benefit from the superior drainage at the top of this sloping garden. Bachelor buttons, dwarf zinnias and marigolds provide non-stop summer color.

Nature often furnishes slopes with rocks and water—an idea well worth imitating with "planted" boulders or small spill rock. Here sedums, ferns and wildflowers amplify the site's natural beauty.

Steep Slopes

Properties in very hilly or mountainous terrain may include slopes that are too steep for stablilizing with plants, stone or retaining walls. On the positive side, a precipitous slope often offers sensational views. In this case, your goal may not be to tame the slope but rather to make your property's inclines more accessible and easier to enjoy.

Wood decks are a simple way to expand outdoor level areas, especially if the land slopes away from the house. Try to shape your deck so that it fits your house and the hillside while making the most of panoramic views. Hire professional help when building a deck on a steep slope; two factors—the height of the deck and the natural instability of mountain land—may require that posts be set so deeply that heavy equipment will be needed to do the job right.

For upward slopes, a small attached deck might lead toward a series of broad landings or terraces built into the hillside. Each level spot can become a small shade garden, relaxation spot or informal wildlife viewing area.

A stone retaining wall with daylilies at its base sets the stage for a broad palette of perennials including liatris, goldenrod, achillea and purple coneflower.

Building a Filled Terrace

If you don't mind a long-term undertaking, you can stack boxes made of landscaping timbers into a moderate slope, and then fill them with soil and plants. Begin at the bottom of the slope and work upward. As you excavate soil to level the site for each box, use the soil to fill the boxes beneath it. Overlap the back of each box and use rebar stakes to reinforce all the corners.

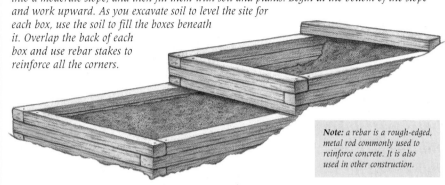

Note: a rebar is a rough-edged, metal rod commonly used to reinforce concrete. It is also used in other construction.

LANDSCAPE FABRIC AND LANDSCAPE MESH

Landscaping companies often use landscape fabric to control weeds and erosion. It is rolled over the prepared ground before planting, and holes are cut to make  places for plants. It is best used on slopes that are being planted with permanent shrubs such as those listed below. Because it does not decay, landscape fabric prevents spreading groundcovers from sending out runners and filling in. You must also use a straw or pine needle mulch over landscaping fabric; bark quickly washes away from a slick surface. When soil gets on top of landscaping fabric, weeds will manage to gain a foothold.

The best choice for holding soil while spreading groundcover plants become established is called landscape mesh. The mesh holds soil and young plants but allows plants to spread through the loose weave. It also breaks down approximately two years after being installed; by this time most groundcovers are fully mature and able to keep a bank from eroding.

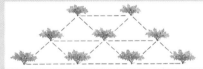

Know how far your plants will spread, then space them the correct distance apart so they'll fill in the gaps.

Hemp netting will hold the soil in place until these strawberries grow together into a groundcover.

GROUNDCOVER SHRUBS FOR SLOPES

Groundcover junipers.

Gold broom 'Vancouver Gold'.

	Bearberry cotoneaster	(*Cotoneaster dammeri*)	Zones 5 to 8	Lustrous evergreen leaves; bright red berries.
	Gold broom	(*Genista pilosa* 'Vancouver Gold')	Zones 5 to 8	Tiny green leaves; loads of yellow flowers in late spring.
	Juniper	(*Juniperus* spp.)	Zones 3 to 10	Evergreen, fine textured foliage; insignificant flowers.
	Heaths and Heathers	(*Erica* and *Calluna* spp.)	Zones 5 to 8	Bushy mounds covered with flowers in summer and fall.

Bearberry cotoneaster.

Heaths and heathers turn a slope into a billowing mound of color.

GROW A SHADE GARDEN

Gardening in the shade presents unique opportunities. Shade gardens aren't as weedy or thirsty as full sun areas, so they tend to require little maintenance. You can tend a shade garden on a hot day without getting sunburned. Best of all, a shade garden has a restful aura that almost whispers that you should rest awhile amidst a hundred shades of green.

As you assess your shady garden spots, look at the plants in the immediate vicinity. Large trees have massive root systems that spread at least as far as their branches. The roots are both shallow and deep ... and they aggressively

To turn a shaded edge into a garden, plant shrubs and trees that thrive in the shelter of larger plants. Here, rhododendrons do the job.

compete for soil, water and nutrients. If you are gardening under large trees you will need to supply added soil moisture and fertilizer.

Some trees such as maples, crabapples and beeches have shallow roots which often break the surface of the soil. Between these roots, cover the ground with drought tolerant groundcovers such as barrenwort (*Epimedium* spp.) and variegated bishop's weed (*Aegopodium podagraria* 'Variegata'). Under better conditions these plants can get out of hand and become invasive, so be careful where you put them in your garden.

Types of Shade

As any walk in the woods shows, different types of shade support different kinds of plants. Survey the shade in different areas of your yard, and note the time of day that each area is shaded.

- **Full Shade (3):** Sun is obstructed for most of the day. Full shade occurs in wooded areas with a mixture of tall trees and understory trees. Full shade may become partial shade in winter when the trees are bare. Plants that make much of their growth in late winter and early spring will grow in full shade.

- **Dense Shade (4):** Dark shade that lasts all day, year-round, as is found under evergreen magnolias, large spruces and other evergreen trees. Few plants will grow in dense shade.

- **Filtered Shade (1):** A lightly shaded area where shafts of sunlight filter through tall trees to the ground. Tall pines and trees that have been pruned or thinned usually give filtered shade. The most vigorous and diverse shade gardens are grown in this type of shade.

- **Partial Shade (2):** An area gets bright light or direct sun for half the day and shade for half the day. A house or other building or a dense tree is usually associated with partial shade. Full afternoon sun is usually too much for shade-loving plants, but they are often happy with morning sun and afternoon shade.

Consider texture when selecting plants for a shade garden. Hostas, iris and ferns are all green plants, but they have very different forms and textures that work well together.

Thin out low tree branches to admit more light to your shade garden. High filtered shade is better for gardens than heavier shade from low tree branches.

Starting a Shade Garden

1 Prune off low branches to let in more light. Also thin out unwanted saplings, damaged or unattractive trees and undesirable brush.

2 Amend the soil with organic matter to hold soil moisture and give the new plants' roots an easy environment in which to become established. If possible, dig in a 4- to 6-inch layer of organic matter each time you plant something. Plant around large tree roots rather than trying to cut through them.

3 Water each plant as you set it in place and mulch immediately with an organic material such as bark, wood chips, pine needles or rough compost.

BULBS FOR SHADE GARDENS

Fill spaces behind perennials with clusters of spring-flowering bulbs including aconites, snowdrops, crocus, daffodils, hyacinths and scillas. When the bulb flowers are gone but the foliage remains, later-blooming plants will provide needed cover.

A shade garden planted with spring-flowering bulbs reaches its color peak just as the trees overhead develop new leaves.

Choosing Plants for a Shade Garden

Adding Shade

All shade-loving plants thrive in the close company of trees. If you need more shade, add small trees such as Japanese maples, dogwoods, redbuds and serviceberry (*Amelanchier*). If your shady area is large, you can give it needed structure with shrubs such as azalea, hydrangea, sweet spire and witch hazel.

Hundreds of different hostas offer subtle or radical differences in leaf color and texture. Here are Hosta fortunei *'Gold Standard',* H. ventricosa, H. Sieboldiana *'Elegans' and* H. fortunei *'Frances Williams'.*

"Greens" to Choose From

The main color you work with in a shade garden is green, with a little help from bronze-red and white. Green comes in hundreds of shades which contrast, harmonize or play off of each other. Bright chartreuse plants, such as hosta 'August Moon' or green and white variegated Solomon's seal, instantly brighten dark corners. Light gray-green or blue-green foliage (such as hosta 'Krossa Regal') make small spaces seem larger.

Deciduous Shrubs

Winter sun is often beneficial in the shade garden, so use large evergreens with restraint. Deciduous shrubs that produce berries such as winterberry (*Ilex verticillata*) help keep the shade garden lively in winter, as do plants with interesting bark such as birches or crape myrtle.

Perennials

Colorful perennials for a shade garden include hundreds of native wildflowers as well as showy cultivated plants such as astilbe and bleeding heart. Hellebores (also called Christmas rose) provide exciting form and color in winter, as do many types of moss and hardy perennial ferns.

When planting tulips in a shade garden, choose cultivars that vary in both height and bloom times to have a long display of color.

Summer Color

In the summer, add light-colored impatiens, wax begonias and variegated coleus to your shade garden for even more color. To avoid digging around delicate perennials, grow your annuals in low containers and slip them into bare spots where extra color is needed.

Whether in pots or beds, impatiens are unsurpassed annuals for the shade garden.

When forced to behave itself and kept restricted to a defined space, variegated bishop's weed (Aegopodium) is a fine groundcover for shade. If allowed to become invasive, the same plant often goes by the unflattering name of goutweed.

❧ CHAPTER 3 ❧

SOIL:
CREATING A SOLID FOUNDATION

Soil is the natural element most critical to gardening success. Soil supports and feeds plants as it provides water and oxygen to roots.

"No occupation is so delightful to me as the culture of the earth..."—Thomas Jefferson

Soil preparation may not be the most glamorous part of gardening, but the time and effort you devote to improving your soil is repaid many times over with healthy plants, abundant harvests, reduced weeding and easier planting. Good soil drains faster when rain is heavy, and holds more moisture during times of drought. No amount of additional water, fertilizer or plant coddling produces the same positive results as does good garden soil.

Before you dig a planting hole or a new garden bed, become familiar with basic soil properties and get to know the kind of soil in your yard. Then you will know how to best use your time and energy to make your soil as good as it can be. You need to know the type of soil you have and whether or not it contains basic plant nutrients, in order to make improvements. Finally, you will need to know your soil's natural pH. Each of these topics is discussed in the following pages.

The more you work with your soil, the better you will know how it responds to changes in moisture, air and organic matter.

Understanding Soil Type and Character

Soil is composed of four main elements: mineral matter, water, air and organic matter. Grains of sand, finely pulverized rock or pebbles are mineral matter. The size, proportions and type of mineral matter give the soil its basic texture, which determines its type. Broadly defined, the four soil types are sand, clay, silt and loam.

- **Sandy soil** is light and easy to dig, warms quickly in the spring and is rich in oxygen. However, sandy soil doesn't hold much moisture or many plant nutrients.

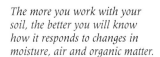

Sandy soil.

- **Silty soil** has a lighter texture than clay but is heavier than sand. Small silt particles travel easily in water, so soil in low places near rivers and streams often has a silty character. Poor drainage and surface crusting are the main problems you will have when gardening in silty soil.

Silty soil.

- **Loam** is the term used to describe soil with a good balance of clay, silt and sand, and a generous amount of organic matter. It is the type of soil everyone wants to have.

Loam.

- **Clay soil** is heavy and difficult to dig and has little pore space for oxygen. Clay often contains plenty of plant nutrients, but the nutrients may be not be available to plants because of the soil's tight texture. Clay soil tends to stay wet for a long time after heavy rains, and may drain poorly. When clay dries out it becomes rock hard. It is encouraging to know that clay soil becomes terrific garden soil if a sufficient amount of organic matter is added.

Clay soil.

LEARNING YOUR SOIL TYPE

Working with the soil is like any long-term relationship: It helps to know who you are dealing with and how they will react to a variety of circumstances. Once you know what kind of soil you have, you can judge how it will react to various practices involving soil amendments, water and fertilizer.

The "Jar Test"

There are a couple of good ways to determine your soil type. The jar test lets you look at the mineral components in your soil and their relative quantities, which indicates soil type.

Dig down 4 inches to get a ¼-cup soil sample. Place the soil and 2 cups water in a clear glass quart jar or plastic drink bottle and add a few drops of dishwashing detergent. Shake the jar vigorously for one minute, and then set the jar aside and let the contents settle. After the water clears (up to 24 hours), look at the layers under bright light. Coarse sand particles settle on the bottom. The next layer is silt and the top layer, some of which may still be suspended in water, is clay (yellow-brown, red or tan). Organic matter will float to the top.

Here's how to analyze what you see:

Sand: If over half of the total is sand, you have a light, sandy soil.

Silt: If over half of the total is silt without much clay, you have heavy silt.

Clay: If one-fourth of the total is clay and you have a fair amount of silt, you have clay soil.

Loam: A good loam will show as two-fifths sand, two-fifths silt and a narrow band of clay.

As soil and water separate into layers, you will be able to see what proportions are sand, silt, clay and organic matter.

Evaluating Soil Fertility

For about $10, you can purchase a soil test kit at a garden center or through a mail order catalog. Choose a test that includes separate test tubes and chemical solutions to determine pH as well as nitrogen, phosphorus and potassium levels. Home tests give only approximate measurements, but this is probably all you need.

You can get a more accurate soil test done through your local university extension service. The test results will tell you what kind of soil you have, pH, nutrient levels and suggested amendments for improving soil. The only disadvantage is that you may have to wait several weeks for test results, especially if you send your sample in during the busy spring season. To avoid a wait, submit your soil sample in the fall. Besides, fall is the best time to add many soil amendments such as lime and organic matter, because they have time to work on the soil prior to spring planting.

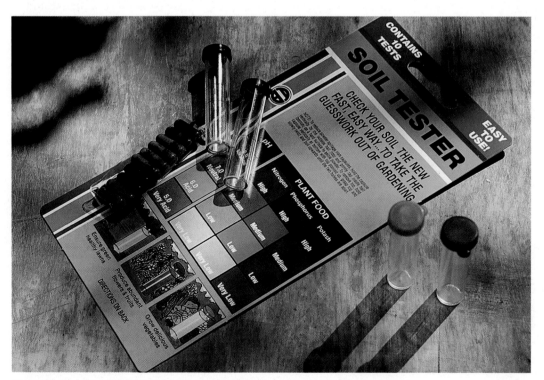

Use an inexpensive soil test kit to get an approximate idea of your soil's fertility.

Basic Facts on Soil Fertility

Rich soil that can meet the needs of most plants is well endowed with the three major plant nutrients—nitrogen, potassium and phosphorus—as well as a broad range of micronutrients. Here is what each major nutrient does for growing plants.

• **Nitrogen** helps plants produce new leaves and stems. You might think of it as the "new growth" nutrient. Plants vary in their need for nitrogen. Heavy feeders need an ongoing supply, while most other plants need nitrogen most when they are making new growth. Too little nitrogen results in slow growth, stunted plants and pale leaves. Too much may make plants grow so vigorously that they flower poorly or do not set fruit. Nitrogen moves through the soil easily, so it also leaches out during heavy rains or watering.

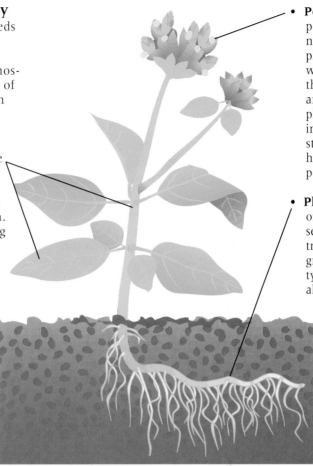

• **Potassium** (sometimes called potash) is closely linked to nitrogen. Potassium aids in photosynthesis, the process by which plants derive energy from the sun. It also helps fruit ripen and is important for developing plump, full seeds. Potassium improves disease resistance, stress tolerance and general plant health. Like phosphorus, apply potassium at root level.

• **Phosphorus** promotes the growth of healthy roots. It helps give seedlings a rapid start and lends tremendous strength to plants that grow from bulbs, tubers and other types of storage roots. Phosphorus also promotes heavy blooming in flowers. Because this nutrient does not move through the soil readily, it needs to be incorporated at root level.

If your garden's soil is full of nutrients, and loose enough to let roots penetrate deeply, you're giving your plants the best possible home.

WHAT'S YOUR pH?

The term pH refers to a numerical scale (from 1.0 to 14.0) used to describe the acidity or alkalinity of soil. The neutral point on the pH scale is 7.0. A pH reading more than a half point lower (below 6.5) is acidic. A higher reading indicates alkaline soil.

The soil's pH strongly influences the availability of many minerals that plants use as nutrients, including phosphorus, boron, copper and zinc. Some plants prefer rather extreme soil pH levels. Azaleas, blueberries and plants native to the East often thrive in slightly acidic soil. Plants native to the Southwest often prefer alkaline conditions. Most plants, however, prefer a near-neutral pH.

How do you raise your soil's pH? Work agricultural lime into the soil. Use sulfur to lower the pH of alkaline soil. Fertilizers and soil amendments also change the soil's pH over time. Test kits for pH are available at garden centers. Keep one on hand for checking the pH of new garden soil and for monitoring the pH of beds planted with finicky plants.

Blueberries are particular about pH. They like an acidic soil between 3.5 and 5.5 pH; around 4.5 is optimum.

Pomegranates adapt easily to alkaline soils with a pH above 7.0.

Like most other garden plants, tomatoes grow best with a near neutral pH between 6.5 and 7.0.

IMPROVING YOUR SOIL

Cultivating the soil can be one of gardening's tremendous pleasures. If you are not blessed with deep, rich soil, you may spend as much time "growing" good soil as you do catering to the needs of your plants. In some soils, simply digging the earth to break up the subsoil and incorporate air results in a noticeable improvement in how well the soil behaves when it is put to work in a garden. But most of the time, simply digging is not enough. Whether your soil is clay, sand or somewhere in between, you can make it better by adding organic matter, minerals (discussed here) and fertilizer (discussed on pages 30-31). Of these three, organic matter is the ingredient that will turn frustrating soil into black gold.

Adding Organic Matter

Organic matter is decomposed plant and animal material that turns to "humus"—sticky soil particles left behind after living things decay. Organic matter and humus will improve any soil's structure. Enriched sand will stick together in loose clumps and retain moisture better. In clay soil, organic matter creates tiny air pockets that greatly improve the soil's drainage.

The best way to get organic matter into the soil is to dig in a little compost each time you cultivate your soil. You can make your own compost (see pages 32-33) or buy it from a local source. Check the classified section of your newspaper to find local sellers of compost or call your extension office to inquire about possible sources.

Quality Compost

The quality of compost varies according to what it's made of, how it is made and how it has been stored. For example, mushroom compost is so rich in nitrogen that you can consider it a fertilizer. However, municipal composts made from leaves and other types of yard waste often contain little in the way of plant nutrients.

Mulching

Mulching your garden with biodegradable materials such as shredded leaves, pine needles, straw or hay also boosts the soil's organic matter content, as does turning under withered plants or weeds.

Pine needles make a neat, fine-textured mulch for front-yard foundation beds.

Decomposing Matter

Several sources of organic matter are listed on the right. Allow raw materials to decompose before you add them to your soil. Sawdust and wood chips actually use soil nitrogen to help them rot if they are mixed into the soil before they have rotted. Fresh manure may burn plant roots.

Manure and other types of rich organic matter improve the soil's texture while boosting its fertility.

SOURCES OF ORGANIC MATTER

Rotted manure
Chopped leaves
Cover crops
Grass clippings
Kitchen waste
Straw
Peat moss
Rotted sawdust
Wood chips

Minerals: Hard Stuff Made Easy

As long as you are cultivating your soil, why not dust on some rock powders? These inexpensive minerals work as both soil amendments and fertilizers. Because they are basically pulverized rock, they condition the soil slowly, over a period of several months or even years. For best results, add minerals to your soil in the fall so they will have time to work before spring planting. Following are some mineral amendments you can add.

- **Lime** raises the soil's pH and increases the availability of micronutrients. Test your soil's pH before adding lime, and recheck it after 6 months. Apply 1 to 10 pounds per 100 square feet.

A light dusting of lime helps keep slightly acidic soil in the neutral range. Always test your soil's pH to determine if and how much lime is needed.

An inexpensive mineral, gypsum helps break up clay soil and provides calcium plants can use as a nutrient.

- **Greensand** is mined from ancient marine deposits, and is a good source of slow-release potassium. Apply 5 to 10 pounds per 100 square feet.

Greensand.

- **Rock phosphate** enriches the soil with slow-release phosphorus that persists in the soil for up to 5 years. Apply 5 pounds per 100 square feet.

Rock phosphate.

- **Gypsum** supplies calcium and breaks up compacted, heavy clay. In areas with high rainfall, reapply gypsum every 3 years. Apply 5 to 15 pounds per 100 square feet.

- **Soil sulfur** lowers the pH of alkaline soil. Use it only in very small amounts. Test your soil's pH before adding sulfur. Start with 1 pound per 100 square feet.

Soil sulfur.

SOIL AMENDMENTS VS. FERTILIZERS

Enriching your soil with soil amendments and fertilizers will improve your garden plants' performance, but there is an important difference between the two types of materials.

Things you add to your soil to improve its texture, drainage and overall quality are called soil amendments. Soil amendments may contain no actual plant nutrients (for example, sand or peat moss) or they may be low in major nutrients yet well endowed with minor nutrients (compost, rotted mulch).

Fertilizers provide nutrients that plants can use when they need them, but they do not necessarily improve the quality of the soil. Most organic fertilizers—including manure and cottonseed meal—are both fertilizers and soil amendments. After the plant nutrients they provide are gone, they persist in the soil as organic matter.

Good Soil Takes Time

Adding large amounts of organic matter and appropriate mineral amendments in one fell swoop will make a big difference in your soil. But remember, improving garden soil is not a one-time thing. In your vegetable garden, where you cultivate and replant at least once a year, you will see steady improvement if you add organic matter each time you renovate a row or bed. With long-lived shrubs and trees, cover the soil around the plants with compost and mulch at every opportunity. Earthworms and other creatures will carry these riches deep into the earth, ensuring that the plants have long and healthy lives.

CHOOSING AND USING FERTILIZERS

The best way to supply your plants' nutritional needs is through a nutrient-rich soil, so improving your soil by adding organic matter should be a top priority every year.

In excellent soil, many plants will grow well with no additional fertilizer—particularly shrubs, trees and wildflowers. But vegetables and showy flowers are another story. In most soils, these and other plants will grow better if you fertilize them.

Spreading granular fertilizer, and working it into the soil near young plants, can give them a boost at transplanting time. Always read the product label to see whether you'll need gloves for such tasks.

Before setting out bedding plants or bulbs such as shallots, mix a little fertilizer into the prepared soil.

Choosing Fertilizers

Garden centers offer a mindboggling selection of fertilizers. There is no single best fertilizer for every plant, though you will certainly find some products more to your liking than others. If you want to use fertilizers that will benefit both your soil and your plants, try to use organic fertilizers whenever they are practical. Then switch to a synthetic fertilizer to meet plants' special nutritional needs.

Plants don't recognize the difference between organic and synthetic fertilizers, but many organic fertilizers serve as soil conditioners, improving soil structure as they feed plants. Synthetic fertilizers are generally easier to handle and give fast results. Each type may have a logical place in your growing plans.

Organic Fertilizers

Fertilizers that supply plant nutrients the natural way, by releasing nutrients as the tissues from once-living plants and animals decompose, are called organic fertilizers. This process speeds up under warm conditions and slows when the soil is cool. After soil microbes finish processing organic fertilizers, tidbits of organic matter are left behind in the soil.

Rotted manure builds good soil texture and provides nitrogen and other important plant nutrients.

POPULAR PACKAGED ORGANIC FERTILIZERS

Alfalfa meal
Animal manure
Compost
Cottonseed meal
Feather meal
Fish meal
Soybean meal

Types

You can use the classic organic fertilizer, manure, gathered from stables or barns; or you can buy new products made of pelleted poultry manure. Allow fresh manure to decompose before using it in your garden, and watch out for the possibility that the manure might carry noxious weed seeds. To kill these seeds, put raw manure through a hot composting process (as described on pages 32-33).

Uses

Other organic fertilizers are listed above, or you can shop for blended fertilizers made from a variety of organic ingredients. The main disadvantages to using organic fertilizers is that they are bulky and may not give you the fast action you want in some situations. In vegetable and flower beds, their best use is as a pre-plant fertilizer worked into the soil at the beginning of the season. Elsewhere in the landscape, use organic fertilizers as an annual top-dressing for established perennials, shrubs and trees.

Blended organic fertilizers will not burn plant roots. Many are as easy to handle as chemical fertilizers.

Granular fertilizers are made to dissolve quickly as rainwater moves through the soil.

Although they cost more, coated time-release fertilizers release nutrients slowly over a specified period of time. The label should tell you how long a given product is designed to last, as well as whether or not the fertilizer contains micronutrients such as calcium, magnesium and copper.

Controlled-release fertilizers are covered with different types of biodegradable coatings. As the fertilizer is moistened through rainfall or irrigation, some of the fertilizer seeps out until the fertilizer is used up. This is the ideal type of fertilizer to use on lawns, shrub groupings and other plants that need a steady supply of nutrients.

Synthetic Fertilizers

The most widely used (and inexpensive) synthetic fertilizers are granulated fertilizers such as 10-10-10 or 20-20-20. The three numbers stand for nitrogen, phosphorus and potassium (abbreviated N-P-K). They reflect the relative abundance of each nutrient in the fertilizer. A 100-pound bag of 10-15-20 fertilizer contains 10 pounds of nitrogen, 15 pounds of phosphorus and 20 pounds of potassium. The remaining 55 pounds is filler. These types of fertilizers release their nutrients as soon as the granules dissolve in water, and their effects last for about six weeks. They are most often used to prepare soil for spring vegetable planting.

Time-release fertilizers, coated with various materials that dissolve slowly, release nutrients to plants faster in warm temperatures than when the weather is cool.

Special-Purpose Fertilizers

There are a variety of special-purpose fertilizers available to cater to very specific needs.

- **Nitrogen-only fertilizers** such as ammonium nitrate are used to side-dress sweet corn and other crops that benefit from a booster feeding of nitrogen.

To grow great peppers, try using a fertilizer specially blended for tomatoes. These products are relatively low in nitrogen, so they do not push plants to develop thick canopies of leaves at the expense of flowers and fruits.

- **Specific plant foods** such as rose food and tomato food are similar to other complete fertilizers, but their N-P-K content is tailored to meet the target plant's needs. Products for acid-loving plants such as rhododendron and azalea food produce a strong acidic soil reaction as their nutrients are released.

- **Instant fertilizers** come as concentrated liquids, powders and pellets that you dilute with water. They are commonly used on container plants and on plants that need a quick boost in midseason.

Fertilizers come in many forms, including pellets, stakes and tablets.

- **Foliar fertilizers** are sprayed on leaves. The nutrients are immediately absorbed and available for plant use. See page 34 for more information on this approach to fertilization.

- **Stakes and tablets** are used to feed trees, shrubs and houseplants. They must be pushed or hammered into the soil near roots. Add water and these products release nutrients directly into the plants' root zones.

CREATIVE COMPOSTING

Composting harnesses the power of nature to make dead things rot into a nutrient-rich soil amendment. Of course, leaves and grass clippings and weeds and bruised tomatoes and all kinds of garden refuse will rot on their own if you let them. With compost, the difference is in the mix. Finished compost is a complex mixture of organic matter, bacteria, enzymes and minerals. But the process of making compost is not complex in the least. In addition, composting is a great way to do something useful with waste from your kitchen and yard.

Some people call it "gardener's gold," but compost tends to become darker as it ages. Whatever the final color, it's great for your garden.

Compost—What Goes In

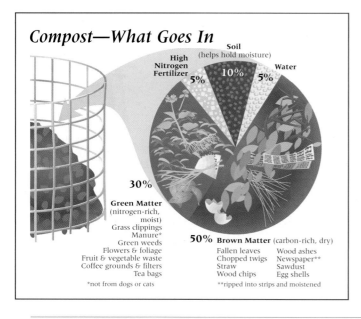

Soil (helps hold moisture) **10%**

High Nitrogen Fertilizer **5%**

Water **5%**

30%

Green Matter
(nitrogen-rich, moist)
Grass clippings
Manure*
Green weeds
Flowers & foliage
Fruit & vegetable waste
Coffee grounds & filters
Tea bags

*not from dogs or cats

50% Brown Matter (carbon-rich, dry)

Fallen leaves   Wood ashes
Chopped twigs   Newspaper**
Straw   Sawdust
Wood chips   Egg shells

**ripped into strips and moistened

COMPOST—WHAT DOESN'T GO IN

Meat scraps, bones or fat	Attracts rodents and other pests.
Diseased plant debris	Can spread garden diseases.
Pesticide-treated plants or wood	May kill beneficial organisms.
Noxious weeds or weeds that have set seed	Can spread into garden.
Charcoal ashes	Much too alkaline.
Pet droppings	Often contain parasites.

The Composting Secret

The only key to making good compost is getting a proportioned mixture of materials and keeping the mass of stuff evenly moist. In mixing materials, your goal should be to have about a 2:1 ratio of brown material rich in carbon to green material rich in nitrogen (see illustration above). Then add water; this promotes activity by insects, earthworms, fungi and other microbes. Finally, add a little fertilizer to make the heap start simmering with microbial heat.

Make compost from almost any type of organic material. Dampened hay with stable manure is a classic combination that yields rich, dark results.

Double Heap Composting

Double heap composting is a slow but practical way to compost. Start by building one compost heap to which you gradually add kitchen scraps, weeds that haven't gone to seed, prunings and garden wastes until the heap stands 3 feet high. This may take several weeks. Turn the heap to mix and moisten the materials, and then start a new heap next to the old one. Each time you add material to the new heap, cover it with a shovelful or two of almost-finished compost from the first heap. This way, you are constantly adding your own custom-grown "activator" to your compost. When you need compost for your garden, harvest what you need from your oldest heap.

The double-heap method takes up little space, and offers you "constant composting" to take care of everyday kitchen and garden scraps.

Hot Composting

The very best way to make compost is through a process called hot composting. A hot compost is made all at once and it absolutely must have plenty of nitrogen-rich materials such as fresh grass clippings or manure. The best time of year to try this method is summer, when the right materials are available, the weather is warm, and the microorganisms that give compost its heat are naturally active.

The temperature in a hot pile should rise above 130°F, which will kill most weeds, insects and plant pathogens. This is the main reason to go to the trouble of making and maintaining a hot heap. Here's how to do it:

Accumulate Material

To make hot compost, carefully blend equal amounts of brown and green matter until you have a pile at least 3 feet tall and equally wide. For example, you might take the slow compost pile you've been accumulating during late winter and spring and mix it with a quantity of fresh green grass clippings. Moisten the pile as you build it and allow it to sit for three days.

"Cook"

Use a digging fork or pitchfork to turn and re-moisten the pile. As you turn it, try to move the material from the outside of the pile to the inside. Turn the pile again five days later. At this point you should feel heat radiating from the heap as you turn it. Wait one week and turn the pile again. After the third turning the temperature of the pile should drop. The composting process should be finished after one or two more weeks.

On cool mornings, you can see the steam that shows your compost is working. In all types of weather, working compost should be warmer in the center than near the exterior of the pile.

QUICK CURES FOR COLD COMPOST

If you make a compost pile and it just sits there, try these remedies to "rev" it up:
- Turn the heap and add water to dry pockets.
- Add nitrogen-rich materials such as grass clippings, or add some high nitrogen fertilizer (some organic gardeners use cheap dry dog food for this).
- Make the pile bigger until it is at least 3 feet high and wide.
- Cover the renovated heap with black plastic to trap solar warmth.

Other Composting Methods

Composting appliances include barrels that mix materials for you when they are rotated. Some gardeners like to compost within bins made of wood, wire or even concrete blocks. Indeed, there seem to be as many ways to compost as there are gardeners, and any method that produces finished compost is a good one.

Compost is ready to use in the garden when its temperature is cool to the touch. Finished compost has an earthy smell and a crumbly texture.

To retain the enzymes and micronutrients in your compost, store it in covered containers or cover the heap itself with a sheet of plastic or an old blanket.

A barrel type composter makes short work of mixing ingredients. You may want to keep large, coarse materials in a wire bin where they will not attract rodents or other pests.

WHAT'S THAT SMELL? CURING COMPOSTING PROBLEMS

Problem	Cause	Solution
Pile smells like sulfur	Too wet, lacks oxygen	Aerate pile by turning, let pile dry out, add more dry material.
Pile smells like ammonia	Kitchen scraps are not covered	Turn pile and add carbon-rich brown material such as leaves.
Pile smells like sewage, attracts flies	Too much nitrogen	Bury scraps in center of pile, cover with soil or brown matter.

FOLIAR FEEDING

Plants take up nutrients mostly through their roots, but they also can absorb nutrients through their leaves. When water-soluble fertilizers are dissolved in water and applied to the leaves of plants it is called foliar feeding. Foliar feeding of plants is similar to humans taking vitamin supplements: It should not be the primary way of providing nutrients, but is a good way to make sure plants never run short of the food they need for healthy, energetic growth.

Foliar feeding gives fast results. Plants can absorb soluble nutrients immediately through their leaves, so nutrients are available right away. But the effect of foliar feeding is short-lived because there is no residual material that continues feeding plants once the soluble nutrients have been taken up by plants or percolated through the soil. Foliar feeding is a good way to solve pressing nutritional problems but it is not a substitute for rich, healthy soil or other fertilizers.

How to Foliar Feed

Apply foliar fertilizers to plants using a watering can, any sprayer or mister, a hose-end sprayer, or a siphon and watering wand. Just about any type of instant fertilizer that can be diluted with water makes a good foliar feed. You can also use kelp-based organic sprays developed specifically for this use.

Always follow label instructions for diluting and mixing water-soluble fertilizers. Adding a mild liquid soap (¼ teaspoon per gallon) helps spread the solution evenly over leaves. Water-soluble plant protectants (including fungicides and oils) can be mixed with foliar feeds and applied at the same time if needed.

Foliar feed early in the morning or early evening to avoid burning foliage. Pick a day that's not extremely hot and when rain is not expected. Spray both upper and lower leaf surfaces until the solution drips from leaves. Of course, you'll want to avoid foliar feeding when rain is likely, as well as days you'll have to water extensively.

Do your foliar feeding in the early morning or evening on a day that's not extremely hot. Choose a day when rain is not expected.

A hose-end sprayer saves time because it automatically mixes liquid fertilizer with water.

FEEDING MASS QUANTITIES

An easy way to feed a large number of plants is to attach a brass siphon mixer between your outdoor water faucet and your hose. A small siphon tube drops down into a bucket of concentrated liquid fertilizer. Attach a watering wand to the other end of the hose and you are able to foliar feed a great number of plants without having to stop and refill a sprayer or watering can.

This is especially useful if you grow a lot of plants in containers potted in soilless mixes that don't contain any nutrients.

Notes of Caution

Foliar feeding is a great way to feed container-grown plants, to temporarily fix acute nutrient shortages or give plants a quick mid-season boost. But it is not a substitute for feeding the soil that feeds your plants.

The other potential hazard of foliar feeds is that they can burn leaves if the mixture is too strong or if they are applied in the heat of the day. If in doubt about potential burn, apply half the recommended amount twice as often. When wetting leaves for any reason, do it early in the day so that the leaves will not remain wet all night.

You can apply any water-soluble fertilizer to plant leaves, but it's important to make a weak solution and apply it on a cloudy day.

ORGANIC FOLIAR FEED

2 Tbsp. concentrated fish emulsion
1 Tbsp. liquid seaweed extract
1 Tbsp. concentrated insecticidal soap
1 gallon water

Mix together and apply to the upper and lower surfaces of plant leaves in the morning or early evening. The fish emulsion provides nitrogen, the liquid seaweed provides trace nutrients and the insecticidal soap helps the mixture spread while deterring insects.

FOLIAR FEEDING FORMULATIONS

Type	Formulation	Uses	Plants
General Purpose	15-30-15 or 20-20-20	Relatively high nitrogen. Use early in season to promote fast leaf growth, also through mid-season for leafy vegetables. Caution: Do not use on perennials after mid-season because succulent growth does not harden off properly prior to the onset of colder temperatures.	All plants grown in containers. Leafy vegetables such as lettuce, spinach and greens. Roses benefit from foliar feed in late summer, to promote fall bloom.
Fish Emulsion	5-2-2 or 4-2-2	Organic source of nitrogen. Use diluted at half strength to fertilize young seedlings. Drench over any plant to provide nitrogen quickly. Many gardeners alternate all-purpose liquid fertilizer with fish emulsion when growing all types of plants in containers.	Vegetables and flowers.
Acidifying Soluble Fertilizer	30-10-10 or 31-11-11	Organic source of nitrogen for plants that prefer acidic soil conditions. Apply soon after blooms fade.	Azaleas, blueberries, camellia, citrus, crape myrtle, many evergreens, ferns, holly, magnolia, rhododendrons.
Liquid Iron	15-4-6	Iron is needed to make chlorophyll, the green pigment in leaves responsible for photosynthesis. Plants may be iron deficient due to compacted or poorly drained soil. Alkaline soil makes iron less soluble. Soil pH and/or drainage needs improvement if yellowing (from iron deficiency) continues.	Pin oak, camellia, citrus, gardenia, any plant in highly alkaline soil.
Bloom Booster	10-50-10 or 10-60-10	Promotes flowering but not production of new leaves and stems. Use after plants have reached half their mature size.	Flowering plants grown in containers, and annual flowers in the garden.

Spinach is a heavy feeder that benefits from extra helpings of nitrogen via foliar feeding.

Be generous when providing foliar fertilizer to plants grown in containers. Twice a month is not too often.

GREAT WAYS TO WATER

Seemingly a simple garden task, watering is actually a critical part of gardening—too much and plants drown, too little and plants bake. But once you get the hang of it, a sixth sense seems to develop and you instinctively know when and how much to water.

The first step to becoming a proficient waterer is getting to know your soil's water-holding capabilities. Clay soil holds more water than sandy loam and takes longer to dry out. Clay soil also produces more runoff than sandy soil because the soil surface is tighter and doesn't allow water in as quickly as loosely-knit sandy soil.

In addition to the general water-holding habits of your soil, you will probably find that some parts of your yard tend to be wet—and others dry—due to influences by slope, large trees, fences and of course your home. There also may be sweet spots, where the soil is unusually rich in organic matter, that stay lightly moist most of the time.

Watering a garden by hand takes time, but it gives you a chance to slow down a bit and enjoy your plants.

Conserving Water

Water conservation is an increasingly important concern in many parts of the country. Limited water supplies and periodic droughts often cause water districts to place restrictions and bans on watering lawns and gardens. It is in everyone's best interest to conserve water in the garden by selecting plants that are well adapted to natural moisture conditions and by using conservative watering methods. Here are some details.

Select Plants Appropriate for Your Moisture Conditions.

Most vegetables, annuals and perennials will need supplemental water through the summer months as will shallow-rooted shrubs such as azaleas and rhododendrons. However, many trees and shrubs grow well with nothing more than natural rainfall. Talk with your local nursery owner to select woody plants that don't need water after they are established.

Desert plants are adapted to areas that get little rainfall. Too much moisture will make them prone to rot.

If you live in a region that receives high levels of rainfall, experiment with moisture-loving plants such as impatiens, ferns and mosses.

Place Plants with Similar Moisture Needs Together.

Place thirsty plants together and drought-tolerant plants together so that no plant receives too much or too little water. Place less drought-tolerant plants in areas where they are protected from drying winds and hot afternoon sun.

Use Mulch to Conserve Water.

A 2- to 4-inch layer of organic mulch placed over the ground around plants helps keep the soil cool and conserves moisture. Mulched plants can go longer between waterings than unmulched plants.

Water Early in the Day or at Night.

Wind and sun can cause supplemental water to evaporate before it moves into the soil. Water when the air is still and the sun is not hot.

Use Efficient Watering Methods.

Soaker hoses, drip irrigation pipes, hand watering and sprinklers that cover a specific area waste very little water when they are properly used. Keep reading for more details on these methods.

Even the simplest mulch—here, shredded leaves—will keep plant roots cooler and help prevent weeds and disease.

Smart Watering Options

Good watering equipment is not expensive, but you can't use it unless you have it. Prepare yourself for drought conditions by having watering equipment ready to meet the needs of your soil and garden.

Drip Irrigation Pipes

Drip irrigation systems are generally made from plastic pipes studded with special devices that emit water a drop at a time. Drip systems work at low water pressure similar to soaker hoses. You can easily design a drip system tailored to meet the needs of your garden.

Because it is a semi-permanent watering system, drip irrigation works best in long-lived plantings of fruits, shrubs or groundcovers.

A long-handled watering wand makes it easy to provide water to hanging baskets or other high containers.

Soil Soaker Hoses

Soaker hoses weep water through small holes in the walls of the hose, so they deliver water at a slow, even rate. Soaker hoses are ideal for watering rows of plants or you can lay them on the ground in a circle around trees or shrubs. If you always need to water shrubs and trees in the summer, you can place a soaker hose between the soil and mulch and leave it there permanently. Or simply lay the hose on the ground around plants. These hoses are much lighter in weight than regular hoses, so they are easy to move from one area of the garden to another.

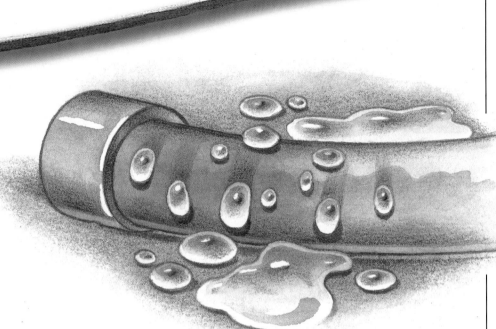

Drip-type emitters are an easy way to target moisture to widely spaced plants. Some systems are specially made for use in container gardens.

Overhead Sprinklers

When you're trying to coax seedlings out of the ground, there is no better way to maintain even moisture than to use an overhead sprinkler that emits a fine spray. But because sprinklers are notorious for watering sidewalks and driveways in addition to garden beds, look for more efficient methods for routine watering. Impulse sprinklers that work by pushing a powerful jet of water through the head and deflecting it are water wasters, too. They are most appropriate for watering large expanses of lawn or groundcover.

Hand Watering

If you must do a lot of hand watering, invest in an adjustable nozzle that emits water in different patterns—a gentle shower for watering containers, a light mist for moistening seedbeds, and a strong stream for filling buckets and watering cans. These types of nozzles also have a shut-off valve so you can turn the water on and off without walking back to the faucet.

A soaker hose slowly weeps water out through tiny pores.

A sprinkler dampens the top of the soil very well, which is exactly what you want when you are coaxing new seeds out of the ground.

Install a T-junction shut-off valve at your faucet. Then you can channel water to different hoses, say one to a soaker and one to your regular hose.

MARVELOUS MULCHES

Looking for a way to save yourself from hours of weeding and watering? Mulch is the answer. Mulch benefits both the gardener and the garden. How? It provides a buffering layer between the soil and the wild world above. Mulch keeps weeds from getting the light they need to grow. Weeds that do get a foothold in mulch are easy to pull out.

Anything used to cover the soil and improve plant growth is considered a mulch. Inorganic mulches such as sheet plastic or landscaping fabric covered with decorative stone reduce weed problems, keep the soil cool and moist, and reduce erosion. Organic mulches—including chopped leaves, bark, straw or thin layers of grass clippings provide the same benefits and much more. As organic mulches decompose into humus, they also improve the soil's structure and fertility.

Bark nuggets are a good low-maintenance choice for mulching woody plants and evergreens .

Go light on mulch if slugs and snails are a problem. Slugs and snails love moist, dark places, and mulch provides a perfect hiding place. Wood chip mulches are especially appealing to slugs and snails and should not be used where slugs are a problem.

Climate Control for Soil

Mulch insulates the soil from summer temperature extremes by shading the soil and conserving soil moisture. As temperatures drop, mulched soil stays warmer than unmulched soil, and extends the growing season by several weeks. Consider this for fall-planted perennials, which need extra time to establish roots before the soil freezes. In winter, mulch moderates soil temperature fluctuations. Once soil is frozen it will stay that way instead of freezing and thawing with temperature changes.

Heavy rains have no trouble penetrating mulch to moisten the soil below. But if you live in a climate where dry spells or droughts are not unusual, install soaker hoses in beds before you mulch them. In the vegetable garden, water the soil thoroughly before applying mulch.

Dried grass clippings make a good temporary mulch. They decompose quickly and can be worked into the soil or covered with a more persistent material.

Before using them as mulch, chop leaves slightly by running over them with your lawn mower. Chopped leaves decompose faster and are less likely to blow about.

THE MULCH-RAIN CONNECTION

Mulches keep the soil moist longer by slowing the evaporation process to almost a standstill. But there's more to the way mulches and water work together.

- **Mulch softens the impact** of pelting rain. This reduces soil compaction, erosion and nutrient leaching.

- **Mulch keeps mud from splashing** on plant foliage, reducing the chance of infection from many plant diseases.

- **Mulch may filter out** fungal spores that are washed to the ground by heavy rains, including the fungus that causes rose blackspot.

- **Mulched soil stays loose** and crumbly instead of becoming hard-packed and crusted like unmulched soil, so shallow surface roots have more soil in which to grow.

 TIP

Allow Breathing Room

Leave a 1- to 2-inch space between mulch and a plant's main stem. Mulch smothering the base of a plant increases the chance of disease and pest problems.

MULCHING MATERIALS

As you select mulching materials, consider where they will be used. Ornamental plantings look best when mulched with attractive materials such as chopped bark or pine needles. Vegetable gardeners often use newspaper or straw.

Material	Primary Benefit	When and How to Apply
Lawn clippings	Builds soil structure. Moderates soil temperature. Conserves moisture.	Allow clippings to dry before applying. Apply a 1- to 4-inch layer that doesn't form a dense mat.
Chopped leaves	Suppresses weeds. Builds soil structure. Reduces soil temperature.	Chop or compost before using because whole leaves mat down. Mulch in winter or spring with a 3-inch layer.
Pine needles	Builds soil structure. Suppresses weeds. Increases acidity, good for acid-loving plants.	Apply a 2- to 4-inch layer around shrubs and trees. Pine needles tend to acidify the soil.
Bark nuggets	Conserves moisture. Suppresses weeds.	Apply a 2- to 3-inch layer around shrubs and trees, preferably over a roll-out mulch.
Straw or hay	Builds soil structure. Suppresses weeds. Moderates soil temperature. Conserves moisture.	Apply a 6-inch layer at planting time and as needed through the growing season. Straw usually contains fewer weed seeds than hay.
Paper, newspaper	Suppresses weeds. Conserves moisture.	Use between vining vegetables or in pathways between beds or rows. Cover with a thin layer of more attractive mulch. Turn under when partially decomposed.

Roll-Out Mulches

Material	Primary Benefit	When and How to Apply
Plastic weed barrier	Suppresses weeds. Conserves moisture.	Use beneath straw or grass clippings in places that are renovated at the end of the season. Reusable.
Plastic sheeting	Black plastic warms the soil and suppresses weeds. The light reflective patterns that accompany red plastic mulch benefits tomatoes and some other crops, and deters nematodes.	Lay down plastic and anchor with rocks or soil at planting time. Can also be laid down to warm the soil so you can plant earlier in spring than you normally would. Use heavyweight reusable products.
Landscape fabric	Suppresses weeds.	Lay down at planting time and cut slits for plants. Can be difficult to cut and doesn't allow plants to spread beyond the cut hole.

Grass clippings.

Leaves.

Pine needles.

Bark nuggets.

Straw.

❦ CHAPTER 4 ❧

LAWNS:
GROWING GRASSES AND
GROUNDCOVERS

*Carpet your landscape's floor with finely textured grasses, and fill
shady pockets with lush plantings of spreading groundcovers.*

Like outdoor rugs or carpets, lawns and ground-covers furnish the floor of the landscape. Their fine textures are unmatched by other garden plants. And the contrast in texture between your landscape's floor and other features makes a mutually flattering partnership.

Yet most people do not grow a lawn simply for its looks. Lawns are unsurpassed for outdoor play or entertaining. When located adjacent to driveways, patios or other large hard surfaces, a lawn also can serve as a natural filter for excess rainwater as it flows toward lower ground.

Lawn Basics

Granted, maintaining a good lawn requires time. So instead of thinking of lawn grass as something you grow where nothing else is planted, design a lawn that pays you back for all the time and trouble you devote to its upkeep. Use the basic characteristics of your site and your personal tastes to decide where and how much lawn you will have and where you can best use comparatively low maintenance groundcovers. There are three major considerations.

1. **Light.** Grass grows best where bright sun is available for at least half a day in summer, when deciduous trees are in full leaf. Because evergreen trees cast shadows year-round, they can limit a site's suitability for lawn-grasses. Many groundcovers thrive in substantial shade.

English ivy blankets the ground beneath a large tree. Other groundcovers used here include liriope and hosta.

Framing a lush lawn with groundcovers reduces the time required to mow and maintain the lawn. Masking the bases of trees with ground-covers also makes mowing easier, and protects the lower tree trunks from injuries caused by mowers and string trimmers.

2. **Maintenance.** Growing a quality lawn requires regular fertilizing and mowing. You may need to renovate a lawn every few years. In comparison, groundcovers require close attention for the first year or two after planting, yet need little ongoing maintenance after they become established.

 Designer's Tip

The fine textures of grasses and groundcovers can be used to direct the flow of your landscape's design. For example, you might use lawn to connect different parts of your yard and groundcovers to fill areas that are seldom used yet constantly in view.

RAISING SHADE

One of the simplest things you can do to enhance the growth of both lawn grasses and groundcovers is to prune off the lowest limbs from the shade trees in your yard. Even shade-loving ground-covers like high shade better than low shade. Begin by removing limbs that are less than 10 feet from the ground. Higher pruning to about 15 feet will admit even more light and fresh air.

Too much lawn creates too much work, but you need enough grass for what's important!

3. **Traffic.** Healthy grass can with-stand moderate traffic, but no grass can handle constant wear.

Groundcovers have even less tolerance for traffic from people and pets.

CULTIVATING YOUR LANDSCAPE'S FLOOR

Climate will determine which grasses and ground-covers are best for your yard, but also consider the depth and quality of your soil. Like other culti-vated plants, most lawn grasses require at least 4 to 6 inches of good topsoil. Some grasses have clear pref-erences for soil pH too. Test your soil before under-taking major lawn projects and add soil amendments to get it in good condition for growing grass.

If you have a failed lawn on your hands, inves-tigate why it's in such sad shape before deciding what to do next. Neglect is a problem that is easily cured with fertilizer, water and a bit of fresh seed. But poor drainage or lack of sufficient topsoil are serious problems that must be corrected before you can expect a new or old lawn to grow as it should.

Nurturing Your Lawn—Fertilizing and Watering

With the notable exceptions of buffalo grass and centipedegrass (described on pages 44-45), all lawn grasses require regular fertilizer. The best fertilizers for lawns are high nitrogen formulations such as 22-4-14 or 18-5-12. Fertilizers that release their nutrients slowly help support steady growth, and are available in both organic and synthetic formulas.

When to Fertilize

As a general rule of thumb, you should fertilize your lawn when new growth appears and again about 10 weeks later. Too much fertiliz-er can lead to water pollution, and you may need to mow it more often, too. With creeping grasses, overfertilizing may make the grass grow so vigorously that a layer of dead stems, called thatch, accumu-lates at the soil's surface. Follow the application rates on the fertilizer you choose. If possible, apply fertilizer to your lawn just before rain is expected.

Applying fertilizer with a drop spreader ensures even distribution and eliminates problems with uneven grass growth or color.

To fertilize your lawn, measure the amount of fertilizer you will need, and then divide it in half. Place one of the halves in the hopper of a fertilizer spreader, and apply it to the lawn in parallel lines. Then change directions and criss-cross the area in the opposite direction to apply the second half.

A Good Soaking

Lawn grasses willingly soak up as much water as you care to give them, but they often can get by with only occasional watering. The biggest mistake you can make is to lightly water your lawn so that only the top inch or two of soil becomes moist. This encourages the growth of shallow roots and shallow-rooted lawns are easily stressed by dry conditions. When you water your lawn, use a sprinkler to soak it thoroughly. The eas-iest way to gauge water is to place empty tuna cans on the lawn and turn off the sprinkler when they are almost full.

Measure the amount of water applied to your lawn with any container that has straight sides. In a pinch, even a tuna can works well.

When grass does not spring back when you walk on it, it's a sign that the lawn is becoming too dry.

Planting a New Lawn

You can plant a new lawn yourself if the area is less than 1,000 square feet, which roughly translates into a 20 by 50-foot rectangle or a 30 by 30-foot square. To plant a lawn larger than this, either rent the heavy equipment you will need or hire a landscaping company to grade and cultivate the soil.

1 Begin by getting rid of existing vegetation. Scrape away scattered weeds with a spade or treat the area with a herbicide. If you prefer, till under weeds and grasses with a rototiller, then go back three weeks later and do it again. Remove large rocks, tree roots, and other obstructions.

2 Add topsoil or organic soil amendments to create a fertile 6-inch-deep layer of topsoil. Check the pH, too, and add lime if needed to make it less acidic. If your soil is heavy clay, working in a few pounds of powdered gypsum will help improve its texture.

3 By this time the soil should be very finely cultivated. Rake or grade it until it is very smooth, and then compact it with a water-filled roller (you can rent small ones that you push). For very small lawns, finish preparing the site by walking over the soil repeatedly and raking it smooth.

Red fescue is a cool-season grass that often gets mixed with Kentucky bluegrass for a good, all-purpose lawn.

Prepare your lawn properly (see above) and you'll salute the results.

Planting Seed

Grasses that have an upright tufting habit will not knit themselves together into a sod, so they are best planted from seed. You can also save money by planting seed of some creeping grasses, including bluegrass. Step-by-step instructions for reseeding an old lawn (the steps also apply to a new lawn) are given on pages 46 and 47.

Planting Sod

Grasses that have a spreading growth habit are often sold as sheets of sod. Sod can be a single species or a mixture of different grasses. Although it can be costly, the obvious advantage to planting sod is that you have an instant lawn.

Prepare the site as outlined above (Planting a New Lawn) before you buy your sod. Make advance arrangements for the purchase and delivery of sod, because freshly harvested sod is much more likely to flourish than sod that has languished on a hot sidewalk for several days. Schedule the project to coincide with the grass's most active period of growth—fall or spring for cool-season grasses, or early summer for warm-season grasses.

Tools, Materials & Timing

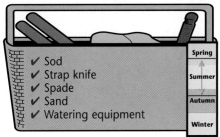

✔ Sod
✔ Strap knife
✔ Spade
✔ Sand
✔ Watering equipment

Spring
Summer
Autumn
Winter

1 *Begin laying your sod along a straight edge, laying the pieces of sod end to end without stretching them.*

2 *Use a sharp knife or spade to trim pieces to fit curves or small corners.*

3 *When you're finished laying the sod, fill the joints between pieces with sand, and water the sod thoroughly.*

CHOOSING GRASSES FOR YOUR LAWN

Turf-quality grasses are divided into two groups: Cool-season grasses, which grow best when air temperatures are below about 75°F, and warm-season grasses, which remain dormant during cool weather and begin growing actively after night temperatures rise above 55°F. The descriptions below include the seasonal classification of each grass, as well as site and soil conditions that affect their growth. The grasses are listed in order of most hardy to least tolerant of cold temperatures.

Many high-quality grasses can be established from seed, including bluegrass, turf-type tall fescue and perennial ryegrass.

Kentucky Bluegrass (*Poa pratensis*)
Type: Cool-season
Where it grows: Zones 3 to 6 and parts of Zone 7 where night temperatures often dip into the 50's and 60's.
Description: Beautiful and fine textured, bluegrass is the lawngrass of choice in any area where it can be grown. Lustrous bluegrass spreads by shallow rhizomes. It needs deep, fertile topsoil with a near neutral pH (7.0) in full sun or very limited shade. In dry areas, water is needed in summer. You can plant bluegrass from sod, or sow 2 to 3 pounds of seed per 1,000 square feet. Mow bluegrass at 2 to 3 inches.

The queen of cool-season grasses, bluegrass turns a vibrant green very early in the spring.

Fine Fescue (*Festuca rubra*)
Type: Cool-season
Where it grows: Zones 3 to 6; may be combined with bluegrass and tall fescue in Zones 6 and 7.
Description: This creeping grass tolerates shade better than bluegrass and its narrow blades give it a fine texture. Fine fescue forms a very dense turf when grown in fertile soil. It may become semi-dormant during periods of hot weather. Fine fescue can be planted from seed or sod; it is often mixed with other cool-season grasses. Mow at 2 inches.

Perennial Ryegrass (*Lolium perenne*)
Type: Cool-season
Where it grows: Zones 3 to 7. The annual form of ryegrass is often used to overseed dormant warm-season lawns in Zones 8 and 9.
Description: Although it is seldom used as a lawngrass by itself, perennial ryegrass brings extra winter hardiness and shade tolerance to mixed lawns that include tall fescue and bluegrass. It shows great green color as long as the weather is chilly. Several named cultivars are available, or they may be combined with other grasses in seed mixtures. Sow the fast-germinating seed at 5 pounds per 1,000 square feet. Mow at 2 inches.

Tall Fescue (*Festuca arundinacea*)
Type: Cool-season
Where it grows: Zones 6 and 7; shallow soils in Zone 5 that will not support bluegrass also are good candidates for tall fescue.
Description: There are many named varieties of this adaptable tuft-forming grass. It is the most heat-tolerant of cool-season grasses. Tall fescue grows well in sun or partial shade, in well-drained soil with a pH between 6.0 and 7.0. Tall fescue is occasionally sold as sod in combination with bluegrass and fine fescue, but it is most often planted alone from seed. Plant in early fall or late winter, using 5 pounds of seed per 1,000 square feet. Fertilize in fall and late winter. Overseed every 2 years. Mow at 2 to 4 inches.

Bermudagrass (*Cynodon dactylon* hybrids)
Type: Warm-season
Where it grows: Zones 6 to 10, but best in warm areas of Zone 7 and most parts of Zones 8 and 9.
Description: Hybrid bermudagrass is a tremendous improvement over more primitive strains, but it is still a high-maintenance lawn grass. Full sun, excellent drainage and regular fertilization are needed. While it is dormant in winter, monitor this grass closely to prevent problems with winter weeds. Bermudagrass looks best when mowed at least once a week with a reel type mower. Mow it low at 1 to 2 inches.

Improved varieties of tall fescue are ideal for climates where summer is too hot and humid for bluegrass, but winters are too cold for warm-season grasses.

A warm-season native grass, buffalo grass thrives in dry areas. To prevent problems with weeds, cut this grass infrequently and let it grow at least four inches high.

Buffalo Grass (*Buchloe dactyloides*)

Type: Warm-season

Where it grows: Zones 4 to 7 in areas where the soil is alkaline and predominantly dry.

Description: This native prairie grass will grow without irrigation after it is established. You can grow buffalo grass in full sun or slight shade, but it does need slightly alkaline soil with a pH above 7.0. Plant buffalo grass from plugs or seed; sod is also available in some areas. Provide water for two months after planting. Fertilize very lightly in late spring, after the grass begins to turn green. Mow buffalo grass high, at 3 to 5 inches, because mowing too low will open the lawn to weeds.

Centipedegrass (*Eremochloa ophiuroides*)

Type: Warm-season

Where it grows: Zones 8 to 10

Description: Low-maintenance centipedegrass grows in poor acidic soil with a pH between 4.5 and 5.5, tolerates extreme heat, and adapts to full sun or partial shade. It is naturally a light to medium green color. Centipedegrass is sold as sod, sprigs (rooted stems) and seed; many people plant both sprigs and seed at the same time. Plant centipedegrass in late spring, using 1 to 2 pounds seed per 1000 square feet. Mow at 2 inches.

Centipedegrass grows beautifully in the sandy acidic soils of the lower South. It requires very little fertilizer and thrives under hot, humid conditions.

Zoysia (*Zoysia* species)

Type: Warm-season

Where it grows: Zones 6 to 8

Description: The most luxurious of the warm-season grasses, zoysia has a very fine texture and grows into a dense carpet. The site should have topsoil at least 6 inches deep with a pH between 6.0 and 6.5 and receive full or almost full sun. Plant zoysia from sod in late spring. Because of its cost and maintenance requirements, zoysia is best used in small spaces where a very fine-textured lawn is a high priority. Mow at 1 to 2 inches.

Zoysia turns a buff brown color in winter. To have a year-round green lawn, you can sow annual ryegrass over zoysia in early fall, just as the zoysia becomes dormant.

St. Augustinegrass (*Stenotaphrum secundatum*)

Type: Warm-season

Where it grows: Zones 8 to 10

Description: This grass is always at its best in filtered or partial shade. St. Augustinegrass spreads by vigorous stolons, and the large folded blades are very dark green. Plant St. Augustinegrass in late spring from sod, sprigs or plugs. Fertilize in late spring. When growing this grass in very sandy soil, fertilize again in late summer. Mow at 3 to 4 inches.

Understanding the Difference: Tufting vs. Creeping Grasses

TUFTING GRASSES, such as tall fescue, divide into bunches of upright crowns.

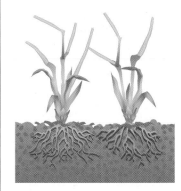

CREEPING GRASSES spread out by developing rooted stems, rhizomes, or tillers (ground-level lateral shoots).

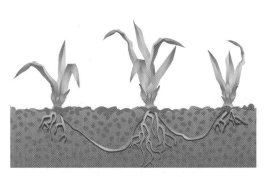

Improving an Existing Lawn

Y ou can renovate a lawn that is plagued by weeds, or simply does not grow well, without actually cultivating the soil. Soil cultivation always invites new problems with weeds, so it makes sense to first try the steps outlined below for reconditioning and overseeding a struggling lawn.

A Lawn Make-Over: Preparation

Begin this project in early fall or early spring, just before your lawn enters a period of new growth.

- **First test the soil** for pH and major nutrients. Also survey your weeds. You will need to remove deeply rooted weeds such as dandelions by hand, and hoe out spreading weeds that shade the soil and prevent grass from growing as it should.

- **Next, use a lawn mower** equipped with a bagger to mow the existing vegetation very close to the soil's surface. Dispose of the material you collect in your compost heap.

- **After "scalping" your old lawn**, rake over the area with a heavy dirt rake to loosen the top half inch of soil between the clipped crowns of grass plants left behind.

- **Using your soil test** as a guide (see pages 26-27), amend the soil as needed with lime and fertilizer. Because you will be planting seeds, use a high phosphorus "starter" fertilizer such as 5-10-15, 6-12-12, or an organic fertilizer with a similar analysis. Follow label directions for application rates.

- **If your soil consists of heavy clay**, improve its texture by poking holes in it and filling them with good topsoil. Make the holes with aerator sandals (worn over your shoes) or by pushing the tines of a digging fork into the soil about 3 inches deep. To aerate a large lawn, you can rent a power-driven core aerator to make quick work of the job.

When mowing near entryways or pools, use a bagger to eliminate problems with scattered clippings.

- **After the holes are made**, spread enough good topsoil over the area to fill the holes and form a ¹⁄₂-inch-deep layer over the surface. Aerating and topdressing will mix in the fertilizer, lime or other amendments you applied after you scalped the old lawn.

Removing Deep-Rooted Weeds

A special tool called a dandelion puller is perfect for prying deeply rooted dandelion plants from a well-established lawn.

Reseeding in Season

Lawn grasses that don't spread– like tall fescue and perennial ryegrass– benefit from reseeding every other fall. To overseed an established lawn, mow the grass very low, rake the area lightly to expose bare soil between grass plants. Then broadcast seed at half the recommended rate for planting a new lawn. Water the site for a few minutes each day until new seedlings appear.

A mixed lawn of tall fescue and perennial ryegrass tolerates partial shade and extreme winter cold.

A hand-cranked seeder is a good tool for reseeding or overseeding an established lawn.

Use a drop spreader to evenly distribute grass seed in a new lawn. Later, you can use the same tool to spread fertilizer.

Planting Seed

Use a drop spreader or hand-cranked seeder to distribute the seed evenly over the area. When planting grass seed, use the same criss-cross method used to apply fertilizer (see page 42). Rake over the seeded area very lightly to mix the grass seed with the top ¼ inch of soil. Then walk over or roll the surface to firmly press in the seeds. On sloping sites, a very light sprinkling of weed-free straw will help hold the seed in place. One bale of wheat straw will cover 1,000 square feet.

Set up as many sprinklers as you need to get water to every part of your overseeded lawn. Turn them on as often as needed to keep the area constantly moist for two to three weeks—the usual germination time for grass seed. Unless the weather is very hot and dry, watering the site for about 10 minutes twice a day should be sufficient.

Begin mowing when the young grass is 3 inches tall. Because some seeds germinate faster than others, frequent mowing ensures that the late sprouters will get the light they need to prosper.

To keep the surface of a newly seeded lawn level, press the seeds into the soil with a weighted roller, or lightly rake in the seeds if the site is very small.

Tools, Materials & Timing

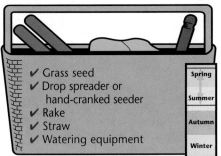

- ✔ Grass seed
- ✔ Drop spreader or hand-cranked seeder
- ✔ Rake
- ✔ Straw
- ✔ Watering equipment

| Spring |
| Summer |
| Autumn |
| Winter |

BUYING GRASS SEED

When shopping for seeds, carefully examine the label on the bag before you buy. Look for percent germination, date of germination test and purity, as well as exactly what cultivars are included in the package. Bargain-priced grass seed may be old, of low quality or might contain unwanted weeds.

The best values in grass seeds are often blends of several named cultivars, or special mixtures of several different species. For example, if you want a beautiful bluegrass lawn, look for a blend of several named bluegrass cultivars (there is usually a little perennial ryegrass added to help hold the soil in place while the bluegrass germinates). For a problem site, you might opt for a blend that includes bluegrass, tall fescue, fine fescue and perennial ryegrass. Just be sure to buy the highest quality seeds you can find.

Dethatching and Topdressing

Zoysia, bermudagrasses and other grasses that form a tight sod are renovated by removing the layer of dead stems that accumulates near the soil's surface, called thatch, and then topdressing the thinned-out turf with compost. Rent a power dethatcher to renovate a large lawn or use a rake or manual aerator to dethatch small areas. Then follow up with fertilizer and water. Always dethatch in late spring, just as the grass turns green. If crabgrass has been a problem, choose a fertilizer that includes a crabgrass preventer. These fertilizers contain a pre-emergent herbicide that keeps crabgrass seeds from germinating. Apply in mid to late spring, the prime season for crabgrass emergence.

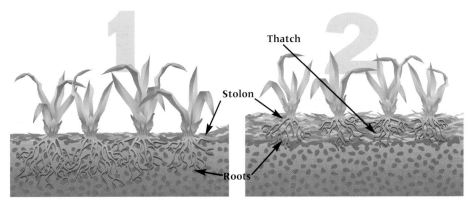

If your lawn is of a thatching-type grass, you'll encourage good, deep root growth if you dethatch in late spring (1). If thatch accumulates, roots can't penetrate into the soil (2).

FRAMING A SMALL LAWN

The fine texture of lawn grass makes a small yard feel more spacious while providing beautiful contrast for nearby flowers, shrubs and trees. If you add a neat frame to a small lawn, it becomes a peaceful oasis that unifies the landscape and provides open space for outdoor activities.

To make the most of a small lawn, choose a high-quality turfgrass and give it the best of care to bring out its color and texture.

When designing a small lawn, keep the lines as simple as possible. Use broad curves or a long straight edge to visually exaggerate the lawn's limited size. Circular or rectangular lawns surrounded by flower or shrub beds often look much larger than they really are when they are finished off with a frame of brick, stone, or evergreen plants. Besides giving a small lawn a tailored appearance, a frame reduces maintenance by making the grass simpler to mow and edge. Details count in a small lawn, so edging is as important as regular mowing.

Edging Materials

Bricks are an ideal edging material for lawns that adjoin flower beds because you can make the back of the strip higher by laying bricks on their sides. The high side keeps soil and mulch from washing out of the beds.

A broad edging of stone and brick works as a mowing strip and a clean visual frame that separates mulched beds from the lawn.

Flat stone creates a broad frame that can double as a narrow walkway. The stone's light color is easily seen at night.

Plastic edging deters grasses that try to spread into beds. This edging is most effective with grasses that spread slowly. However, some edging labor is usually needed after the grass is mowed.

Plastic edging retains fine mulch and defines the lawn's edge.

A brick edging defines the lawn and reduces edging chores.

Plants such as clump-forming groundcovers or dwarf ornamental grasses can be used to form a soft, natural frame that defines the edge of the lawn.

Planted in a broad band, liriope frames the lawn and eliminates the need for edging the grass.

Installing a Mowing Strip

A mowing strip serves three purposes: It visually frames the lawn, provides a level track for lawn mower wheels and the wheels of edging tools, and it can help retain the soil and mulch in adjoining flower beds. You can make a mowing strip using bricks, small 12-inch-wide preformed concrete pavers or flat stones. See page 54 for more information about these and other materials you might choose for your mowing strip. Here's how to build it:

Tools, Materials & Timing

- ✔ Spade
- ✔ Sand
- ✔ Bricks or pavers
- ✔ Rubber mallet
- ✔ Broom

Spring
Summer
Autumn
Winter

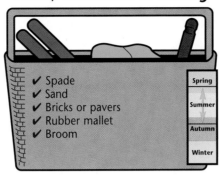

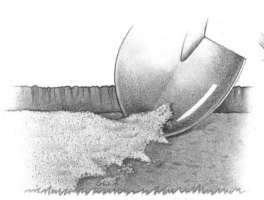

1 Excavate a flat-bottomed trench ½ inch deeper and ½ inch wider than the depth and width of your bricks or other pavers. Pack down the bottom of the trench to make it as level as possible. Then spread ½ inch of sand in the bottom of the trench.

2 If using a single row of bricks or pavers, place on a bed of sand, checking often to make sure the bricks are level. The tops of the pavers should be only ¼ to ½ inch higher than the soil line of the lawn. Use a rubber mallet to make stones or pavers fit tightly together because weeds are likely to sprout in open crevices.

3 If using a double row of bricks, set 4 bricks on their sides in the back of the trench so their tops are 1 inch above ground level. Then set foreground bricks (see step 2) in place at right angles to the back bricks. With any type of brick or stone, complete small sections before going on to the next area.

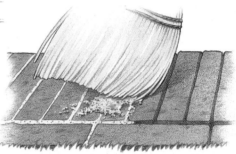

4 After the frame is complete, sweep clean sand into the crevices between bricks.

Tools for Edging

Choose edging tools based on the size of the job and the type of grass you need to trim.

Hand Tools

For small areas planted with a grass that spreads slowly such as tall fescue, use a spade or a simple hand tool called an edger/scraper. Or buy manual edgers that include a wheel attached to a rotating blade. These are ideal for

Sometimes all you need for small edging jobs is a spade and a little elbow grease.

Most string trimmers can handle small edging jobs. Some models can be outfitted with special blades for edging lawn grass.

edging lawns that are level with concrete curbs, walkways or driveways. If the lawn and adjoining hard surfaces are not level with each other, a string trimmer works best.

Power Tools

Manual tools may not pack enough muscle for strong-stemmed Bermuda or St. Augustine and they are a slow way to edge a large lawn. For about $50 you can buy a light-weight electric edger that will trim any type of lawn grass quickly and efficiently. Should the electric cord prove too confining, many models of gas-powered string trimmers can be equipped with edging blades.

Gas-powered walk-behind edgers cost about $200. These are what professional lawn care services use to maintain the edges of commercial landscapes.

Consider investing in a power edger if your lawn includes long edges that adjoin concrete walkways or driveways.

Low-Tech Mowing

One of the secrets of keeping a small lawn that looks like green velvet is mowing it often. A push reel mower may be all you need if your lawn is truly tiny. Be sure to keep the blades sharp to get a smooth, even cut. Lightweight electric mowers are ideal for small lawns too. Electric mowers are easy to start, fold away for easy storage and make only a little noise. Choose a gas-powered rotary mower if your lawn is more than 1,000 square feet in size. Lawns of more than ½ acre justify the use of a riding mower.

USING GROUNDCOVERS

Use vigorous groundcover plants to fill shady spots, areas that are too steep to mow or places where you want to reduce maintenance to occasional watering and pruning. Evergreen groundcovers bring color and texture to the landscape year-round and require less than half the upkeep needed to maintain a nice lawn. Flowering groundcovers usually grow best in sunny areas.

To ensure strong growth, take the time to improve soil before planting groundcovers. Most groundcover plants need two to three years to fill in, so you will also need to mulch and weed the area while the plants are getting established. In areas that are difficult to dig because of tree roots or slopes, prepare planting pockets for groundcover plants. Species that spread by developing vining stems will cover the spaces atop the roots.

A lush planting of fragrant sweet woodruff blankets the ground beneath a nicely sculpted river birch.

Fertilizer and Maintenance

Groundcover plants make most of their new growth in spring, so that's the ideal time to prune and fertilize established plantings. Here's how:

- **Begin by trimming** off ragged stems and old leaves. In large plantings, set your lawnmower blade at its highest cutting height and mow over the swath.

- **Trim smaller plantings** with pruning shears, being careful to trim back only to 3 to 4 inches from the ground.

- **Gently rake off the trimmings** and broadcast a balanced organic fertilizer or slow-release synthetic fertilizer over the area at the rate recommended on the package.

- **Topdress the planting** with a 1-inch layer of weed-free compost or a 50-50 mixture of peat moss and good topsoil.

- **In young plantings** that have not yet filled in completely, mulch over bare spots with finely shredded bark or another weed-free material.

- **Water the area deeply** when your renovation is complete, and expect to see vibrant new growth within one month.

EVERGREEN GROUNDCOVERS

English ivy (Zones 5 to 9). Wide beds beneath big trees are perfect spots for swaths of ivy. To keep it in bounds, trim the edges of the planting twice a year.

Variegated English ivy (Hedera helix).

Liriope (Zones 6 to 9). Often called lilyturf or monkey grass, liriope is a top choice for broad edgings that receive partial shade. Blue flower spikes appear in summer.

Liriope (Liriope muscari).

Pachysandra (Pachysandra terminalis).

Pachysandra (Zones 3 to 8). Give this groundcover rich, well-drained soil in partial shade. Use variegated forms to fill in dark corners.

Periwinkle (Vinca minor).

Periwinkle (Zones 5 to 9). Let these plants pave the ground around azaleas or other shade-loving shrubs, or use it to cover shady slopes.

Colorful Spreaders for Sun

Where winters are mild, these groundcovers hold their foliage year-round, but in cold climates they become dormant in winter. Think of them as vigorous spreading perennials. Weed and fertilize the plants when new spring growth appears. If old plants become tattered, pull them out to make room for healthy young ones.

Ajuga.

Ajuga (*Ajuga reptans*) Zones 3 to 9. Green, red-bronze or white variegated foliage is highlighted by brilliant blue flowering spikes in late spring. Also known as carpet bugle, this plant is great for gentle slopes or broad edgings.

Creeping phlox (*Phlox subulata*) Zones 2 to 9. Thick mossy green foliage is covered with pink or white flowers in early spring. Other colors are not as vigorous. You can mow creeping phlox back to 3 inches in summer to stimulate growth of new branches.

Stonecrop (*Sedum acre*) Zones 4 to 9. This super succulent can take dry soil and strong sun better than any other groundcover. Fine show of yellow flowers in spring. Wonderful when partnered with attractive rocks or stones.

WEED WATCH: POISON IVY

Poison ivy often turns up in the same shady niches where groundcovers grow.

All parts of this plant cause painful itching that can persist for 2 weeks or more. You can suddenly become allergic to poison ivy even if you have never reacted to it before. Here's how to avoid a run-in with this unwelcome garden invader:

- **Identify poison ivy** by its "leaves of three" leaflets.
- **Wear gloves** and protective clothing when working around this plant.
- **Wash soiled gloves** and clothes in hot water with plenty of detergent.
- **Spray large colonies** of poison ivy with a broad-spectrum herbicide.
- **When individual plants pop up** in a groundcover planting, either clip them off at the soil line or carefully paint the leaves with a systemic herbicide. Cover nearby groundcover plants with plastic or newspaper to protect them from herbicide damage.

Poison ivy.

Planting Groundcover Near Trees: Making a Planting Pocket

To find pockets of soil among large tree roots, pound a 2-foot long steel stake into the ground to determine where you can dig holes.

In spots where the stake will go down at least 6 inches, use a narrow spade to dig out a 6" x 6" hole, and fill it with a 50:50 mixture of soil and compost. Plant a groundcover plant in the prepared pocket, then water it. Water all newly planted groundcover plants regularly during their first summer in the ground.

◆ CHAPTER 5 ◆
WALKWAYS:
PAVING YOUR WAY WITH MULCH, CONCRETE, STONE AND BRICK

Secure walkways keep your garden accessible in all types of weather, and enhance its natural beauty.

Gardens are made of plants and soil, but a good landscape also provides an easy way for people to pass through it. Garden walkways range from cozy mulched paths that meander through a wooded area to broad landings paved with brick right outside your front door. You can tailor the size and type of pathway to the area it is designed to serve, and make your garden more practical and beautiful at the same time.

Four areas benefit most from constructed walkways: entry areas; commonly-used traffic corridors that connect different parts of the yard; pathways into and through places where you grow special gardens; and activity areas where you like to work or your children like to play. Furnishing the floors of these walkways with a clean, stable material makes them more enjoyable to use and goes a long way toward keeping mud off of your shoes.

Designing a New Walkway

A walkway is meant to facilitate easy foot travel. Visually, a well-designed walkway will pull you along your way and give you the subtle feeling that you have been invited to make this little journey. It is free of obstructions, offers sure footing and has an interesting texture that works well with nearby structures and plants. Many walkways broaden as the destination nears—another subconscious hint that something special is about to be discovered.

Landscape Additions

Walkways draw lines in a landscape, strongly influencing its style. Straight, symmetrical lines are formal and neat. Curving lines suggest a more informal, relaxed feel. Straight walkways make distances seem shorter, which is a real asset to a walkway that connects your back door to your garbage cans. Curving walkways flanked with attractive plants invite you to take it slow and enjoy the view.

Plan your path to be as wide as possible. A walkway must always be at least 30 inches wide to accommodate a single person, but a 48- or 60-inch-wide path allows two people to walk side by side.

Budgeting for a Walkway

Time and money are important design considerations, for no plan is a good one if it's impossible to carry out. As you will see in the following pages, some kinds of walkways are inexpensive and easy to install while others may turn into disasters if you don't hire professional help. But if you take time to study your site, carefully consider materials and jot down a written plan, you can probably solve most walkway problems on your own.

Curved walkways and beds add an element of relaxed flow to any garden or home entryway. Here, the neutral tones of a flagstone walk bring out the bright colors of the adjacent border planting.

MATERIALS FOR WALKWAYS

Choose materials that will blend with your yard's existing features and buildings. This helps create a cohesive, well-planned landscape which you will continue to enjoy throughout each season.

The drainage situation in your yard will also affect what materials you choose. Whenever you alter the surface of a site by adding a walkway, you also change the way rainwater filters

Use a cushiony mulch beneath children's play equipment.

and drains. Before starting work on your walkway, observe the site in dry and wet conditions. Any type of paved surface will produce runoff rather than allowing water to percolate into the soil. Plan hard-surfaced paths so that they channel water away from structures and entrances to buildings. A slight slope across the path will direct water to one side or the other.

Brick pavers.

Brick Pavers

Special bricks made for walkways, called pavers, are more dense than regular bricks; pavers absorb less water and are less prone to breakage due to freezing and thawing. The standard size for a brick paver is 4 inches wide by 8 inches long, and $1\frac{1}{4}$ to $1\frac{1}{2}$ inches thick (regular building bricks are at least 2 inches thick). You will need about $4\frac{1}{2}$ pavers for every square foot of walkway space, but work with your dealer to estimate how many bricks

you will need to work any of the popular patterns (shown on pages 65). To reduce the need for cutting pavers, choose a simple pattern and make the dimensions of your walkway even multiples of the dimensions of the pavers you choose.

Straight walkways exaggerate distance and often appear longer than they really are.

Interlocking Pavers

When shopping for bricks or stone, also look at preformed interlocking pavers. Available at home supply centers in a variety of patterns and colors, interlocking pavers are handled and installed like unmortared brick or stone. The pieces must fit together very tightly to keep the pattern even and symmetrical. Interlocking pavers cost more than regular brick pavers but may be worth it for small areas where looks are important.

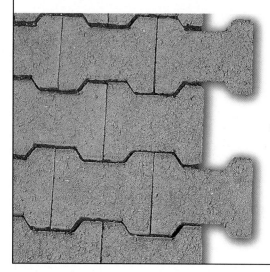
Interlocking pavers.

Flagstone comes in a wide range of colors.

Stone

In landscaping, flagstone is one of several types of rock available in flat pieces with irregularly shaped edges. Very high-quality flagstone suitable for indoor use is expensive, but landscape-grade material, customarily sold by the ton, costs much less. Flagstone seldom cracks in a properly constructed walkway, but the stones do shift so that some areas may become uneven. Weeds often find their way into the crevices between stones too. Because flagstone varies in its thickness and weight, it is best to work with a dealer to determine exactly how much you need. Flagstone's greatest advantage is its natural beauty.

Stone.

Concrete

Concrete is made of four ingredients: Portland cement, sand, gravel or pieces of stone (called aggregate) and water. Most do-it-yourselfers use pre-mixed products to which only

Part of the appeal of this concrete walkway is its width. Two people can approach the entry walking side-by-side.

water must be added. Some large home centers sell pre-mixed concrete in 20-pound bags. However, heavier 60 or 80-pound bags are more common and practical. A 60-pound bag of dry mix will yield enough concrete to cover about 2 square feet of walkway 4 inches thick. Botched concrete can be a very heavy mistake. Do not undertake large jobs if you have no experience with concrete. Good projects for beginners are described later in this chapter.

Wood chip mulch ensures firm footing in the central corridor of a lush flower garden.

Pine needles decompose slowly, seldom host diseases, and have a rich color that works well with many different plants.

Mulch

Simple mulched pathways can work very well in areas that are not subjected to heavy traffic. Materials for mulched paths include wood chips, straw, pine needles, gravel and various types of shredded bark. Mulched walkways are inexpensive to construct, but they must be raked, weeded and replenished from time to time. You will also need to install a solid edging of 2 by 4 lumber, landscape timbers, closely spaced plants or stones to keep the mulch in place. Some types of mulch offer little traction and may not be appropriate for walkways that will be used by toddlers and senior citizens. A 2- to 4-inch-deep, fairly fine-textured mulch forms a soft, resilient surface ideal for children's play areas.

Redwood bark nuggets.

MATH FOR MEASURING MATERIALS

To make the design process easier, take measurements and draw a diagram of the finished project. This helps with layout and estimating materials. Mark out the new path with wooden stakes and connect the stakes with string or twine. Determine the square footage of the surface area of the path by multiplying the length by the width.

Measure both the surface area and the depth of the various layers to determine the volume of material required to construct a walkway. For example, a walkway 4 feet wide and 30 feet long equals 120 square feet. If you want to fill or cover it with 4 inches of gravel, you would multiply 120 by 4. Then divide by 12 to convert the measurement to cubic feet. To convert

cubic feet to cubic yards divide by 27.

Here's an example: For the amount of sand needed for a 2-inch-deep bed beneath bricks for a 120-square-foot path, the numerical equation would be 120 (square feet) x 2 (depth in inches) = 240. Divide by 12 to convert this measurement to 20 cubic feet of sand or about ¾ cubic yard (20 divided by 27).

IMPROVE YOUR ENTRYWAY

Before you launch into any building project, carefully study your entryways.

Every entry involves some kind of walkway, which is typically made of a hard material like concrete, brick or stone. A clean, all-weather walking surface right outside the door goes a long way toward keeping indoor floors free of outdoor debris.

Entryways should be safe, clean and welcoming. Because the entry is the first place that you or a visitor will stop to look around, the entry helps set the style and mood for the rest of the landscape.

However, several other factors are important elements in developing a pleasing entryway, including the seven discussed here.

A sure way to keep garden soil out of your house: Park your shoes outside the door.

How to Create a Welcoming Entrance–7 Guidelines

1. Keep It Clean

Choose entryway plants that produce minimal litter and have a naturally neat form. Small evergreen shrubs, groundcovers and flowers that have compact growth habits will not crowd the entryway. Never plant shrubs or trees that shed berries or nuts near a door. Smashed berries will surely turn up on your carpet and walking on nuts is not much different from walking on marbles. Also take care to place flowerpots, benches or other objects where they will not take up needed walkway space or become obstacles to foot traffic.

2. Finish the Edges

Edge your walkway with low plants or lawn. To make a cramped entry seem more spacious, use plants on the house side of the walkway and let the other side open into lawn with no edging plants between the walkway or the lawn. Dwarf flowers that bloom white or pale pastel bring light to a walkway at night and also tend to make small spaces seem larger. To make the edge interesting year-round, you may want to plant a series of widely-spaced dwarf shrubs. In summer, place containers planted with annuals between the shrubs.

An effective entryway: An edging of lawn that expands the area, while soft pastels contrast with the lawn and white picket fence.

3. Improve Lighting

Unless you want to meet guests at their car with flashlight in hand, make sure your entries are well lit at night. Lampposts, small spotlights and low area lights that emit a soft glow are some of the options available. See page 140 to learn more about outdoor lighting.

You probably already know where you most need secure walkways. Worn places in the lawn, spots where you find yourself tiptoeing through flower beds or frequently-traveled passageways that feel like obstacle courses are the first problem areas to identify and set right.

A well-lit entryway welcomes guests and makes them feel safer. It also dramatizes the contours of bordering shrubs and other "Welcome!" plants.

When placing containers near entryways, allow plenty of open space near corners or steps.

4. Check Your Steps

Entryway steps deserve close scrutiny. If existing steps are too few or far between, replacing them may be in order. Entries that include more than three steps should have a sturdy handrail.

5. Add a Landing

In addition to a walkway, most entries benefit from a broader area near the front door called a landing. You can greatly enhance a lackluster entry walkway by adding a large, flat landing at the base of your front steps. In the back of your house, a deck serves the same purpose as a landing.

6. Unify with Color

Use color to link your front door with another point farther away, so that the two points unify the landscape and subtly underscore the door as a destination. For example, you might paint your front door a rich green or wine red and repeat the color near the street—perhaps with your mailbox or a small entry gate. Planters filled with flowers provide numerous opportunities to use this design trick during the summer.

7. Add a Focal Point

As the entry draws near, install a small piece of statuary, etched boulder or other minor focal point to bring a little excitement to the area. Keep the focal point simple to avoid a cluttered look.

The front fence and gate echo the style and color of this house, giving the entryway a feeling of solid unity.

Buried Bricks

Older homes often have hidden surprises an inch or two below the soil—forgotten walkways made of old brick. Should you discover such an asset in your yard, use a hammer and ½-inch rebar stake to explore the size of the walkway. If it is within ½ inch of the surface, you may be able to restore it by giving it a good going over with a high-pressure power washer and vacuuming up the mud with a wet-dry utility vacuum. If the walk is deeply buried or badly buckled, dig up the bricks and reset them in a new-old walkway. See page 64 for information on working with unmortared brick.

A well-maintained brick walkway behind an older home.

A WALKWAY MAKEOVER

Many homes already have concrete walkways that connect either the parking area or the sidewalk to the front door. These may not be attractive or functional. Perhaps the concrete has cracked or discolored, the walkway may be too narrow, or shrubs may have grown so large that they take up important walkway space.

If this sounds like your house, try a series of small improvements before resigning yourself to a renovation that involves jack-hammers, bulldozers and concrete trucks.

Rent a high-pressure power washer to clean the concrete, trim back the shrubs or replace them with more compact species. Open up the area on either side of the walkway with a broad band of mulch or stone.

If you want a more attractive texture, another option is to use old concrete as a foundation for laying brick pavers, interlocking pavers and various types of outdoor tile. You will need mortar to hold the new paving in place, so you may want to hire an experienced mason to do this job.

Sometimes a good cleaning is all that is needed to improve the appearance of weathered concrete.

NATURAL PATHWAYS AND PLAY AREAS

In keeping with the notion of matching the paving material with the site in which it is used, mulched pathways are a simple solution when you need a safe passageway through a shade garden or woodland area. Walkways paved with natural mulch allow air, water and nutrients to pass through to tree roots below. Because they form natural cushions, mulch is the preferred paving for areas around children's play equipment where lawn grass has worn away and left muddy holes. Pet pens and the ground around your compost pile also are prime areas for covering with mulch.

Mulching Pathways

Any site where mulch is used as a pathway paving must be reasonably level, or the material will wash away in heavy downpours. Mulch is not the best choice near entryways, as you will undoubtedly track the material indoors on your shoes, especially in wet weather.

Edge a mulched path with stones or landscape timbers, or you could use clump-forming plants. Ferns, liriope and hosta grow well in partial shade and look very natural when placed right next to a mulched walkway. Mulched pathways are inexpensive to construct and easy to maintain, even when you factor in the cost of edging materials or plants.

Landscape timbers help stabilize a sloping section of a mulched pathway.

Finely-shredded wood chips pave a pathway in a woodland garden. Featured: rhododendrons and dainty blue phlox.

TIP   Special Effects

When a walkway from one part of your garden leads into another, switching from a tailored hard surface to a more relaxed mulch paving signals a change in mood and style. For example, you might use brick or stone to pave your primary walkway, then switch to a softer natural mulch as the walk nears a shady area or water feature. To emphasize this change, install a small gate or flank the transition point with specimen shrubs or clumps of ornamental grasses.

Materials for Mulched Paths

Save money by using locally available mulch materials. Some are even free if you are willing to gather and transport them yourself. Some examples of locally available materials include cocoa shells, pecan shells, peanut shells, roughly ground corncobs, spent hops and ground tobacco stems.

The following materials may be easily purchased at large garden centers. Or, maybe you'll be lucky enough to find a local source!

Pine needles.

- **Pine straw** has a waxy coating that makes it naturally resistant to decay. It has a fine texture that is visually pleasing and is comfortable when you walk on it barefoot. You can often gather free pine needles in the fall, or buy them in compressed bales at large garden centers. Pathways covered with pine straw will need to be replenished at least once a year.

- **Pebbles** bring a light color and fine texture to mulched pathways, but they are not maintenance free. Weeds often spring up in pebble mulches, but they are easy to pull out when young. Pebbles shift underfoot, so they offer very little traction. When using pebbles to pave frequently-traveled pathways, you may want to combine them with pre-cast steppingstones.

- **Bark nuggets** come in varying sizes, and the smaller ones are best for mulched pathways. Bark decomposes slowly, but its light weight makes it wash away easily if it is not enclosed by a secure edging. Bark is sold in bags containing either 2 or 3 cubic feet, or you can buy it by the truckload. When covering pathways, apply bark about 3 inches thick.

Bark nuggets.

- **Straw** is inexpensive and widely available. It has the ability to "knit" itself into bare soil, which helps it stay in place. Wheat and oat straw naturally deter weeds, weather to a buff tan color, then to gray. Because dry straw can be a fire hazard, use it primarily in damp areas of your garden. Straw compacts over time, so start out with a 4- to 5-inch-deep layer.

- **Wood chips** decompose slowly, and you can often get them free for the asking from tree-trimming crews. These will be rough pieces of differing sizes, so they will form a rustic surface that weathers to gray. Purchased cedar or cypress hardwood mulches have a reddish color and finer texture, so they may work better in high-visibility areas. Cedar or pine chips naturally deter fleas, so they are ideal for covering bare soil in dog pens.

Pebbles or river gravel.

Straw.

SUPPRESSING WEEDS

If your mulched pathway is in a shady area, you will probably have few problems with weeds. But weeds have a nearly supernatural ability for establishing themselves in any type of mulch used in the sun, including pebbles and wood chips. Reduce weed problems by laying a piece of landscape fabric, weed barrier or perforated black plastic under the mulch. Be sure to cover the smooth "undermulch" with at least 3 inches of coarse natural mulch. If the top layer of mulch becomes thin, the walkway may become dangerously slippery in wet weather.

Landscape fabric keeps weeds from sprouting through pathways made of loose materials like gravel. All the same, lay gravel deeply enough—2 to 4 inches, in most cases—to make your pathway firm underfoot.

Landscape timbers form a natural-looking utility ramp that links this driveway to the yard beyond. It is sturdy enough to carry wheelbarrows, lawn mowers and other heavy equipment.

WORKING WITH CONCRETE

Concrete, the most widely used construction material in the world, provides a hard and permanent walking surface. Concrete is heavy and permanent, so think carefully before putting it to work in your landscape. Large expanses are prone to cracking and are best installed by professionals. However, anyone can complete the simple projects described in the following pages.

Concrete is a simple, inexpensive and permanent walking surface that coordinates well with colorful flowers and rustic stones.

When mixing concrete, add water a little at a time. Begin with 3 quarts of water per 60-pound bag of pre-mixed concrete.

> **TIP Save Your Hide**
>
> Wear heavy rubber gloves, sturdy boots and clothing that will keep wet or dry concrete from contacting your skin. Concrete is caustic enough to burn your skin. It's also a good idea to wear safety goggles and a dust mask to avoid contact with dry particles of cement.

Mixing Concrete

Mix small batches of concrete in a wheelbarrow by using a shovel or a special tool called a mortar hoe (a hoe with two round holes in the blade). Renting a power mixer is a good idea with projects that need more than 500 pounds of dry mix.

To mix concrete to the right consistency, add water to the dry mix a little at a time. If it becomes soupy you have added too much; correct this by adding more of the dry mixture. If the mixture is stiff and crumbly it needs more water. Well-mixed concrete should be of a uniform color. It will slide off of a spade or mason's trowel rather than run.

Work quickly when placing wet concrete into a mold or form, because it begins to harden within minutes. By the time you work out any air bubbles and level the surface, it should be firm enough to round off the edges and start working on the finish. Several interesting finishes are described later.

HOW CONCRETE CURES

Concrete hardens through a chemical reaction. The chemical reaction continues as the concrete cures, so concrete becomes harder with age. For example, new concrete which has set for 24 hours may support 1,000 pounds per square inch. Five-year old concrete will bear 8,500 pounds per square inch.

It is important to "cure" concrete slowly by controlling the loss of moisture, which prolongs the chemical reaction. Concrete that dries too fast will be weak and may crumble away with traffic. Cover wet concrete with plastic for 3 days, or lightly sprinkle the surface with water several times a day for 3 days. Curing may take a little longer in colder weather.

In-Ground Concrete Steppingstones

In a single afternoon you can use concrete to make permanent steppingstones in an eroded pathway. This is also a good way to learn how to handle concrete before moving on to bigger projects.

Concrete will take the shape of any mold into which it is poured, so you can choose any shape that suits you.

Tools, Materials & Timing

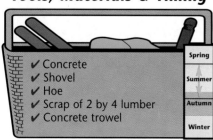

✔ Concrete
✔ Shovel
✔ Hoe
✔ Scrap of 2 by 4 lumber
✔ Concrete trowel

Spring
Summer
Autumn
Winter

1 Remove enough soil to allow a depth of 2 to 3 inches of concrete—the minimum depth needed for strong, durable steppingstones. Lightly dampen the excavated area.

2 Use a shovel and hoe to spread wet concrete in the earthen form. Tamp and compact the concrete at corners and edges to fill all crevices.

3 Use a scrap piece of 2 by 4 lumber to "screed" the surface—a process that compacts and levels concrete at the same time. Move the board across the surface with a rapid back-and-forth sawing motion. Use a shovel or trowel to remove or add extra wet concrete as needed.

4 Smooth the surface of the concrete with a concrete trowel. Arc the back of the trowel back-and-forth over the surface using smooth motions, and add a little water if needed to keep the surface wet. Wait a few minutes, and smooth the surface again. If you want a rough non-skid finish, use a stiff broom as the final finishing step.

Deposit concrete, screed the surface, finish with a trowel.

Dig hole in the shape you want.

When imaginatively used, concrete can imitate flagstone, which is much more costly.

Personalized Finishes

There are many ways to finish a concrete surface to make it more interesting and personal.

Patterns

Use a piece of ½-inch bent copper pipe to produce a pattern of impressions to make your concrete resemble mortared stones. When the water sheen disappears, go over the tops of the "stones" with a trowel. Then clean out the tooled impressions with a paintbrush.

With a little hand finishing, a concrete surface looks like cut stones.

Concrete steppingstone styled into a huge sand dollar.

Concrete with aggregate and inlaid stones.

Concrete with pebble surface.

Impressions

Leaves, shells, seeds, hands, feet and many other objects make lasting impressions in concrete. Coat the surface of leaves and other small objects with an all-purpose spray lubricant before pressing them into wet concrete with a piece of wood. When the water sheen disappears, remove the objects and smooth the surface. You may need to use a fine paintbrush to improve the detail of the impressions.

Seeding

Add a layer of smooth pebbles, glass marble or other decorative stones to the wet concrete as soon as you have screeded the molded concrete. Place the "seed stones" into the concrete in an attractive pattern and press them in with a flat piece of wood until they are flush with the surface but still visible. Finish the surface with a wet rag.

Lay out larger walkway sections by framing with 2 by 4 lumber.

Make a Molded Concrete Walkway

You can make a small concrete walkway or utility ramp by using molds you build yourself. Or use pre-formed molds sold at building supply stores and mail-order catalogs. Concrete walkways

Tools, Materials & Timing

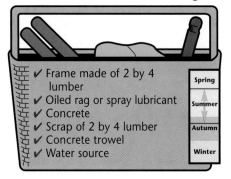

✔ Frame made of 2 by 4 lumber
✔ Oiled rag or spray lubricant
✔ Concrete
✔ Scrap of 2 by 4 lumber
✔ Concrete trowel
✔ Water source

Spring
Summer
Autumn
Winter

must be at least 2 inches thick, so use inexpensive pieces of 1 by 2 lumber to make your own mold. When properly blended with water, a 60-pound bag of premixed concrete will fill a 24- by 24-inch mold. Larger expanses of concrete also need to be thicker and are best molded in frames made of 2 by 4 lumber. When making a mold from wood, screw the corners together instead of using nails.

This style of concrete mold makes a walkway that resembles smooth river rocks. Use the same mold to make a broad landing or a small patio.

1 Measure and mark the site where the concrete will be installed. Remove weeds, grasses and other vegetation by slicing them off at ground level. Do not dig or cultivate the soil, because this softens the foundation. Fill depressions with small rocks or sand and rake it roughly smooth. Compact the site thoroughly by walking over it several times.

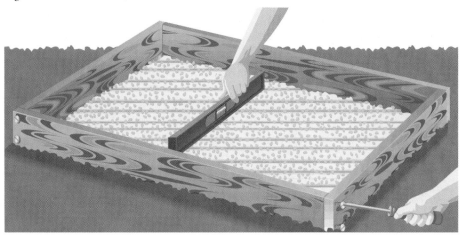

2 Lubricate the mold: Wipe it with an oiled rag or spray the inside with an all-purpose spray lubricant. Place the mold on the prepared ground and secure it in place with two wood stakes. Mix the concrete in a wheelbarrow, mixing only enough to fill the mold one time. Add only as much water as is needed to mix the concrete to a smooth consistency. A 60-pound bag of premixed concrete usually requires a little more than 3 quarts of water.

This concrete mold creates a walkway that looks like it is made of stone. The mold is sized so that it can be completely filled with one 60-pound bag of premixed concrete.

3 Pour the concrete into the mold. Use the tip of a concrete trowel to make diagonal slices into each corner (see diagram). This helps to eliminate air pockets, as does running the trowel through the concrete just inside each edge or mashing the mixture into the corners of the mold with gloved hands. Style the top of the concrete with a piece of scrap lumber (see diagram) to make it smooth and level, or simply use your hands. Work back-and-forth over the surface and the top of the mold. Then smooth the surface with a trowel, adding a light spray of water if needed.

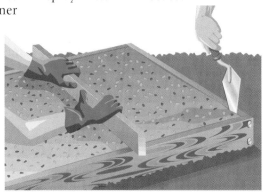

Eliminate air pockets in corners with a trowel, then screed the top of the mix level with a board.

4 After two to three minutes, remove the mold by twisting it slightly and lifting straight up. Immediately begin smoothing the edges and corners with a trowel, gently rounding all edges (sharp corners will easily chip off). Stop briefly to rinse off the mold with a strong spray of water and set it aside to dry. Oil the dry mold again before using it to pour additional molded pads.

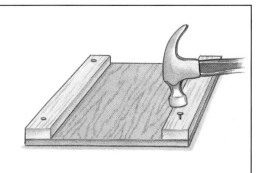

1 Cut the plywood into a square that is 12 inches on each side. Nail two 12-inch-long pieces of 1 by 2 to the bottom of the mold, placing the 1 by 2's parallel to each other 8 inches apart. Cut the 1 by 4 lumber into pieces for the sides. Two sides will be 12 inches long and two sides will be 13½ inches long. Drill 2 guide holes in each end of both of the longer pieces.

Molded concrete turtles with flat backs make fun and functional steppingstones.

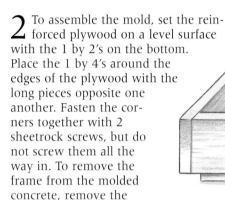

2 To assemble the mold, set the reinforced plywood on a level surface with the 1 by 2's on the bottom. Place the 1 by 4's around the edges of the plywood with the long pieces opposite one another. Fasten the corners together with 2 sheetrock screws, but do not screw them all the way in. To remove the frame from the molded concrete, remove the screws.

Placing Movable, Molded Steppingstones

If you like the idea of personalized steppingstones described on page 61 but don't want to leave your children's footprints behind when you move on to a new home, you can make movable concrete steppingstones in a special mold. This is an easy way to permanently preserve family memories in stone.

Begin by building a box type mold. A 12-inch square is a good size to work with. Use ½-inch exterior grade plywood for the bottom and pieces of 1 by 4 lumber for the sides. You will also need to reinforce the bottom of the mold with 2 pieces of 1 by 2 lumber. Construct the box as shown.

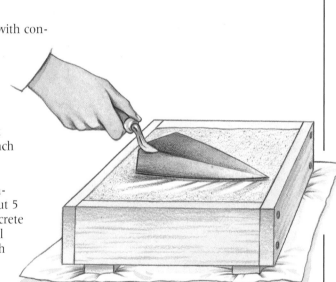

3 Before filling the mold with concrete, place it on a level surface covered with sheet plastic. Lubricate the inside of the mold with vegetable oil. Mix concrete as previously described and place it inside the mold. Each 12-inch steppingstone will require approximately half of a 60-pound bag of premixed concrete. Begin by mixing about 5 shovelfuls of premixed concrete with 1 quart of water. Level the top of the concrete with a scrap piece of lumber, then smooth the top with a trowel. When children make their handprints in the concrete, make sure they wash their hands with soap and water right away. You can use a pencil or a small stick to write dates and name in the concrete, if desired.

Tools, Materials & Timing

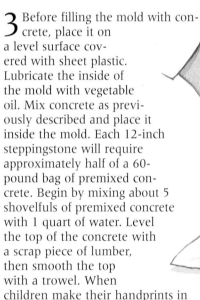

✔ Plywood
✔ Lumber: 1 by 2 and 1 by 4
✔ Concrete mix
✔ Hammer
✔ Water
✔ Trowel
✔ Scrap lumber
✔ Sheetrock screws
✔ Nails
✔ Screwdriver

Spring
Summer
Autumn
Winter

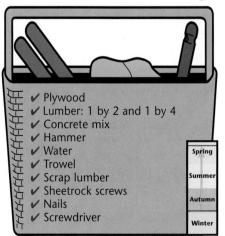

4 Allow the concrete to cure for two days before removing the mold. After disassembling the side pieces, slide the concrete onto a level surface, spray it with water and allow it to cure for three more days. The steppingstone is now ready to move to the landscape, where it will be a family attraction for years to come.

WALKWAYS OF BRICK AND STONE

Brick and stone surfaces are versatile, durable and within the reach of any gardener willing to invest their time and muscle. Both materials are handled in similar ways, though they bring very different textures to the garden. Since individual bricks are small and easily handled, working with brick requires

The richness of unmortared brick is ideal for patios and courtyards. A bonus: Brick is simple to install.

more time than strength. Larger pieces of flat flagstone are sufficiently heavy that you may want to lift a few in the sales yard before committing yourself to installing several hundred. Working with either brick or stone, you can construct a nice walkway gradually or all at once, depending on your preference.

Making Brick and Stone Walkways

The simplest way to make a brick walkway is to set unmortared pavers in a level bed lined with 2 inches of sand. If the walkway abuts an area of lawn, you will need to excavate the site to make your walkway level with the soil's surface. Walkways that separate beds may be constructed so they are higher than surrounding soil.

Some sites benefit from a "settling bed" made of a 2-inch layer of fine gravel or crushed rock. If you have soft, sandy soil that shrinks and swells as the seasons change, excavate an extra 2 inches and fill it with crushed rock before laying down the bed of sand. In any site, if you accidentally dig

Simple yet elegant, a stone walkway is easy to fit into many different types of landscapes. Make sure stones are laid so that the tops are as smooth and level as possible.

too deeply, fill in with gravel or rock instead of soil. Backfilled soil tends to settle over time and may cause cracks and dips in the finished path.

Framing Your Walkway

If you are working with brick pavers, frame the area with lumber held in place with sturdy stakes before you lay in a settling bed or a bed of sand. You will be able to remove the frame if the top of the bricks will be level with the surface, but a raised brick walkway needs a permanent frame. Use treated lumber if the frame is to be left in place indefinitely.

Whether temporary or permanent, make sure the frame

fits your brick pattern perfectly. To get exact measurements, arrange a dozen or so brick pavers on a smooth concrete or asphalt surface and measure the width of the pattern after it is assembled.

A wood frame does not complement stone, so it is customary to lay a stone pathway in a slightly excavated site so that it is level with surrounding surfaces when it is finished. However, you can build a raised frame for a stone walkway using small broken stones set on their sides. This is usually done only when stone walkways are designed as level plateaus on sloping ground. Dig a narrow trench down both sides of the walkway, and fit in the framing stones as tightly as possible. Then proceed to make a sand bed and start laying the paving stones.

Making the Bed

1 With the frame in place, fill the bottom of the site with a settling bed of crushed rock (if needed) and 2 inches of sand.

2 Make a special screed from 2 scrap pieces of lumber—one a foot longer than the width of the walkway, and another 1/4 inch shorter than the walkway's width.

3 Nail the short piece of lumber to the long piece so that when you place the screed over the frame, the short piece will rake over the sand 1½ inches below the top of the frame, or the exact depth of your brick pavers or flagstone. The objective is to use the screed to level the sand so that when the pavers or stones are set on top of the sand bed, they will be even with the top of the frame or surrounding surfaces.

For larger beds, use a 2 by 4 to smooth the sand to an even 2-inch depth.

Fitting the Pieces

1 Begin laying the bricks in your chosen pattern along a straight edge. Use a rubber mallet or the end of a hammer handle to tap the bricks together tightly. If uneven places develop in your work area, smooth the sand with your hand. Stop after completing each tier and tap the top of the bricks to settle them in place.

2 Lay stones in the same way, stopping to rearrange pieces as needed so they fit together well. Some people leave a few large gaps in a stone walkway on purpose, and fill these large crevices with soil and small plants. However, you will get a cleaner look and safer level surface by building a solid level walkway out of stone.

3 With either brick or stone, the last step is to fill the crevices with sand. Scatter sand over your new walkway and use a broom to work it into the crevices. Walk over the bricks, lightly dampen them with water, and add more sand if needed to fill any small holes. It's a good idea to go back after a few weeks and refill the crevices again. If soil rather than sand is allowed to seep into the joints, tough little weeds may appear. Should their roots break off when you pull them, you can steam them to death with boiling water.

TIP   Be Prepared

Especially when laying bricks, keep a small piece of scrap plywood or broad board handy to lay over the sand bed in case you need to step onto the prepared space.

Popular Brick Walkway Patterns

Basket 1.

Basket 2.

Basket 3.

Herringbone.

Running.

Stacked.

◆ CHAPTER 6 ◆

BOUNDARIES:
FENCES, SCREENS AND WALLS

*Add security, definition and drama to your landscape by
furnishing its edges with fences, screens or walls.*

Because humans are territorial creatures, it naturally follows that we find our outdoor spaces more comfortable and enjoyable when those spaces feel like they are uniquely our own. Enclosed spaces feel more private and intimate, and the enclosures themselves may define outdoor living areas or serve more practical purposes. For instance, fences can mark boundaries attractively *and* ensure the safety of pets or children. Use screens to hide unsightly objects from view or create walls made of plants or stone that serve as backdrops for colorful flowers.

Property Survey

Before investing your time and money enclosing any part of your yard, study your property survey. If you own your home, you probably have a survey among the paperwork you received in the purchase. In addition to the exact location of the property lines, you need to know about any easements or setbacks that affect your use of the property's boundaries. Also find the locations of buried utility lines.

Study zoning restrictions and building codes before making elaborate plans for your landscape's boundaries. In many cities, you must obtain a construction permit before building a fence or wall on or near your property line.

Even if your property lines are clearly marked with stakes or markers, it's a good idea to place a fence a few inches inside the property line. Allow more setback space for shrubs and trees. In most situations, plant parts that protrude into your neighbor's space are legally under their control.

As your plans develop, talk them over with neighbors if the changes you want to make will affect their views or the drainage on their property. Potential problems then can be addressed and solutions found before work gets under way.

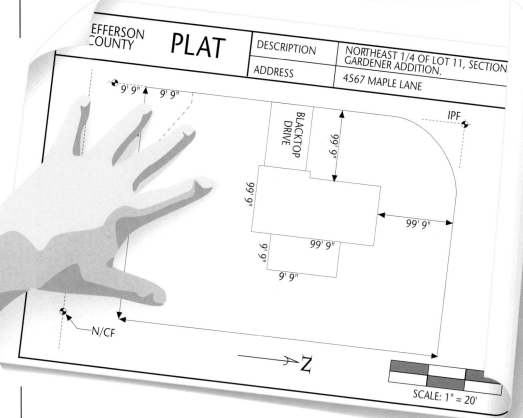

JEFFERSON COUNTY **PLAT**

| DESCRIPTION | NORTHEAST 1/4 OF LOT 11, SECTION GARDENER ADDITION. |
| ADDRESS | 4567 MAPLE LANE |

BLACKTOP DRIVE

IPF

9' 9" 9' 9"

99' 9"

99' 9"

99' 9"

99' 9"

9' 9"

9' 9"

N/CF

N

SCALE: 1" = 20'

OVERHEAD SCREENS AND STRUCTURES

Trees planted along your property's boundary will add a new overhead feature to your home. As sunlight penetrates the trees' canopy, it will change your landscape's floor and ceiling.

Instead of planting trees, you can copy this natural pattern by adding constructed shade-giving structures to your landscape. For example, a lath house with open sides nestled into a group of shrubs is an irresistible shady retreat. Or you might construct a pergola or lattice overhead screen that matches the style of an existing wood fence. A free-standing gazebo becomes an instant focal point that can double as an outdoor dining room, or you can simply use it as a cool and tranquil place to relax.

No matter what kind of structure you use, consider adding plants to it: either hanging baskets, or flowering vines. You'll increase the amount of shade produced, plus make the environment even more relaxing and hidden away.

Silky wisteria forms a fragrant canopy above a wood fence trimmed with decorative lattice work.

MATERIALS FOR BOUNDARIES

When designing boundaries, think of your garden's walls as geometrical extensions of your home. As you study the many different materials you might use to define and enhance your boundaries, imagine how each might coordinate with your house's architecture. Think about scale, too—the size relationship between the boundary and your house.

A low picket fence will look charming with a small house, while massive trees and bushes add substance and elegance when used near a large, tall home. To further focus your planning, think about what you want your boundary to do. Perhaps there is a nice view from your deck that would look even better framed with evergreens. On the other hand, you may want to totally block from view the gas station on the corner. If you have pets or small children, the security of the boundary may be your top priority. One of the approaches discussed below should meet your needs.

A concrete wall fence is camouflaged beneath a thick blanket of firethorn (Pyracantha). Fall fruits follow the spring flowers.

Natural Boundaries

Trees

Shade trees cool a yard on a hot day and continuously dramatize wind, rain and the changing seasons. Closely spaced evergreens planted along your property's boundary can form a windbreak. You can also leave the space between trees open to admit more air and light. Pines are popular for planting along property lines because they grow fast. You can also choose from many smaller ornamental trees including dogwoods, crabapples and other ornamental fruits, as well as numerous other species that grow to less than 30 feet tall.

Superior shrubs for informal hedges include winged euonymus and Hydrangea arborescens. *Both need only casual pruning.*

UNUSUAL TREES FOR SUBURBAN YARDS

These trees grow to less than 30 feet tall, so they fit easily into small yards:

Fringe tree (*Chionamthus virginicus*), Zones 4 to 9
Japanese maple (*Acer palmatum*), Zones 5 to 8
Japanese snowbell (*Styrax japonicum*), Zones 5 to 9
Pistachio (*Pistacia chinensis*), Zones 6 to 9
Redbud (*Cercis canadensis*), Zones 4 to 9
Smoke Tree (*Cotinus obovatus*), Zones 3 to 8
Sourwood (*Oxydendrum arboreum*), Zones 4 to 9

Shrubs

Large shrubs—or groups of smaller shrubs—form walls infused with texture and color while providing habitat for wildlife. Some shrub or shrub combinations will work well with any architectural style. You may need only a few shrubs to showcase your entryway, improve the privacy in your backyard or block out an unwanted view. Evergreen shrubs form a barrier year-round, while deciduous shrubs let in sun during the winter. Clipped hedges always look formal, while unpruned shrubs set a more relaxed mood. Thorny shrubs such as roses and hollies deter two-legged and four-legged intruders. The drawback to using shrubs to define your boundaries is that shrubs need time to grow. Fast-growing shrubs may fill in within 3 years, but 5 years is a more realistic time frame for a good hedge. See page 70 for more information on boundary planting with shrubs.

Electric pruning shears are required equipment for maintaining an evergreen hedge like this one.

A wood fence and gate add a private courtyard to an older home.

Metal Fences

Metal fences are strong and functional. They include chain link, aluminum, wrought iron, electric fencing and barbed wire. The last two are used mostly to control the movement of animals and are not often used in urban or suburban settings. Wrought iron is expensive and requires regular painting, which leaves us with good old chain link—the most popular type of fencing in America. Chain link (and other types of wire fencing) are unsurpassed for keeping pets and small children from wandering too far. In many neighborhoods, the addition of a chain link fence raises the property value by more than the cost of the fence—especially if you use various landscaping tricks to make the fence more attractive (see page 74).

Clematis clings daintily to an iron fence.

Man-Made Boundaries

Wood or Vinyl Fences

If your goal is to create privacy, you will probably be happiest with a wood fence. Solid wood fences take heavy battering from wind, while open or lattice fences filter the wind. With any type of wood fence, you will need gates. Wood fencing varies in price and you will probably need help installing one. Finish a wood fence with water-resistant stain or paint.

Vinyl fencing is made from white PVC vinyl. A vinyl white picket fence costs more than one made of wood, but vinyl does not require painting and it never rots. Whether wood or vinyl, you can turn an open style fence (such as split cedar) into a barrier by planting it with shrubs such as junipers or landscape roses. If you live in a neighborhood, you may want to match the type of fence used in nearby yards.

Stone Walls

Garden walls made of stone or brick are almost maintenance free and give the landscape a sense of permanence. Low walls that are flat on top can double as sitting benches. You can also plant large containers with vines or cascading plants to give the wall more color and texture. Building a stone wall is slow work, but because placement of the stones is imprecise, this is a project that's easy enough for the inexperienced do-it-yourselfer (see page 78). Building a brick wall, however, is best done by a professional.

The formality of a brick wall is emphasized with the symmetry of English ivy and repetitious placement of mealycup sage and marigolds.

PLANT A LIVING FENCE

The most natural type of boundary is a thicket or hedge comprised solely of plants such as shrubs and small trees. Shrubs are texture plants in the garden. When used in a boundary planting, shrubs filter and deflect winds while providing habitat for small birds and other creatures.

Boundary Planting

Use your house's style as a starting point for planning this type of boundary. Clipped hedges planted in a straight line have a strong formal look, but you will need to trim them up to four times a summer to keep them looking neat. In comparison, a boundary that includes a mixture of evergreen and deciduous shrubs is interesting to observe every season and needs little upkeep beyond yearly pruning and mulching.

Pruned boxwood.

Using Shrubs in Boundaries

A single straight row is only one of several ways to use shrubs in a boundary planting. For more depth, consider planting two layers of shrubs in offset

Most shrub cultivars come with tags that suggest proper spacing between plants. To get your hedge or shrub grouping to look fuller, quickly fill the spaces between shrubs with fast-growing ornamental grasses for a year or two or until the shrubs are ready to take over the space.

lines, with evergreens in the background and flowering shrubs in front. If you want to leave open spaces in the planting to allow easy movement through the boundary, plant your shrubs in planned groups that include several different species and repeat the groups between openings. For example, you might weave evergreen and deciduous shrubs together into flowing braids of color, texture and fragrance, and connect them with corridors of open lawn.

THE LANGUAGE OF LEAVES

Needle evergreen shrubs remain green year-round. Many evergreens that are hardy in cold climates have this leaf type, including junipers, dwarf hemlocks and dwarf arborvitaes. Although prickly to touch, needle evergreens have a dense texture and hardly ever need pruning.

Broadleaf evergreens are usually evergreen only in mild winter climates, though they may drop their leaves during an unusually cold winter. When grown in colder climates, broadleaf evergreens such as privet, nandina and abelia become deciduous.

Deciduous shrubs often turn yellow or red in the fall before dropping their leaves. The majority of flowering shrubs are deciduous. Species that develop numerous twiggy branches can work as a screen even in winter.

Juniper, a needle evergreen.

Boxwood, a broadleaf evergreen.

Forsythia, a deciduous flowering shrub.

DEPENDABLE SHRUBS FOR HEDGES AND SCREENS

Boxwood *Buxus sempervirens*, Zones 5 to 10

Dwarf boxwoods frame formal rose beds.

Evergreen. Boxwood is always a top choice for a formal hedge in areas where it will grow. Prune 3 times a year to keep the plants shapely. Common boxwood takes decades to reach its mature height of 15 feet, while dwarf varieties mature to only 2 feet tall after 10 years. Grow boxwoods in full sun or partial shade.

Burning bush, winged euonymous *Euonymus alatus*, Zones 4 to 8

Winged euonymus in fall.

Deciduous. Elegant lateral branches give this shrub a layered look. Famous for its brilliant red fall color, burning bush also has unusual flat "wings" attached to its stems and twigs. Plants look best unpruned. Compact forms grow 6 feet tall, while native types may reach 20 feet. Thrives in sun or partial shade.

Japanese holly *Ilex crenata*, Zones 6 to 9

Evergreen. Prune this tough and flexible shrub into a hedge or allow it to grow into a naturally rounded shape. Japanese holly tolerates drought after established, and some cultivars have reddish leaves. Mature size ranges from 5 to 10 feet. Plant in sun or partial shade.

Juniper *Juniperus* spp., Zones 2 to 9

Versatile junipers.

Evergreen. Junipers come in a variety of sizes and shapes and adapt to many different soils. The prickly, needle-like leaves come in varying shades including blue-, gray- and dark-green, and bright yellow-gold. Plants have strong natural silhouettes and usually require no pruning beyond clipping off injured branches. Size ranges from 2 to 20 feet. Junipers grow best in full sun.

Border Privet *Ligustrum obtusifolium*, Zones 4 to 10

Young privet shrubs.

Deciduous. This fast-growing shrub is virtually indestructible and needs little maintenance. Trim the bushes only to shape them; they are too vigorous to use as a formal clipped hedge. Plants grow 10 to 12 feet high, and thrive in sun or partial shade.

Rugosa Rose *Rosa rugosa*, Zones 2 to 10

Deciduous and thorny. Root suckers form new plants, so a rugosa hedge will grow into a broad thicket. Most cultivars bloom heavily in late spring and set colorful hips by fall. Plants grow 5 to 6 feet high. They can adapt to partial afternoon shade if they get full morning sun.

Lilac *Syringa vulgaris*, Zones 3 to 7

Lilac.

Deciduous. Some lilacs are tall enough for the back of a boundary grouping, while others are much more compact. All produce fragrant flowers in spring. They grow 8 to 15 feet high, depending on cultivar, and prefer full sun to partial shade.

BUILD A WOOD FENCE

Wood's natural look blends easily into any garden. For almost total privacy you can enclose your backyard with a solid wood fence. Or use small sections as backdrops for special plants or to block a small yet undesirable view such as your garbage cans or utility meters. Short picket fences can help frame and unify a small front yard, or use them as partitions between activity areas in other parts of the landscape.

Investing in a Wood Fence

There are three parts to any wood fence: posts, rails and infill. All are available pre-cut and ready-to-install at large building supply stores. Price varies according to the type of wood and amount of shaping and detailing that has been done to create pickets (upright infill pieces) with special designs. For a broad estimate, figure on spending about $150 for materials to build an 8-foot-long section of solid privacy fence 6 feet tall. Materials for a 4-foot-tall picket fence will cost considerably less.

Posts

A wood fence's sturdiness depends on its posts, which may be made from 4 by 4 treated pine, cedar or locust. Cedar, locust and redwood naturally resist rotting and can be set in the ground without concrete. Treated pine posts work best when set in concrete (see pages 60-63 for information on working with concrete). Space posts no more than 8 feet apart and use a level to make sure they are perfectly plumb (straight up and down).

Rails

A wood fence can have either two or three horizontal rails attached to the posts. Lightweight fences, such as 4-foot-tall picket fences, need only two rails, but a solid privacy fence gains strength from a third rail. Treated pine is the most common wood used for rails; hardwoods tend to sag. Attach rails to posts with screws rather than nails.

Infill

Fence style is determined by your choice of infill. For a light, airy look, space horizontal pickets 2 inches apart or use lattice panels for infill. Solid privacy fences utilize flat picket boards made from cedar, fir, spruce or treated pine. To avoid streaks and stains, use aluminum nails to attach cedar pickets to rails, or galvanized nails if you are working with treated pine or redwood.

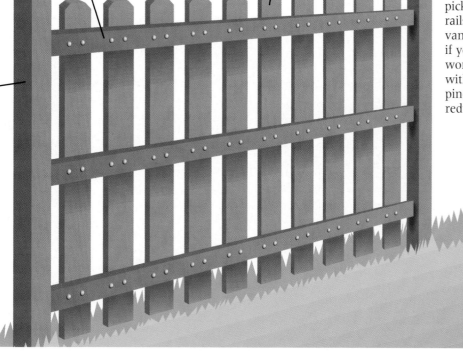

FINISHES FOR WOOD FENCES

The Natural Look

When exposed to sun and rain, wood naturally weathers to a gray or brown color. Cedar and redwood turn such a pretty shade of gray that they are often allowed to weather, but pine and other woods last longer and look better if you paint them with waterseal—a watery substance that's easier to apply than regular paint. Many products are available that tint the wood with a stain and waterseal them at the same time.

Stained wood can hold different types of attachments such as shelves or hayrack planters like this one.

Painting

If you plan to paint your fence, you will need to seal or prime it first. Otherwise the paint will crack and peel as the wood expands and contracts due to changes in moisture and temperature. Use high quality exterior enamel to paint a wood fence, and paint when the weather is warm and dry.

Salvias and rudbeckia flank a decorative white wood fence.

Installing Fence Posts

The most challenging part of building a fence is installing the posts. Decorative 3-foot fences can be attached to posts set only 18 inches deep, but you will need to set posts 36 inches in the ground if you are building a solid privacy fence or panel. If you are setting fewer than five holes, use a posthole digger to dig holes 3 times the width of the post. Rent a power auger to dig more numerous postholes.

A Fence Builder's Toolbox

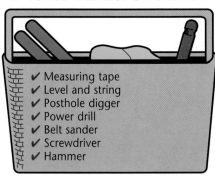

✔ Measuring tape
✔ Level and string
✔ Posthole digger
✔ Power drill
✔ Belt sander
✔ Screwdriver
✔ Hammer

1 Dig a 36-inch-deep hole, 3 times the width of your post. Place a flat stone at the bottom of the hole, set the post on it and then place sufficient gravel in the hole to cover the base of the post.

2 Fill the hole with concrete or a mixture of soil and gravel. Tamp soil thoroughly while adjusting the post to make it perfectly plumb.

3 When setting posts in concrete, bring the concrete up above the soil line and slant it away from the post. You may need to temporarily brace the post with a piece of scrap lumber to hold it plumb while the concrete sets. Let the concrete cure for at least two days before installing the rails.

4 Don't worry if the tops of your posts are not absolutely level. You can trim these back with a power saw after the posts are installed.

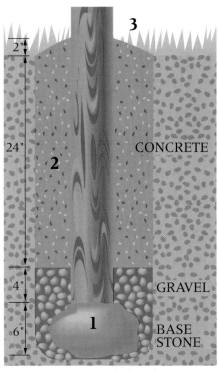

Properly installed postholes will provide a solid, straight base for your fence for years and years.

Popular Posthole Diggers

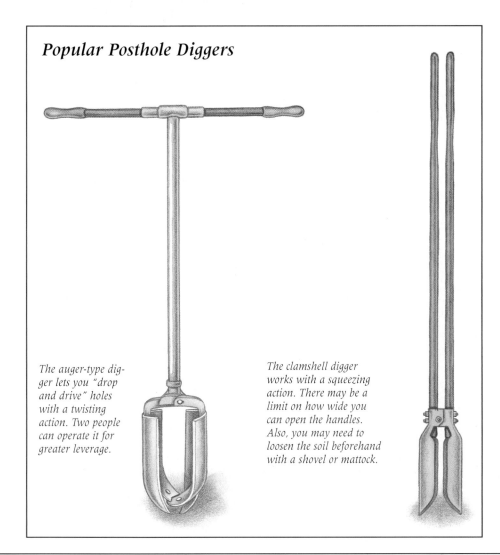

The auger-type digger lets you "drop and drive" holes with a twisting action. Two people can operate it for greater leverage.

The clamshell digger works with a squeezing action. There may be a limit on how wide you can open the handles. Also, you may need to loosen the soil beforehand with a shovel or mattock.

TIP Sanding Savvy

If you want a refined look for your fence, go over each infill piece lightly with a sander using a medium-grade sandpaper. Smooth down rough spots and large splinters, but do not attempt to make the wood furniture-quality smooth. The easiest way to sand is to lay the pieces out on sawhorses at waist level. Wear a dust mask and protective goggles when sanding, especially if you are working with treated pine. Sawdust from treated pine is toxic: Do not dispose of it in your compost heap.

CHARM YOUR CHAIN LINK FENCE

Chain link fencing is so durable and long lasting that it is sometimes called hurricane fencing, for that's what it might take to destroy one of these fences. Ideal for keeping pets safe (or keeping neighboring pets out), metal chain link is the most common type of fencing in America. Used near garden areas, chain fencing admits air and light, and can be used as a ready-made trellis for climbing plants. Another bonus: Chain fence does not block the view to other areas. The challenge: Chain link is not an especially attractive fencing option. But we offer some tune-up ideas here.

Fence Installation

Professional installation of a chain link fence is a good deal. Posts must be absolutely secure and straight, and are usually set in concrete. As the fencing goes up, it must be tightly stretched to keep it from sagging. Fencing companies have the special equipment needed to do the job right.

Morning glories dress up even the plainest chain link fence.

TIP Painted Chain Link

To improve your chain link fence's appearance, paint it black or dark green. This makes it look less utilitarian and helps blend the fence into the rest of the landscape. Painted chain link also makes any flowers you grow next to the fence look a little better. Use a deep pile roller to paint the fence, then finish off the posts and poles with a brush, or use an electric spray painter. Paint stores sell special rust-retardant self-priming paints that give good coverage with one coat. For one coat, you will need a quart of paint per 20 feet of standard 4-foot-tall fencing.

How do you make a chain link fence beautiful? Paint it dark green or black and surround it with beautiful plants.

Bringing Chain Link to Life

Put chain link to work as a trellis for any type of vine that twines or clings to support with tendrils. Hardy perennial vines such as clematis and honeysuckle produce beautiful flowers, or you can go with vines grown primarily for their foliage such as dutchman's pipe (*Aristolochia*) and five leaf akebia (*Akebia quinata*).

Before you plant a vigorous perennial vine on your fence, it's a good idea to experiment with annual vines first. If you're so delighted with your annual vines that you decide your fence deserves coverage year after year, move on to locally adapted perennials.

Clematis gets just the right amount of support from chain link, which has been painted dark green. Shown here is Clematis montana *var.* rubens.

LOW-MAINTENANCE PLANTING

Skirting the base of a fence with clump-forming plants such as daylilies or iris reduces maintenance chores because the plants form a thick mass that weeds cannot penetrate. Mulching the base of the fence with a thick layer of leaves will also help control weeds. Without some sort of mask or skirt along its base, you will need to use a string trimmer to clean up the base of your fence frequently during the summer. This can be a slow and frustrating task because chain link fencing has a tremendous talent for eating up string trimmer line.

Lemon yellow daylilies suppress weeds at the base of the fence and are lovely to behold.

SIX FINE ANNUAL VINES

These vigorous vines often reseed themselves, and may become weedy if the fence adjoins fertile garden beds. To be on the safe side, grow morning glory and other reseeding annuals along a section of fence bordered by lawn that is regularly mowed.

Morning glory.

Morning glory
Ipomoea tricolor
Tremendously heat tolerant, showy morning glory flowers open in the morning and close at midday. White moonvine (*I. alba*) is strongly fragrant at night. Cardinal climber (*I. quamoclit*) has ferny, soft-textured foliage and seldom becomes weedy. Soak the hard seeds overnight before planting to improve germination. Direct sow or transplant morning glories.

Sweet pea.

Sweet pea
Lathyrus odoratus
Sweet peas are the ideal fence vine for cool climates. The blossoms make fine cut flowers, and some varieties are highly fragrant. Soak the seeds overnight before planting: After hot weather comes, expect your sweet peas to stop flowering and die.

Black-eyed Susan vine
Thunbergia alata
Grow this vine as much for its lush green foliage as for its flowers. In warm weather, black-eyed Susan vines will completely hide a chain fence. Yellow, orange or white flowers with dark throats appear until frost. Start seeds indoors in spring and set out the plants after the last frost has passed. This vine is a strong reseeder, and may be perennial in mild winter climates.

Black-eyed Susan vine.

Scarlet runner bean
Phaseolus coccineus
This vigorous, fast-growing summer vine produces bright red blossoms that attract hummingbirds. Pods are edible when very young and tender, but the main reason to grow scarlet runner bean is its flowers. Sow seeds where you want them to grow after the last spring frost has passed.

Scarlet runner bean.

Cup-and-saucer vine.

Cup-and-saucer vine
Cobaea scandens
Perennial in Zones 8 and 9, cup-and-saucer vine thrives in hot sun. By midsummer, the thick foliage is punctuated with large bell-shaped lavender flowers. Start fresh seeds indoors in spring and set out the plants two weeks after the last frost has passed.

Hyacinth bean.

Hyacinth bean
Dolichos lablab
Another warm weather wonder, hyacinth bean is similar to a pole-type lima bean, but much prettier. The purple flowers coordinate beautifully with the reddish purple stems and leaf margins. Soak seeds in water for a few hours before planting them in warm, sun-drenched soil.

ENRICH A WOODLAND EDGE

I f part of your property has shade trees or woods along its edge, you have a special microclimate that's ideal for a unique group of plants. The ecology of a woodland edge is well represented in nature—think of the banks of a stream or the rim of a natural meadow. Because of this, a number of low-maintenance native plants find such spots much to their liking.

Light becomes brighter along the front edge of this woodland garden. The color of the painted wood fence makes the most of available light toward the rear.

Creating an Understory

Any shrub that grows naturally as an "understory" woodland plant is a good candidate for an enriched woodland edge. It's wise to place emphasis on natives because this microclimate can cause problems for cultivated plants. Native or not, to thrive in a woodland edge a plant must be able to use light and moisture during the winter, when trees are bare, and tolerate shade and dry soil during the summer. Above all, they must be able to get along peacefully with tree roots.

Make footpaths through the area so you can enjoy being in your woodland garden. Don't be surprised to find yourself in the company of birds, chipmunks, frogs and other wildlife. You can work in a woodland garden, too. Perhaps a hidden pocket of shade is the perfect place for composting leaves or there's a nice tree branch that would make the ideal summer canopy for a potting table.

Placing Plants: Layers

"Stacking" plants in layers according to their sizes and light requirements maximizes the growing space along a woodland edge and looks good as well.

If your edge is a straight line, you will be able to enlarge your growing space by pulling the front of the woodland garden out into a broad curve.

- **Tall pine or hardwood trees** (layer one) might give way to ...

- **Smaller trees** like dogwoods or redbuds (layer two) that stretch out into ...

- **Azaleas or hydrangeas** underplanted with crocuses or other little bulbs (layer three).

- **The front edge** (layer four) is the place for colorful woodland perennials like those described on the next page.

The approach to this woodland garden: A soft blanket of mixed hardy ferns.

Neat Native Ferns

You can grow many native ferns in a woodland garden, but you'll need to prepare a special place for them. Before setting out container-grown ferns, dig a 2-inch layer of peat moss into the site along with an equal amount of composted manure. Then, unless the site is naturally damp, snake a soaker hose or drip irrigation pipe over the bed and barely cover it with soil (see pages 36-37 for more information on this watering method). Although most native ferns will survive droughts, they will look much better if their roots are kept lightly moist at all times.

Azaleas are native to open woodlands, so they adapt easily to limited light and acidic soil.

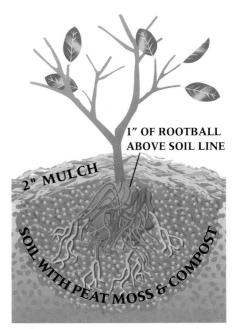

2" MULCH

1" OF ROOTBALL ABOVE SOIL LINE

SOIL WITH PEAT MOSS & COMPOST

A moist, slightly acidic soil amended with peat moss and rotted leaves compost will provide a humus-rich home for azaleas. A constant layer of acidic mulch will insulate the shallow roots and keep them moist.

The Art of Planting Azaleas

Azaleas and rhododendrons are premier shrubs for a woodland garden—provided you can give them moist, acidic soil that drains well. Before planting container-grown plants, enrich the soil with acidic forms of organic matter such as peat moss or rotted leaves. Here's how to plant:

1 Remove the plant from its pot and set in the prepared spot so that one inch of the root ball remains above the soil line.

2 Gently rake up loose soil to barely cover the topmost roots, and water thoroughly.

3 Mulch with at least 2 inches of an acidic mulch such as pine needles, bark or rotted sawdust. The first year after planting, water as needed to keep the shallow roots constantly moist. Renew the mulch regularly to provide excellent insulation for the fibrous roots.

Spring Color from Perennial Plants

Numerous woodland wildflowers will grow in a woodland edge with little care. The spring bloomers described here will stay pretty longer if watered in early summer. Without water, expect the plants to die back when hot weather comes. They will reappear the following spring.

Cranesbill.

Cranesbill (*Geranium maculatum*) puts on a great show of pink flowers in late spring. The plants grow from tough rhizomes and form long-lived colonies. Adapted in Zones 5 to 8.

Blue phlox (*Phlox divaricata*) forms airy sprays of lavender blue flowers on 12-inch-tall plants. Loose colonies form flowing drifts on the woodland floor. Good in Zones 4 to 8.

Blue phlox.

Solomon's seal.

Solomon's seal (*Polygonatum biflorum*) has a brief period of bloom but persists through summer as a dramatic foliage plant. Thrives in rich, moist soil in Zones 4 to 8.

Columbine (*Aquilegia canadensis*) produces showy spurred flowers on long wiry stems. The foliage is also attractive. Established plantings reseed themselves in Zones 3 to 8.

Columbine 'Nora Barlow'.

TIP Hang Up Your Rake

One of the special characteristics of a woodland garden is the mulch that naturally forms when leaves fall to the ground in autumn. So never rake the "floor" of this type of garden! Upkeep consists mostly of pulling or chopping out unwanted plants, and scattering a bit of fertilizer about in the spring.

Leave those leaves! A woodland garden features its own "forest floor," a mulch of fallen leaves and other organic matter.

CREATE A STONE WALL GARDEN

When the boundary for your garden ends in an upward slope, a stone wall will stop erosion while enriching the scene with a look of rugged permanence. Best of all, your wall doubles as a rock garden as you fill crevices with plants that delight in wrapping their roots around rocks.

Tools & Materials

✔ Shovel
✔ Wheelbarrow
✔ Heavy work gloves
✔ Soil amendments
✔ Sand
✔ Stones

Beds and passageways within this elevated garden are held in place with stone. Cascading plants help soften craggy edges.

Building a stone wall garden is not difficult, but it's not a project to speed through quickly. Handling stones is heavy work, and stacking them is an artful process that deserves slow and careful scrutiny.

Building the Wall

1 Dig a foundation for the wall. To help the wall withstand the slope's natural pressure, angle the foundation slightly so the back edge is 2 inches deeper than the front. Place your largest, flattest stones in the foundation to form the first layer. Fill large crevices with a mixture of soil and sand.

2 Set the second tier of stones in an offset pattern so they are centered over the crevices in the previous layer. The wall will tilt slightly into the slope if you set each tier so the front edge is ¼ to ½ inch behind the edge of the tier below it. Use small rocks as wedges to help hold wobbly rocks in place. Stand back and take a look at your work. Rearrange any rocks that appear awkward.

3 Begin planting crevices and backfilling behind the wall as soon as the rocks are in place. Place soil behind the wall and use a broom handle to poke soil into pockets and crevices. Backfill soil a few inches at a time. Stop often to water the loose soil to settle it. Set aside some large, flat rocks and use these for your wall's top tier. Although you may not plan to sit or walk on the wall, any child left to their own devices certainly will.

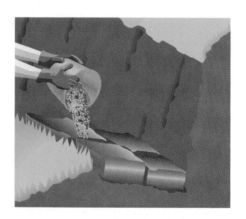

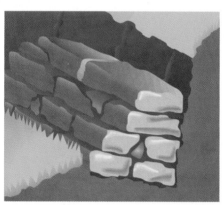

WALL BUILDING TOOLS

You will need a shovel, wheelbarrow and at least two pairs of heavy work gloves. To protect your toes from accidents, always wear sturdy shoes or steel-toed boots when handling heavy stones. Place a piece of plywood over nearby areas of lawn and park your stones on the plywood until you get them stacked. As your wall nears completion and you start filling pockets and crevices with plants, you will also need soil amendments including compost, peat moss and sand.

Heavy gloves are required equipment for building a stone wall.

SLOPING WALLS

A stone wall built into a slope will get plenty of support from the soil behind it, so there is no need to use mortar. The slope will also exert constant pressure on the wall. Low walls (less than 2 feet high) can withstand this pressure, but higher walls may crumble or pop loose after heavy rains. If this is your first time working with stone, stick with a low wall about 18 inches high and 12 to 14 inches deep.

Planting Your Wall

Setting a plant in a stone wall involves stuffing a suitable soil mixture into the planting crevices, then laying in the plant with its roots spread as wide as possible. Top the roots and adjoining rocks with ½ to 1 inch of the soil mixture. Then water thoroughly and go on to the next tier of rocks.

- **For ferns** set near the base of the wall, use a mixture of 2 parts soil, 2 parts peat moss and 1 part each sand and composted manure.

- **For fibrous-rooted plants** such as basket-of-gold (*Aurinia saxatile*) and moss pink (*Phlox subulata*), mix equal parts of soil, composted manure and sand.

- **For succulents** such as sedums and sempervivums, mix equal parts of soil, leaf mold, sand and composted manure.

Three levels of low stone walls give this garden plenty of depth, and allow for the use of lawn, formal plantings of 'Autumn Joy' sedum, and an informal garden where plants can be grown just for the fun of it.

BUYING STACKING STONE

Limestone, sandstone and other types of stratified rock naturally break into flat-sided blocks, so they are easy to stack into a stable wall without the help of mortar. Stone is customarily sold by the ton. Most suppliers will deliver large orders. You will need one ton of stone to build a wall 18 inches high and 20 feet long. Buy extra stone if you can. When building gets underway, it's great to have a big pile to pick through when you're looking for just the right rock.

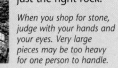

When you shop for stone, judge with your hands and your eyes. Very large pieces may be too heavy for one person to handle.

PERENNIALS FOR A STONE WALL GARDEN

Small plants such as these allow your stone wall's beauty and texture to show through their flowers and foliage. Although these and other rock garden plants do not need constant water, do keep them lightly moist for the first two months after planting. When you water the wall, sufficient water should seep through the crevices to the plants' roots.

Name	Botanical Name	Description	Adaptability
Basket-of-gold	*Aurinia saxatilis*	Cascading green stems covered with gold flowers in spring.	Sun or partial shade in Zones 5 to 10.
Hen-and-chickens, houseleek	*Sempervivum* spp.	Hardy succulents with gray or green leaves.	Full sun to partial shade in Zones 4 to 9.
Moss pink	*Phlox subulata*	Narrow green leaves; spring flowers in pink, white or lavender.	Sun or partial shade in Zones 3 to 9.
Rock cress	*Arabis* spp.	Gray-green leaves; fragrant white or pink flowers in spring.	Sun and gritty soil in Zones 3 to 9.
Stonecrop	*Sedum* spp.	Green leaves, mostly yellow flowers in late spring.	Sun or partial shade in Zones 4 to 9.

Basket-of-gold (Aurinia saxatilis) is an evergreen with colorful late spring flowers. It grows to 8 inches high and spreads to 20 inches wide.

Hen-and-chickens will cover wall areas with new flocks of delightful rosettes.

Moss pink.

Stonecrop.

◆ CHAPTER 7 ◆

FLOWERS:
GROWING ANNUALS,
PERENNIALS AND BULBS

*Colorful flowers become instant focal points in the landscape.
Grow different types to have color all season long.*

Sooner or later, flowers capture the heart of every gardener. There are literally thousands of different ones to try, each with their own distinct colors, forms and fragrances. Whether you grow flowers in containers, beds or even a meadow, you will not have to look far to find species that thrive in your climate and soil.

Flower Categories

Most flowers fall into one of three categories which describe their life cycle and reproductive habits. These are annuals, perennials and bulbs.

- **Annuals** are plants that sprout from seed, then flower and produce mature seeds within one year's time. Many annuals bloom for six weeks or more. Some shed so many seeds that they

One of the easiest annuals to sow and grow, nasturtium flowers are beautiful and the leaves are edible too.

LANDSCAPING WITH FLOWERS

Use flower's vibrant colors to emphasize parts of your yard that are easily seen from both inside and outside your home. Most flowers need at least a half day of sun to bloom well, and all but a few require soil that drains quickly after heavy rains.

come up on their own in subsequent seasons. Starting large-seeded annuals from seeds is fun and economical. Try growing your own seedlings of cosmos, marigold, morning glory, nasturtium, sunflower and zinnia. It's not difficult to start small-seeded annuals either, but they grow very slowly at first. Buy bedding plants of small-seeded annuals such as petunias, impatiens and snapdragons to save several weeks of growing time.

The majority of annual flowers grow from spring to fall, but a few hardy ones are so attuned to cool weather that they can be planted in fall for bloom the next spring. Popular hardy annuals include pansies, snapdragons, some dianthus, corn poppies and larkspur.

- One plant category "in between" annuals and perennials are the **biennials**. Plant a biennial from seed and it will grow the first year but flower the second; then you need to re-plant. Popular biennials include the foxgloves and sweet William (*dianthus*).

- **Perennials** are long-lived plants that die back to the ground in fall and return the following spring. Perennials usually do not bloom for as long a period of time as annuals, but while they are in bloom they are simply spectacular. Some perennials are as valued for the color and texture of their foliage as much as for their flowers—for example hosta, daylily, and heuchera (coral bells). Flowers such as peonies and daylilies grow indefinitely with little attention. However, many perennials need regular dividing and replanting.

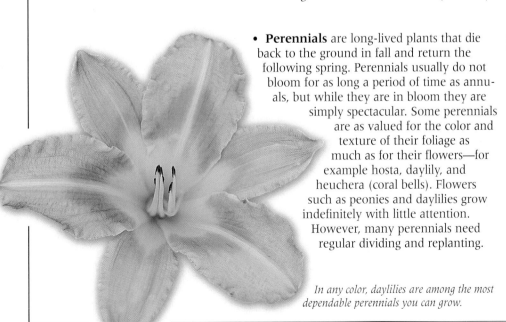

In any color, daylilies are among the most dependable perennials you can grow.

- **Bulbs** are perennials with specialized storage roots. Bulbs bloom at specific times and usually for no more than three weeks. When grown in hospitable climates, many bulbs can prosper for generations. In spring, you can often tell where old homesteads once stood by the presence of daffodils. In addition to true bulbs (which have roots that look like onions) many other flowers that develop thick storage roots are commonly referred to as bulbs. These include dahlias, iris and gladiolus.

Plant tulip bulbs in the fall for a colorful display in spring.

DEVELOP A STYLE

One of the best ways to use flowers is to put them to work defining your landscape's style. To begin, consider your home's architectural style and your personal tastes.

In this formal garden, dahlias, begonias, phlox and verbena are edged with purple lobelia and fragrant white alyssum.

Formal Landscapes

If both your home and your personal taste tend to be symmetrical and neat, you can follow guidelines for formal landscape design when planting flowers. In a formal design, plantings are balanced and often follow straight lines. For example, a formal front yard flower bed might be planted with repetitive groups of naturally tidy flowers such as geraniums, pansies and snapdragons. Flanking your front door with matching containers planted with flowers helps define a formal style as well.

Informal Landscapes

Informal landscapes are less structured, and beds usually have curved edges. Certainly you can grow informal flower beds in your front yard, but also look for promising spots on other sides of your house. If you simply love to garden and want to grow every flower you meet, create a few informal beds in different parts of your yard. This approach opens up great possibilities for experimenting with color schemes and plant partnerships. As any flower lover will tell you, sometimes plants must be grown in the company of other plants to look their best.

This informal cottage garden features annuals, perennials and bulbs. Cool gray artemisia provides a soothing note among marigolds, perilla, four o'clocks, heliopsis, globe thistle, phlox and drumstick allium.

Warm and Cool Colors

Color sets the mood in the landscape. Warm colors such as red, orange and bright yellow will bring life to any space. They are also easily seen from afar. Cool colors like soft pink and lavender suggest a more relaxed mood, and are best viewed up close. The lighter the shade, the better you will be able to see your flowers at night.

One of the most enjoyable things to do with flowers is experiment with combinations of warm and cool colors. Certain colors that are opposite each other on a color wheel team up beautifully when combined in the garden. For example, pink and yellow always look good together and the same is true of orange and purple. Blue and white usually go with everything, but in the garden it seems that no two blues are alike! If you feel nervous about mixing flower colors, play it safe by planting mostly soft neutrals such as lemon yellow, light blue or even silvery gray or white. Bright feature flowers grown near neutral tones look even more enchanting.

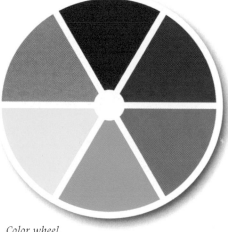

Color wheel.

Yellow 'Moonshine' achillea and purple 'May Night' salvia make a winning combination.

Any partnership of red and white flowers dazzles the eye, as seen here with red geraniums and white alyssum.

The Strongest Hues

Nowadays you can grow flowers in shades that were unheard of only a few years ago—white marigolds, orange impatiens and yellow petunias, for example. If you want to grow flowers that thrive with little care, it's a good idea to stick with the colors that are oldest and strongest within a certain species. For example, annual geraniums and salvias are strongest in red, while marigolds are unsurpassed for rich yellow-orange. The prime color in petunias is pink and few flowers can match the cool blues of campanulas.

For strong visual impact, plant mixed colors of the same flower in a broad band or a large mass.

Vertical Accents

Even if you don't generally like surprises, you might enjoy a few in your flower garden. Tall, upright flowers add a new dimension, giving it more depth and making small mounding flowers appear more interesting. Many of these are old favorites from times past, including delphiniums, hollyhocks and sunflowers. Or you can train vines to scramble up a trellis and use that as a vertical accent.

Don't make the mistake of thinking that tall plants will remain upright without help. Especially after they become top heavy with flowers, it takes only one gusty thunderstorm to tumble a towering plant. To prevent this, provide stakes or some other type of support for any flower that grows more than two feet tall.

TIP When Flowers Wear White

There are plenty of good things to say about white flowers. They never cause clashes and they glow in moonlight or partial shade. White tends to make small spaces seem larger and more spacious. On the down side, white is simply not very exciting. Since many white flowers turn brown as they fade, it helps to choose white flowers that clean themselves, such as impatiens, nierembergia, nicotiana and pansies.

Upright hollyhocks make fine vertical accents. In most climates, hollyhocks grow as perennials.

CONTAINERS AND WINDOW BOXES

Growing pretty flowers in containers is low-labor fun. Heavy digging and weeding are not required and you can move your flowers around at will. And container gardening demands little space, so it's the perfect way to let your gardening spirit soar in a small yard or patio setting.

Starting a Container Garden

Kick off the container gardening season in spring, when bedding plants are widely available. Choose containers that are as large as you can comfortably handle—large containers need less frequent watering than small ones. If weight is a worry, go with featherweight plastic containers. Many are available in earthy colors that mimic the appearance of heavier clay or stone.

Also buy plenty of bagged potting soil. These products contain little (if any) actual soil, so they do not pack down the way real soil does. Purchased potting soils usually are made of pulverized peat moss, composted organic matter, a little sand and perhaps some absorbent perlite or vermiculite. The result is a soft, moisture-retentive medium for pot-grown plants. If you're new to container gardening, try two or three different brands of potting soil until you find a favorite.

Pots of impatiens and begonia provide quiet beauty for a shady deck.

TIP Try Something New

Fan flower, properly known as *Scaevola*, stays covered with elegant blue flowers all summer, and actually grows better in pots than it does in the ground. Look for container-grown plants in nurseries in spring. Grow them in partial to full sun.

Scaevola 'Blue Wonder'.

Creating a Container Bouquet

1 Choose a container with at least one drainage hole in the bottom through which excess water can escape.

2 Fill the bottom half of the container with potting soil. Mix in some loose stones or broken pottery to give the container extra weight and improve drainage. Dampen thoroughly. Add potting soil to within ½ inch of the top. Tamp the pot to help settle the soil into the container.

3 Before planting container-grown plants, break apart the bottom half of the root ball and gently spread out the loose roots.

4 Your composition will be more lush and colorful if you crowd plants so that the root balls are only 2 inches apart. Make sure the highest roots are covered with at least ½ inch of potting soil.

5 Water the planted container thoroughly and allow the excess water to drain away. Drench the pot again after 20 minutes. Place the container in a dish filled with stones or gravel, or set it up on flat stones or bricks. Check to make sure the drainage holes are not blocked.

AMAZING ANNUALS FOR CONTAINERS

FULL SUN
Geranium
Petunia
Portulaca
Sweet alyssum
Verbena

PARTIAL SUN
Begonia
Dusty miller
Lobelia
Pansy
Salvia

SHADE
Coleus
Impatiens
Nicotiana
Polka dot plant
Torenia

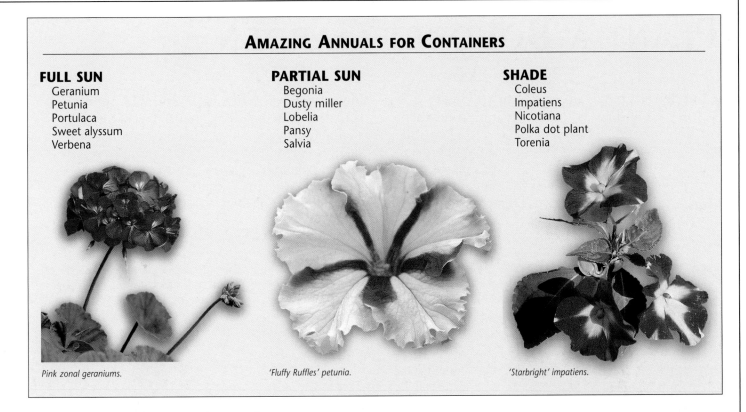

Pink zonal geraniums.

'Fluffy Ruffles' petunia.

'Starbright' impatiens.

Water and Fertilizer

Because their root area is restricted, plants grown in containers need frequent watering and feeding. Each time you water, nutrients in the potting soil leach away. Replace these nutrients by using fertilizer spikes or pellets in the containers. Or mix a small amount of a time-release fertilizer into the potting soil before you fill your containers with plants. You can also simply mix a soluble fertilizer with the water you use for your plants. Add a half-ration of fertilizer to the water each time you moisten the soil in your pots.

Many gardeners alternate synthetic soluble fertilizer with an organic fertilizer such as fish emulsion. Every few weeks, you may want to treat your plants to a compost "tea tonic" (made by mixing a gallon of compost with 5 gallons water). This solution supplements other fertilizers, providing micronutrients and enzymes.

As plants grow larger and their roots fill the container, water may run out through the sides of the container before the roots receive adequate moisture. The best way to tell if this is happening is to lift the pot to see if it feels heavy. If a container still feels light after watering, soak it several times or place it in a tub filled with a few inches of water until the thirsty plants drink their fill.

Mixing and Matching

It's fun to plant different annuals together in the same container. When creating a container bouquet, place upright plants, such as a geranium, near the center and flank with plants that grow into soft mounds, such as petunias. Finally, add small trailing plants such as lobelia or sweet alyssum at the pot's edge.

Layered into a window box, yucca, geranium and trailing stems of vinca make great companions.

PLANT A BOUQUET GARDEN

Cut flowers bring grace and beauty to indoor rooms, but there is another treat in store when you grow your own flowers for cutting. When you meet your flowers eye-to-eye, you will notice details about the blossoms that you may have missed in the garden—a refreshing new way to enjoy flowers, foliage and perhaps even weeds from your yard.

In arrangements, most flowers look best when they are at least twice as tall as the height of the container in which they are displayed. Short-stemmed pansies and nasturtiums are at home in small squat-shaped containers, but taller vessels call for long-stemmed flowers. Many varieties that develop long stems for cutting also are quite tall, so you may need to stake them as they approach their mature height.

Sunflowers and delphinium rest in water after being cut from the garden.

Cut Flower Basics

You will need a spot of good soil that receives at least a half day of sun to grow select flowers for cutting. Some of the finest cut flowers to grow in your garden are described here, but you can use other plant materials from your yard in arrangements too. Foliage from evergreen shrubs, budding tree limbs, browned tops from wild grasses, even strappy leaves taken from iris or daylilies ... all enrich simple flower arrangements with their textures and forms.

Color and Form

Flowers that work well with the colors in your indoor rooms make irresistible cut material. A bunch of a single type of flower always looks elegant when dis-played in a glass container, but it's easy to mix and match flowers in unique arrangements. Here are two important guidelines for flower arranging success.

- **Structure the composition** with upright spikes that help define the arrangement's silhouette. Use branches and long-stemmed grasses. Spike-shaped flowers such as larkspur, veronica or plume-type celosias also work well for this job.

- **Use plants that have neutral colors or soft textures** to meld your composition together. Don't hold back when adding soft neutral plant material such as velvety gray dusty miller, sprays of baby's breath or rounded heads of Queen Anne's lace. Their textures will contrast beautifully with your feature flowers while giving your arrangements a full, lush look.

Larkspur, baby's breath, chrysanthemums, and alliums anchor this softly hued cut flower arrangement.

Will They Drink?

The longest lasting cut flowers eagerly take up water through their cut stems. When experimenting with different flowers from your yard, watch to see if the water level in the vase drops overnight—a sure sign that the flowers are drinking their fill.

Flowers with hard or woody stems will take up water better if you use a sharp knife to make ¹/₂-inch-deep slits in the bottom of the stem. This treatment also works well with shrubs or bud-bearing branches gathered from flowering trees.

Handling Cut Flowers

To keep your stems looking fresh for days, take a container filled with water with you when you gather flowers. Remember to submerge the stems the moment they are cut and immediately bring the stems indoors, out of sun and warmth.

You must seal stems that bleed a white or clear sap after they are cut, to keep nutrients from escaping. Singe the bottom of the cut stems in a candle flame until they barely blacken, then return them to a container filled with water. Flowers that benefit from this treatment include butterfly weed, columbine, iris and poppies.

While it may seem a bit fussy, recutting the stems of cut flowers under water keeps an air bubble from forming (which blocks the transfer of water up the stem), and has a significant effect on the flowers' longevity.

Feature Flowers for Cutting

Chrysanthemums and dahlias are the dynamic duo among devotees of

- **Garden chrysanthemums** (which are different from florists' mums) are hardy perennials that bloom in late summer and fall. In Zones 3 to 5, try pink 'Clara Curtis' or yellow 'Mary Stoker', both of which are super hardy and dependable. Most midseason mums perform well in Zones 6 and 7. The midseason cultivar known as either 'Single Apricot' or 'Hillside Sheffield Pink' is outstanding in the garden and the vase, and the same is true of 'Yellow Jacket'. In Zones 8 and 9 you can grow late-blooming cultivars as well as special warm-natured strains that bloom twice a year, in spring and fall. Look for them at local

- **Dahlias** are tender perennials that grow from tuberous roots. In Zones 7 to 9, leave them in the ground through winter if protected with a good mulch. In other zones, dig the tubers in late fall and store the cleaned roots in a cool, frost-free place until the following spring. Choose your dahlias based on color and flower form, and be sure to stake varieties that grow more than two feet tall. Grow dahlias in rich soil and full sun. Fertilize them in spring and midsummer.

home-grown cut flowers. Both are easy to grow and will last in a vase for up to two weeks when properly handled.

'Ginger' garden chrysanthemum.

nurseries. Dig and divide all mums every other spring, just after new green growth appears.

'Border Princess' dahlia.

CUT-AND-COME-AGAIN ANNUALS

Flowers that develop stem buds that grow into new flowering branches produce more flowers the more often they are cut. To make the most of this growth habit, cut stems just above a robust node—the place on the stem where new leaf buds can be clearly seen. No flower arranger should be without vigorous cut-and-come-again annuals such as these:

Celosia	Snapdragon
Gomphrena	Strawflower
Salvia (*salvia farinacea*)	Zinnia

The aptly named 'Cut-and-Come-Again' variety of zinnia produces new blossoms continuously over a period of two months or more.

BIRD AND BUTTERFLY GARDENS

One could hardly ask for better company in the garden than colorful butterflies or chattering birds. Both types of creatures will find your garden irresistible if you do a few simple things to make them feel welcome.

You can easily develop your landscape into an oasis for birds and butterflies by growing hospitable plants, providing a source of water and offering food when natural sources are in short supply. It is also essential to use no insecticides in a butterfly garden, and to avoid using fungicides and herbicides as much as possible.

Water and Food—Choosing the Right Spot

For a wildlife refuge, choose a spot that is warm and sunny during most of the day. Because butterflies are cold-blooded insects, they are most active in warm, sunny areas. Birds also like an open spot where they have a clear view of possible predators. Make sure you can see the wildlife area from inside your house on days when it's uncomfortably hot or cold outdoors.

Birds and butterflies share a common need for water. A shallow birdbath no more than 2½ inches deep with a few large flat stones placed in the bottom will meet the needs of both. Butterflies like to stand on a dry spot and sip water. Birds will use the same water for drinking, cleaning and raucous play. A broad, shallow watering dish placed on the ground also will work well as a birdbath. You might install a little pocket pond (see page 136) and add fish and frogs to your backyard wildlife brigade.

CHOOSING PLANTS FOR BIRDS

Look for areas where you can grow shrubs and small trees that give birds seasonal food and year-round shelter. The plants listed below are pretty enough to grow as specimen plants, or you can group them together to form a bird-friendly hedge or thicket. All produce flowers in spring followed by berries in the fall.

Small Trees
Dogwood
(*Cornus florida*)
Zones 4 to 9
Ninebark
(*Physocarpus* spp.)
Zones 2 to 8
Serviceberry
(*Amelanchier arborea*)
Zones 4 to 8

Serviceberry (Amelanchier arborea).

Shrubs
Beautyberry
(*Callicarpa americana*)
Zones 5 to 8
Juniper
(*Juniperus* spp.)
Zones 3 to 9
Viburnum
(*Viburnum* spp.)
Zones 2 to 8

Many viburnums are wonderfully fragrant.

HOSTING HUMMINGBIRDS

Any red flowers will attract hummingbirds, and you can provide them with a feeder stocked with sugar water.

flowers. To discourage bees and wasps, place a small amount of vegetable oil around the feeder's feeding holes.

Good Plants for Hummingbirds
Cardinal flower (*Lobelia cardinalis*)
Honeysuckle (*Lonicera* spp.)
Hosta (*Hosta* cultivars)
Bee balm (*Monarda* cultivars)
Sage (*Salvia* spp.)

Like butterflies, hummingbirds sip flower nectar. They will visit the same tubular flowers preferred by butterflies. You can supplement their diet by setting out hummingbird feeders in late spring. Planting red or bright orange flowers will also attract hummingbirds.

Fill hummingbird feeders with sugar syrup (one part sugar to four parts water), and clean them with hot water once a week. Between cleanings, don't worry if you find small insects floating in the feeder. Hummingbirds routinely consume small insects as they feed in

Red monarda or bee balm attracts hummingbirds and butterflies.

When hostas bloom, their tubular flowers host hummers.

Sensational Sunflowers

TIP

Expect to see plenty of bees on any sunflower during the first few days after the blossom opens. Three weeks later, as the seeds begin to ripen, finches and many other birds will promptly harvest them. Or you can cut the ripe old blossoms and save them for winter bird feeding. Sunflower seeds are ripe when the seeds fall out freely when you gently twist the dried flower. Also cut and save faded seedheads from the purple coneflowers you grow for butterflies. Birds love them!

'Park's Velvet Tapestry' sunflower.

Monarch butterflies sip nectar from ornamental alliums. When they find a plentiful food source, it is not unusual for butterflies to feed in groups.

Choosing Plants for Butterflies

Butterflies do most of their eating when they are caterpillars (their larval stage). The plants that the larvae eat, called host plants, include a few garden flowers but mostly weeds and wildflowers. Adult butterflies consume flower nectar from a wide range of flowers, which they sip through a long curling tongue-like organ called a proboscis. Because of the way they feed, flower form is more important to butterflies than flower color. Butterflies (and hummingbirds) flock to plants with short tubular flowers such as the aptly-named butterfly bush and butterfly weed. They also like flat, daisy-

Swallowtails find the tubular blooms of butterfly bush impossible to resist.

shaped flowers. Double blossoms crowded with petals make it more difficult for butterflies to feed, while single blossoms provide a platform for butterflies to stand upon while sipping flower nectar.

Keeping Butterflies Around

To keep butterflies happy all summer, use the seven butterfly favorites, listed at left, in your butterfly garden. Add other flowers both you and local butterflies find attractive. Butterfly populations are always highest in late summer, but they will remain with you well into fall if your garden includes autumnal bloomers such as; asters, chrysanthemums, boltonia, sedum and goldenrod.

BUTTERFLY-ATTRACTING PLANTS

Perennials	Annuals
butterfly bush	cosmos
garden phlox	lantana
purple coneflower	tithonia
	zinnia

Purple coneflowers are fine butterfly plants.

Lantana.

Feeding Birds in Winter

You can feed birds year-round if you like, but many gardeners ease up on bird feeding in summer, when food is abundant. In winter, when the garden's insects and seeds are at low tide, set up feeders stocked with different food to attract a number of different species to your garden. A platform feeder with perches for birds, stocked with sunflower seeds or a mixture that includes sunflower seeds, will attract seed-eaters like cardinals, titmice, chickadees and finches. To attract goldfinches, set up a slender tube-type feeder and stock it with niger thistle seeds.

Not all birds eat seeds. Woodpeckers and nuthatches will dine at feeders stocked with suet. You can buy suet in blocks or bags and hang them from tree branches.

A goldfinch enjoys a nourishing lunch at a seed feeder.

BULBS ON PARADE

True bulbs are the garden's magical plants. Like other long-lived perennials, bulbs grow and flower, and then become dormant. Inside their plump storage roots, each cell is arranged so that the next season's blossoms will appear on schedule.

Types of Bulbs

Bulbs can be neatly divided into spring-flowering bulbs (crocus, daffodil, hyacinth and tulip) and summer-flowering bulbs such as lilies. Here we will concentrate on the three most popular and dependable bulbs for American gardens—daffodils, tulips and Asiatic lilies. Once you master growing these, there is no limit to the bulb-growing adventures you can have in your garden.

Choose your bulbs' planting site with good drainage in mind, for waterlogged soil will cause any bulb to rot. To create bold splashes of color, locate like bulbs together in groups of 3 to 5 bulbs. With a little planning, you can have daffodils in mid spring, tulips a few weeks later and wonderful lilies from early to midsummer. All are dazzling in the garden and also make great cut flowers. To help your bulbs prosper year after year, let them hold onto their leaves until they naturally turn yellow and begin to die back. Then clip off the plants at the soil line.

After tulip bulbs are planted in fall, buttery yellow pansies are added. The pansies will provide color long after the tulip flowers fade.

WHEN IS A BULB NOT A BULB?

Many plants that have heavy storage roots are called bulbs, but they're not. A true bulb has a root like an onion, covered with layers of scales with a thicker inner heart. Corms (gladiolus), rhizomes (iris) and tuberous roots (dahlias) do not have these layers—only a solid mass of starchy flesh that's kept stored in the root until it's needed by the plant.

True bulbs such as tulips and daffodils grow roots during the winter and emerge first thing in spring, ready to bloom.

TIP What's Bugging Your Bulbs?

Holes and notches in leaves are usually the work of slugs or snails, which you can snare in beer traps. Squirrels find tulip flower buds a great delicacy, but you can change the flavor of their treat by coating the buds with hot pepper spray (see page 180). Where gophers dig and consume bulbs, either stick with daffodils (which they do not like) or protect tulip and lily bulbs with a buried wire cage. Another option: Plant the bulbs in plastic nursery liners and then bury the pots in the soil.

Daffodils (*Narcissus* cultivars) Zones 3 to 8

These are the most indestructible of bulbs. You can grow early daffodils that bloom before the last snow, or late cultivars with huge trumpet-shaped flowers. Try naturalizing daffodils in an open woodland area beneath deciduous trees (those that lose their leaves in winter). Daffodils will flourish as long as they receive good light during late winter and spring.

Plant bulbs 6 to 8 inches apart in the fall, after the soil has cooled. Plant daffodils using a bulb planter or a piece of hollow pipe; both tools pull out plugs of soil. Sprinkle a teaspoon of bulb fertilizer or other phosphorous-rich organic plant food into the bottom of the hole, push in the bulb with the pointed end up and cover it with 5 to 6 inches of soil.

If daffodils have a problem, it's that they grow too well. In fertile soil, they often become crowded within 4 years. The only way to restore strong flowering is to dig, divide, and replant the bulbs (see page 164).

Daffodil.

Tulip (*Tulipa* cultivars) Zones 3 to 8

Tulips always bloom beautifully for a year or two, but after that they expend much of their energy nurturing bulblets. As a result, flowers become smaller or the bulbs fail to flower at all. For this reason, you may want to set out fresh tulips every year and dig out and dispose of the older ones. Or plant some comparatively small-flowered species tulips, which often persist as long-lived naturalized perennials.

Plant tulips in mid to late fall. It's fun to mix and match tulips with smaller companion plants such as pansies, perennial candytuft or creeping phlox. In warm climates, plant tulips where they will get partial shade in late spring, when they are in flower. Cool conditions at flowering time helps tulips hold their blossoms longer. Plant tulips so that the bulbs are covered with 5 to 6 inches of soil. When planting groups of tulips in flower beds, mix bulb fertilizer into the soil just under the bulbs.

'Pink Impression' tulips.

Lily (*Lilium* cultivars) Zones 4 to 8

If you choose a good site and plant them carefully, lilies will grace your summer garden year after year.

These large bulbs must have excellent drainage and the soil should be moist and cool. In most areas, lilies grow best with a half day of sun.

Plant lilies in late fall or very early spring. Meticulous planting (as shown below) is a good investment of your time. When a lily is happy, the number of flowers and stems it produces will increase every season. Keep trying new lilies until you find cultivars that perform this way in your climate. Asiatic hybrids are vigorous and dependable in a wide range of climates.

Asiatic lily.

Oriental lily.

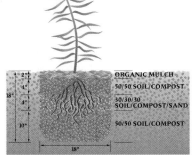

Asiatic lilies adapt to many different climates and come in a wide range of colors.

Give Lilies a Comfort Zone

ORGANIC MULCH
50/50 SOIL/COMPOST
30/30/30 SOIL/COMPOST/SAND
50/50 SOIL/COMPOST

Lilies will thrive and multiply if you give them a "comfort zone." They love a sunny site; a cool, moist, rich soil with good drainage; and at least 2 inches of mulch.

Paint Your Garden
with Wildflowers

To bring color and excitement to your yard without a lot of bother, try turning a forgotten corner into a wildflower meadow. When properly selected and handled, wildflowers will thrive with very little care. With wildflowers, the only secrets to success are choosing species well suited to the site and climate, and planting them at the appropriate time.

Types of Wildflowers

The plants we know as wildflowers include many native species as well as imported plants that have naturalized themselves with great success. Natives enrich the meadow with their dependable natures and natural forms. Introduced wildflowers are valued for their ability to provide riveting color.

A pretty wildflower meadow is always a work in progress. Try a few new species every year, and do not be discouraged if some plants refuse to grow. Over time, you will learn which wildflowers are best suited to your soil and site.

To make a home for both categories of plants, choose a sunny spot that drains reasonably well and is not overrun with persistent perennial weeds (such as bindweed) or invasive grasses (such as quackgrass or Bermudagrass). Also make sure you can reach the area with a mower. You will need to mow down old plants at least once a year. If the soil is very poor, spend a season growing cover crops such as crimson clover or buckwheat before starting your wildflower meadow.

*To improve poor soil, plant your meadow with crimson clover (*Trifolium incarnatum*) before adding wildflowers. As soon as the clover's color begins to fade, mow down the plants to keep them from reseeding. Lightly scratch open "pockets" left in the cut clover mulch and plant them with buckwheat (another soil-building cover crop plant). Mow down the buckwheat in late summer. Turn under or rake up the residue, then start planting wildflowers.*

Seed Selection

To get a long season of color from your meadow, you will need to include annual, hardy annual and perennial species of flowers. If you begin by planting a mixture of many different species, make sure you choose a mixture that has been developed just for your climate. All the mail-order companies that specialize in wildflower seeds sell special regional mixtures.

Starting with packets of individual species has several advantages. If you know exactly what you planted in a certain place, it's much easier to identify wildflower seedlings and to track their success or failure. Working with separate species also simplifies the task of planting them at the right time. It also makes it possible to sow seeds at different times to extend your season of bloom.

In addition to choosing wildflowers that are likely to grow well in your region, pay close attention to the growing conditions in your site. Keep a close watch for wildflower species that appear satisfied with what you have to offer and be prepared for surprises. Black-eyed Susans thrive in dry gravel or moist ditches, and Indian blanket always produces colorful blossoms.

Wildflower meadows evolve season by season. Check the difference between the same meadow in spring (left) and autumn (right). Now that's wild!

But don't expect soil that can barely support scraggly weeds to grow a large collection of different wildflowers. Improved or naturally good soil will greatly expand the list of wildflowers you can grow while enhancing their appearance, health and hardiness.

LEAVE ROOM FOR GRASSES

At least half the plants in your wildflower meadow should be wild grasses that grow into tufts or small bunches— not spreading grasses that will crowd out your wildflowers. Exemplary native grasses will probably spontaneously appear in your meadow. All you must do is skip over spindly tufts when removing unwanted weeds. To help them further, delay fall mowing until after the grasses have shed their ripe seeds.

By their nature, wildflowers are a little bit wild. In this wildflower meadow, rudbeckias and daisies show how much diversity you can expect within each species.

Plugging in Perennials

In the wild, perennial wildflowers spend their first year—and sometimes two years—developing strong roots and crowns beneath the shelter of nearby annuals and grasses. Be patient when direct-sowing them, or start the seeds in flats. Even in carefully tended flats, expect slow growth.

Nurseries that specialize in native plants are gold mines of good starter material. Perennial wildflowers are typically sold in 3- to 4-inch pots; many cost less than $5 per plant. If you plan to buy from a small regional nursery, place your order in advance to make sure you get your plants in time to set them out in early spring,

just as they begin to show new growth.

Many perennial wildflowers resent transplanting, so disturb the roots as little as possible when setting out the plants. After planting, water as needed to keep the soil around the plants lightly moist for at least six weeks.

Every spring, spend a few minutes checking your perennials to discover opportunities to propagate new plants. Look for healthy-rooted growing tips sprouting up around the base of the parent plant. Dig and replant these to other parts of your meadow while leaving the parent plant intact. With luck, the old plant will probably bloom for a few more seasons.

THE NEED TO RESEED

Some of the showiest annual wildflowers—including corn poppies (*Papaver rhoeas*) and cosmos (*Cosmos bipinnatus* and *C. sulphureus*)—simply do not reseed themselves very well, so it's best to sow them anew each season. Or use this weakness as an opportunity to try different "color flowers" in addition to these common ones. You just might find a surprise species that adores your site! Some fun ones to try include scarlet flax (*Linum grandiflorum* var. *rubrum*), pink catchfly (*Silene armeria*, also known as none-so-pretty) and annual candytuft (*Iberis umbellata*).

Corn poppies and bachelor's buttons bloom at the same time in late spring. Where winters are mild, plant both of these species in the fall.

To save wildflower seeds for replanting, snip off the ripened seedheads and store them in a cool, dry place where mice cannot find them. To plant the seeds, simply crush the dried seedheads in your hands over the prepared soil where you want the flowers to grow, then barely rake the seeds in.

Planting Tip

Plant seeds in a pattern or in blocks to make it easier to find and identify seedlings.

How to Plant a New Wildflower Meadow

1 In fall, set the cutting blade on your mower as low as possible and scalp off all existing weeds and grasses. Rake up the clippings. If you prefer, treat the area with a glyphosate herbicide three weeks before planting your wildflower seeds.

2 Cultivate the surface of the soil, but go only 1 inch deep. Deep cultivation often increases weed problems. Rake over the surface.

3 Broadcast seeds of hardy species over the surface, distributing them in an even pattern. Walk over the area to press the seeds into the loose soil.

4 In dry or windy climates, barely cover the seeded soil with a light sprinkling of weed-free wheat or oat straw so that you can see the soil's surface between pieces of straw.

5 In early spring, rake open spaces where wildflower seedlings are evident, and sow them with annuals species as described in step 3.

DEPENDABLE WILDFLOWERS FOR SPRING

Ox-eye daisy
Leucanthemum vulgare
Introduced perennial.
Midwest, southeast.
Sow seeds in fall or spring. To increase your supply, dig, divide and replant colonies in early fall.

Ox-eye daisy.

California poppy
Eschscholzia californica
Native annual.
Northwest, west, southeast.
Sow in fall where winters are mild. Elsewhere sow first thing in spring. Often reseeds.

California poppy.

Fivespot
Nemophila maculata
Native hardy annual.
Northwest, west.
Sow in fall where winters are mild. Elsewhere sow first thing in spring.

Fivespot.

Bachelor's buttons
Centaurea cyanus
Introduced annual.
All regions.
Very easy to grow from seed sown in fall or spring. This reliable reseeder makes a good companion for other spring flowers.

Bachelor's button.

Corn poppy
Papaver rhoeas
Introduced hardy annual.
All regions.
Sow in fall in Zones 6 to 9. Spring planting best in cold winter areas. Responds dramatically to fertile soil. Gather seeds and reseed by hand.

Corn poppy.

Toadflax
Linaria maroccana
Introduced annual.
All regions.
Scatter the tiny seeds in patches first thing in spring. Reliable reseeder.

Toadflax.

Blue flax
Linum lewisii
Native perennial.
Midwest, northwest, west.
Sow in spring, but be patient as plants may not bloom until their second year.

Blue flax.

DEPENDABLE WILDFLOWERS FOR SUMMER

Butterfly weed
Asclepias tuberosa

Butterfly weed.

Native perennial. Midwest, north-east, southeast. Start with young purchased plants, as seedlings are very slow grow-ers that do not transplant well.

Indian blanket
Gaillardia pulchella
Native annual.
Midwest, northeast, southeast, southwest.
Sow in spring or fall south of Zone 6. In all areas, expect strong reseeding. Flowers longer in fertile, moist soil.

Indian blanket.

Lanceleaf coreopsis
Coreopsis lanceolata
Native perennial or annual.
Midwest, northeast, northwest, southwest.
Set out purchased plants, or sow seeds in late summer or spring.

Depending on the cultivar, lanceleaf coreopsis (Coreopsis lanceolata) is a perennial hardy to Zones 3-9.

Annual coreopsis
Coreopsis tinctoria
Native hardy annual.
Northwest, southeast, southwest.
This bright bloomer is ideal for ditches and low spots. Sow in early spring. Good reseeder.

Annual coreopsis.

Purple coneflower
Echinacea purpurea

Purple coneflower.

Native perennial. Midwest, north-east, southeast. Expect first blooms from 2-year-old seedlings, or save time by setting out purchased plants.

Black-eyed Susan
Rudbeckia hirta
Native annual or perennial.
Midwest, northeast, southeast.
Sow seeds of this strong reseeder in both fall and spring to prolong the summer blooming period.

Black-eyed Susan.

Prairie coneflower (yellow or red)
Ratibida columnaris
Native perennial.
Northwest, southwest, southeast.
Sow in spring. Plants larger and flower more heavily in moist soils.

Prairie coneflower.

Cosmos
Cosmos bipinnatus
Introduced annual.
All regions.
Sow in spring for bright summer color. Gather seeds and reseed by hand.

Cosmos (C. bipinnatus).

DEPENDABLE WILDFLOWERS FOR FALL

New England aster
Aster novae-angliae
Native perennial.
Midwest, northeast, southeast.
Start with plants rather than seeds. Dig and divide plants every three years to help retain vigor and strong flowering.

New England aster.

Goldenrod
Solidago spp.
Native perennial.
All regions.
Start with a purchased plant, or dig them from construction sites. Numerous species have subtle dif-ferences in plant, flowers, and bloom times.

Goldenrod.

Care of the Wildflower Meadow

In every climate there are rampant weeds unworthy of the wildflower meadow. Here's how to tame them:

- **Hoe, pull out or chop down** large, aggressive weeds before they shed seeds.

- **Mark the locations** of tough perennial weeds with a stake and dig them out during the winter.

- **Mow down** wildflowers any time there is not a major species on the brink of bloom:
  - In most areas late fall is the best time to mow.
  - Allow time for your favorite species to shower the ground with seeds before you mow.
  - Leave the "wildflower hay" on the ground. It is probably chock full of good seeds.

PLANT AN AMERICAN BORDER

Traditionally speaking, a border is a special flower bed devoted to perennials. Situated so that it dramatizes a property boundary, a "proper" border includes a backdrop such as a fence, wall or evergreen hedge and has a walkway or swath of lawn along its front edge.

This is the English way borders are created, but American gardeners often find that a border comprised entirely of perennials leaves much to be desired. Instead, we give perennials plenty of company in the form of annuals, bulbs, shrubs and small trees.

An American definition of a flower border is this: A special flower bed in which plants of varying heights are planted in layers to create a feeling of depth. Blooming periods are orchestrated to give the longest possible season of color.

Foundation First

If you want your border to support a wide range of plants, you will probably need to spend quite a lot of time digging and amending the soil in your chosen site. Ideally, you should spend a season or two getting the soil in top condition before planting perennials. During this time, use the new bed to grow annual flowers. Add soil amendments, minerals and biodegradable mulch at every opportunity. In especially difficult soils, excavate the native dirt and refill the bed with high-quality topsoil to form a good foundation for a border.

Your border should be at least 5 feet deep. This allows ample room to grow small, medium-sized and tall plants in planned layers. Deeper borders can accommodate more layers of plants. They also require inner pathways, and one at the back of the border, to allow easy access to plants. Your border can be as long or short as you like. Most gardeners start with a small border and enlarge it gradually, in keeping with their growing collection of plants.

The first phase of creating a new border is preparing the soil. Be generous when adding organic matter, and cultivate the ground as deeply as possible.

Anatomy of a Border

Petite edging plants define the front of the border, even if the bed is enclosed with brick or stone. Mounding plants with fine texture such as perennial candytuft or annual sweet alyssum work well. Other fine choices include pansies, dianthus and other dwarf annuals. Where it is hardy (Zones 6 to 9), liriope is hard to beat as an evergreen edging plant.

Thigh-high plants fill the middle of the border and should include annuals and perennials with varying textures and bloom times. Try to arrange plantings in natural looking drifts that flow through the middle of the bed in an undulating line.

Tall plants form a vertical plane at the back of the border. Use tall perennials or shrubs, or let a fence serve as the backdrop. Train a vine or climbing rose on the fence to incorporate it into your border.

In this complex border, different plants and colors are woven together rather than being planted in straight rows. Repetition of white flowers and yellow marigolds give the garden a feeling of wholeness and unity.

Designing Your Border

You will be happiest with a border that showcases the plants you love. Here are four more ways to enhance your border's beauty from the very beginning.

- **Repeat groups of like plants** at regular intervals, particularly near the front of your border. Repetition gives the border a sense of rhythm and helps to unify a diverse collection of plants. Try this technique with light, neutral flowers such as white pansies or silvery-gray dusty miller.

Dusty miller.

- **Locate similar plants together** in flowing drifts rather than lines or squares. Besides looking pretty, plants grown in natural-looking colonies are simpler to renovate or propagate compared to scattered individuals.

- **Include a few small evergreen shrubs** to help structure the border in summer and define its existence in winter. Dwarf boxwoods or small junipers are excellent for this purpose.

- **Utilize foliage plants** such as dusty miller, hosta, heuchera and ornamental grasses.

These are not spectacular bloomers, but they help keep the border lively when colored flowers are in short supply.

Evergreens define the existence of a border in winter. Mounds show where plants have been left untrimmed so that the aboveground parts can provide extra cover for the base and surface roots until warmer weather returns.

Tips for Better Borders

As your border develops and you get to know the site and the plants better, you might want to make use of these secrets:

- **Partner plants** that work especially well together. For example, you might plant daylilies in front of daffodils to hide fading daffodil foliage from view.

- **Pave over any vacant spaces** with mulch. Any unplanted place is an invitation to weeds.

- **Place steppingstones** between plants if you need a place to stand while staking, weeding or gathering blossoms. Small 12-inch-wide steppingstones are easy to move as needed.

Steppingstones interplanted with a creeping groundcover make an attractive and functional pathway surface.

- **Fill holes with pots.** Keep some petunias or impatiens blooming in plastic pots and slip them into spots where other plants have failed unexpectedly.

Geraniums and chrysanthemums in containers enlarge this summer border.

- **Move plants around** as needed to create color combinations that work well together. It's always best to dig and move plants when they are dormant. But bend this rule without breaking it: Move most plants any time as long as soil remains packed around their roots at all times and they never run short of water. In sunny weather, cover plants you move with a cardboard box for three or four days after transplanting.

Delphiniums hold their heads high with the help of slender wood stakes.

- **Support tall plants** with stakes, cages or specially-made support hoops. Use dark green or brown spray paint to make any type of support device less visible.

A Border for Cool Climates: Zones 3 to 5

Plants are listed in order of bloom times

1. **Forget-me-not**
   (*Myosotis sylvestris*)
   Reseeding biennial; blue.

2. **Daffodil**
   (*Narcissus* spp.)
   Bulb; yellow, white, bicolors.

3. **Lilac**
   (*Syringa* spp.)
   Large shrub; lilac, purple or white.

4. **Dianthus**
   (*Dianthus* hybrids)
   Dwarf perennial; pink, rose or white.

5. **Pansy**
   (*Viola wittrockiana*)
   Hardy annual; many colors.

6. **Peony**
   (*Paeonia* cultivars)
   Perennial; white, rose or pink.

7. **Petunia**
   (*Petunia*)
   Annual; many colors.

8. **Rugosa rose**
   (*Rosa rugosa*)
   Shrub; pink, white or red.

9. **Daylily 'Stella D'Oro'**
   (*Hemerocallis* hybrid)
   Perennial; yellow.

10. **Mealycup sage**
    (*Salvia farinacea*)
    Hardy annual; purple, white or bicolored.

11. **Daylily, 'Hyperion'**
    (*Hemerocallis* cultivar)
    Perennial; yellow.

12. **Purple coneflower**
    (*Echinacea purpurea*)
    Perennial; pink or white.

13. **Sedum 'Autumn Joy'**
    (*Sedum* cultivar)
    Perennial; pink to rust.

14. **Chrysanthemum 'Clara Curtis'**
    (*Dendranthema rubellum*)
    Perennial; pink.

15. **Winged spindle tree**
    (*Euonymus alatus* 'compactus')
    Small tree; bright red in fall.

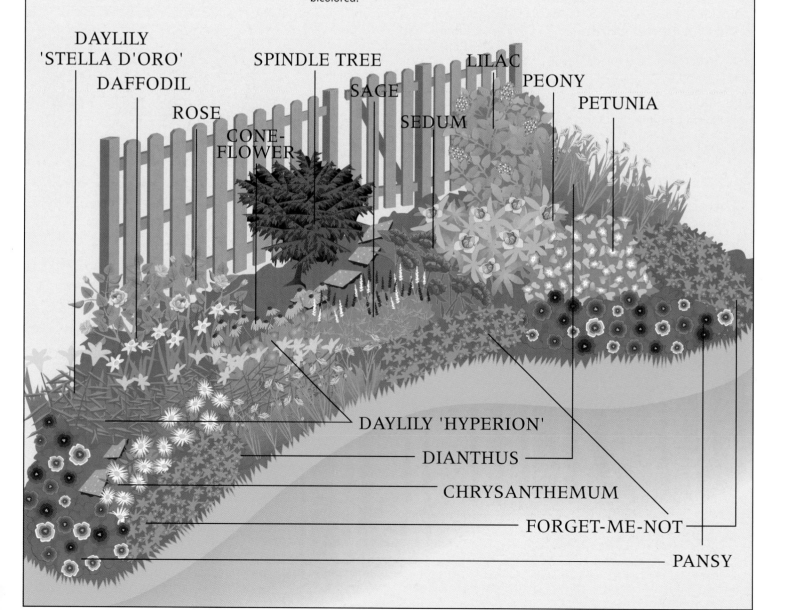

A BORDER FOR WARM CLIMATES: ZONES 6 TO 9

Plants are listed in order of bloom times

1. **Dwarf boxwood**
   (*Buxus sempervirens*)
   Evergreen shrub; dark green.

2. **Azalea**
   (*Rhododendron* cultivar)
   Shrub; many colors.

3. **Petunia 'Pink Wave'**
   (*Petunia* cultivar)
   Hardy annual; medium pink.

4. **English rose 'Heritage'**
   (*Rosa* cultivar)
   Shrub to semi-climber; light pink.

5. **Oak-leaf hydrangea**
   (*Hydrangea quercifolia*)
   Shrub; white to bronze.

6. **Zinnia 'Dreamland'**
   (*Zinnia* cultivars)
   Compact annual; many colors.

7. **Lantana**
   (*Lantana* hybrids)
   Tender perennial or annual; many colors.

8. **Butterfly bush**
   (*Buddleia davidii*)
   Shrub; lilac, purple or white.

9. **Crocosmia**
   (*Crocosmia* cultivars)
   Hardy corms; red, yellow or yellow-orange.

10. **Crape myrtle**
    (*Lagerstroemia indica*)
    Shrub or small tree; many colors.

11. **Mexican sunflower**
    (*Tithonia rotundifolia*)
    Annual; orange or yellow.

12. **Chrysanthemum 'Yellow Jacket'**
    (*Dendranthema* cultivar)
    Perennial; yellow.

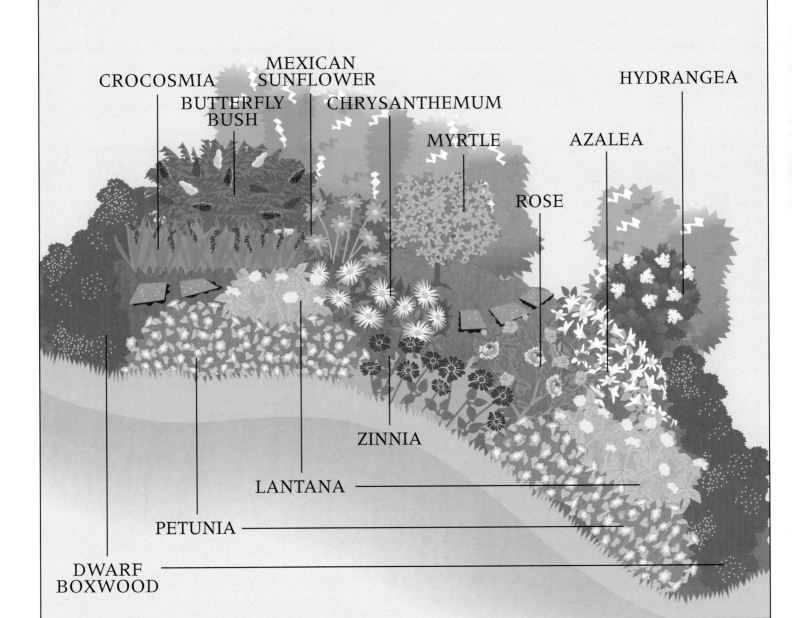

CHAPTER 8

FRAGRANCE:
GROWING SCENTED PLANTS

*Add the dimension of fragrance
to your garden and enter an enchanting world
that is bewitching to your nose as well as your eyes.*

Today's catchword for fragrance may be aromatherapy, but it's not at all a new idea. For centuries people have known about the beneficial effects of fragrance. Ancient Greeks planted the most fragrant plants near the windows of their living rooms. Medieval monks grew the sweetest-smelling herbs near their infirmaries for the benefit of patients. The idea? That beautiful scents are as important to our well-being as the opportunity to feast our eyes on beautiful flowers. All our senses deserve some rewards, and your nose is no exception when it comes to gardening.

Gardening for Fragrance

When planning a garden, we may become so concerned with beds, borders, paths and design styles that we forget to consider plants that will bring the pleasure of fragrance to our days.

Some fragrant plants are obscure and hard to find, so you may not know of the wide range of "smell good" plants. But you can add fragrant flowers to the garden as easily as your sense of smell can be educated. In this chapter, you will see how to plan your garden to maximize fragrance, then discover four simple ways to use fragrant plants in your landscape:

- Structuring your landscape with long-lived, fragrant shrubs and trees.

- Using containers to grow spots of portable fragrance.

- Growing roses and herbs that are famous for their fragrance.

- Planning a garden that is aromatic in the evening and at night.

'Chocolate Mint' scented geranium is a fragrant delight.

The Secrets of Fragrance

Why do plants have fragrance? The most obvious answer is to attract nectar-feeding insects that will pollinate the flowers. Instead of attracting animals, some plants smell disagreeable to repel destructive insects and animals. Others release their essential oils as part of a cooling process on a hot day. Fragrant foliage often needs the warmth of full sun or a brush of our hand to release the essential oils. It takes a rain to release the apple scent of sweetbriar foliage.

Other factors that affect fragrance include the age of the flowers, temperature, humidity and time of day. Many fragrant flowers wait until night to emit strong scents; these are usually pollinated by night-flying moths. In some species, there is a minor association between flower color and fragrance. White flowers are often the most fragrant, but there are many exceptions well worth exploring.

In her 1932 book The Fragrant Path, *Louise Beebe Wilder wrote that the memory of fragrance "...reaches into the heart" and that the sense of smell is "...unmistakably reminiscent of a time and state in which one was something else and possibly something better." Rare is the person who does not associate some pleasant aspect of youth with a fragrance of a particular flower, such as an old-fashioned rose, lilac or lily-of-the-valley.*

Moonvine flowers open at night. Their fragrance attracts nocturnal moths, which serve as pollinators.

MAXIMIZING FRAGRANCE

To make the most of fragrant flowers and leaves in the garden, the air must be fairly still. Slight breezes may gently bring the scents to you, but strong winds quickly disperse them. To shelter a garden area, consider installing a fence or establishing a windbreak of evergreen or deciduous trees or shrubs. Some of these may be specially selected for their fragrance.

Fencing in Fragrance

If you don't have the space for a windbreak, consider building a small south-facing length of wall or fence, which will reflect and radiate heat. In cooler regions such as the Pacific Northwest or New England, many gardeners find that a windbreak surrounding a wall shelters the garden from wind, while the wall is effective in warming the garden. This extra warmth heightens the fragrance of many favorite flowers.

Adding a paved surface helps as well. Include a bench or seat in this area so that you can linger, breathing in the delicious fragrances.

Tarragon's savory flavor is matched by its fresh herbal fragrance.

Scented geraniums are well suited to containers, so you can amass a large collection in a small amount of space.

Location and Height

"The closer the better" is the motto of growing fragrant plants in the garden. Place them near the deck or patio, beside the front and back doors, and in windowboxes. Make sure some of your favorite scented plants are near benches in the garden, the porch swing and around any outdoor dining area.

Furnish outdoor living areas with fragrant plants so that they are always close enough to enjoy at nose level.

Simple Touches

This aspect of touch provides several landscaping opportunities. Plant creeping herbs, like different species of thyme or chamomile, among steppingstones or under and around a garden seat. Let larger plants like lavender, mint, or rosemary spill over a garden path, so that the foliage is easily brushed as you walk along.

Thyme is a tough little herb suitable for growing in crevices among steppingstones.

Containers of Scent

For plantings farther from the house, choose a site in the garden where you'll frequently go. Whenever possible, plant low-growing plants in raised beds or planters so they are a little closer to nose height. Pots of fragrant plants bring mobility to fragrance, plus it's easy to put them on raised surfaces such as the tops of low tables or walls.

The foliage of many plants also brings scent to the garden. The main difference between foliage and flowers is that foliage usually must be touched to release the scent. The main exceptions are the herb garden or an evergreen planting on a hot, still summer day.

Beneath this pergola, there is no question that one should stop to smell the roses—and the wisteria, too.

Surround Yourself with Scent

Arbors, pergolas, arches and tunnels are another way to surround yourself with fragrance. What pleasure to walk or sit under wisteria, honeysuckle, climbing roses or arched laburnum trees. And don't overlook the possibilities of picket fences, trellises or low walls with planting pockets for bringing fragrance closer.

Night and Day

When considering which fragrant plants to grow, keep the time of best scent in mind. A garden overflowing with fragrance might never be appreciated if the gardener leaves the house early in the morning to go to work. For this person, it would be advantageous to plant those flowers that exude their scent during the evening hours. Some evening favorites include flowering tobacco, four o'clocks, evening primrose and dame's rocket. Some plants that you might think are not fragrant, like common garden phlox and some daylilies, become well scented at night.

Conversely, the gardener who is out at dawn wandering among the plants should concentrate on day-scented flowers, which include most of the fragrant plants other than the night-scented varieties.

Lightly fragrant four o'clocks show their festive colors from late afternoon until the following day when the sun shines brightly.

The Language of Fragrance

Through the centuries, people have attempted to create standard categories of fragrances in order to better describe them and remove at least some subjectivity. With these categories, you'll be better able to differentiate floral scents from one another.

Balsamic - Found in leaves that contain menthol or minty essential oils: mints, lavender, sages, rosemary, wormwood, balsam and eucalyptus.

Fruited - Found in flowers or leaves of a wide range of plants: grape hyacinth, magnolia, flowering fruits, sweet olive and fruit-scented geraniums.

Heavy - Found in flowers with strong, penetrating perfume: gardenia, orange blossom, jasmine and tuberose.

Honeyed - Found in many different flowers: hawthorn, barberry, Oregon grape holly and hybrid musk roses.

Rose - The scent that predominates in a few old European garden roses and a few other plants: some peonies, winter honeysuckle and leatherleaf mahonia.

Spicy - Found in leaves and flowers, often combined with other scents: carnations, pinks, azaleas, fennel and nasturtium.

Sweet - Found in flowers, grasses, and ferns: fringe tree, elder, honeysuckle, heliotrope and crinum.

Unique - Similar to heavy scents (described left), but even more distinct and refined: lily-of-the-valley, sweet pea, some iris, wisteria and common lilac.

Violet - Found in the flowers or roots of only a few plants: sweet violet, Siberian crabapple and orris root.

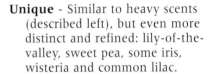
Tansy, chives, lemon balm, tarragon and sage create a mix of fragrances in this herb border.

Scented geraniums release soft fragrance when the leaves are touched.

LANDSCAPING FOR FRAGRANCE

To make fragrance a permanent aspect of your garden, it makes sense to choose plants that are in themselves relatively permanent. Woody plants, such as trees and shrubs, are the first to consider; their longevity and low-maintenance requirements are unmatched by other garden plants.

Whether you're starting with a bare lot or adding to an existing landscape, carefully study your surroundings before buying any plants. As with any garden, determine your soil type, pH, drainage, hardiness zone and available sun so that you can choose plants best suited for your conditions.

The fruity scent of saucer magnolia perfumes warm spring days.

Woodsy Aromas

When planning for fragrant plants, determine the direction of the prevailing summer wind (usually from the southwest). You'll want the plant's fragrances wafting toward your house, not away from it.

Woody plants make it easy to have some fragrance almost year-round. Smaller plants including annuals, perennials and vines usually perfume the air only in spring and summer. Fragrant shrubs and trees fill the fall-to-spring void, but there are also wonderful woody plants for the summer garden. Consider if one season of the year is more important to you than another. And remember that there can be too much of a good thing. An over-

abundance of different fragrances, particularly in a small area, can be overwhelming.

Trees and shrubs form the framework of a garden. Because of their size, they have a major impact on the garden's overall appearance. Besides the season and type of scent you must consider each plant's height, spread, density and shape.

Fragrant old-man's-beard (Chionanthus virginicus) *grows into a large shrub or small tree.*

Woody Plants for Spring Fragrance

Carolina allspice.

Carolina allspice, sweetshrub (*Calycanthus floridus*), midspring. Zones 5 to 9. Slow-growing native shrub bears maroon flowers with a fruity fragrance. Grows best in partial shade with moist, fertile soil.

Daphne (*Daphne* spp. and cultivars), spring to summer. Zones 4 to 8. Fine-textured, semi-evergreen shrubs suitable for use as specimens in mixed shrub groupings. Give them a sheltered but sunny spot with fertile, neutral soil and a good mulch. Plant carefully as daphnes can be tricky to handle.

Daphne.

*Fringe tree (*Chionanthus virginicus*).*

Fringe tree (*Chionanthus virginicus*), spring. Zones 5 to 9. Large shrub or small tree that grows to about 15 feet and blooms in spring on new wood. Fruits develop if both male and female plants are grown. Grow in slightly acidic soil in sun or partial shade.

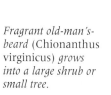

Lilac.

Lilac (*Syringa* spp. and cultivars), spring. Zones 3 to 8. The hardiest of fragrant flowering shrubs, lilacs sweeten the springtime air in millions of yards. Newer cultivars resist mildew, the most common problem with these adaptable plants. Mature height ranges from 9 to 20 feet.

Mock orange (*Philadelphus* spp. and cultivars), late spring. Zones 5 to 8. Fast-growing deciduous shrubs to 9 feet tall are ideal for areas where their white fragrant flowers can be enjoyed in spring but fade into the background for the remainder of the season. Will grow in any fertile, well-drained soil in sun or partial shade.

Mock orange.

Woody Plants for Summer Fragrance

Sweet bay magnolia.

Magnolia (*Magnolia virginiana*), spring to late summer. Zones 5 to 9. This native magnolia tree seldom grows taller than 30 feet. Dwarf cultivars are available. It is deciduous in the north and evergreen in the south. Commonly known as sweet bay magnolia, it bears lemon-scented flowers sporadically all summer. Thrives in wet soils and low spots.

Summersweet (*Clethra alnifolia*), summer. Zones 3 to 9. This native shrub or small tree is perfect for wet, shady areas. White or pink panicles of flowers develop dependably in midsummer and are attractive to butterflies. Be patient, for this plant is a slow grower.

Butterfly bush (*Buddleia* spp. and cultivars), summer to autumn. Zones 5 to 9. Long spikes of yellow, lavender, purple or white flowers with pungent fragrance appear on new wood and attract butterflies and hummingbirds. Prune back hard in winter. Will grow in any sunny, well-drained location.

Woody Plants for Fall and Winter Fragrance

Thorny eleagnus (*Eleagnus pungens*), autumn. Zones 7 to 9. Large thorny bushes produce small white, fragrant flowers in fall. Useful in boundary plantings or as part of a shrub screen. Prune to control shape. Dig or pull out unwanted volunteer seedlings.

Wintersweet (*Chimonanthus praecox*), late winter. Zones 7 to 9. Large shrub to 10 feet tall with big glossy leaves bears fragrant yellow flowers on old wood. Needs good drainage and mulch to keep roots constantly moist.

Winter honeysuckle (*Lonicera fragrantissima*), late winter to spring. Zones 5 to 8. You know spring is coming when the lemon-scented flowers appear on this wide, arching shrub. It makes an excellent accent plant for places that get winter sun but are partially shaded in summer. Mature size is 10 feet tall and equally wide.

Witch hazel (*Hamamelis* spp. and cultivars), late fall, winter or early spring, depending on species and location. Zones 4 to 8. Witch hazel flowers are shaggy clusters of stringy yellow or orange petals that fill shady woodland areas with their sweet aroma. Give these plants good sun in the north. In the south they are better in partial shade.

Butterfly bush.

Witch hazel.

FRAGRANCE IN CONTAINERS

Gardening in containers is easy, and allows you to bring fragrance up close, whether in window boxes, hanging baskets, pots on the front porch or large planters on your deck or patio. The special group of plants that provide strong fragrance and grow well in containers includes annuals, perennials and a few shrubs and bulbs. Here we will provide a sufficient sample so that you can fill your containers with unfussy fragrant plants. Then sit back and reap compliments on your gardening flair and expertise.

Scented Geraniums

Scented geraniums (*Pelargonium* spp.) are grown for their leaves rather than their flowers. They are best handled as pot-grown perennials left outdoors in summer and kept indoors when temperatures drop below freezing. Scented geranium leaves offer an amazing array of fragrances as well as shapes and textures, with over 200 species and cultivars.

Many gardeners enjoy collecting these undemanding plants with fragrances that include rose, mint, lemon and even chocolate.

Scented geraniums do best in pots placed in full sun in spring and 50 percent shade in summer. Water them when the top ½ inch of soil is dry. Feed monthly from spring to autumn. Trim them to maintain the shape and size you want. For additional plants, take root cuttings. Winter plants indoors in bright light with nighttime temperatures of 60°F.

A trio of scented geraniums.

Gardenias

The gardenia is one of the most fragrant plants on earth. It is a tropical shrub that serves well as a summer patio plant, but it needs a cool indoor place to spend the winter. Most cultivars are hardy only to about 20°F. The cultivar commonly known as 'Radicans' (*G. jasminoides radicans*) is ideal for pots filled with potting soil amended with acidic peat moss. The best flowering period is early summer. Salt buildup in pots can be a problem; it is best cured by flushing out the containers with large amounts of water at least twice each summer. Water lightly during winter when the plants are indoors.

Gardenia blossoms.

Forced Bulbs

Plant fragrant hyacinths and paperwhite narcissus in pots in the fall. Dampen well, then place the pots in a cold place for at least six weeks. An unheated garage or trench dug in the ground, or a protected spot next to the side of your house, are good places for bulbs to spend a few cold weeks growing roots. Move the pots indoors in late winter, and treat them as sun-loving houseplants until they flower. Tazetta daffodils need little (if any) cold treatment, but the hyacinths and fragrant daffodils like 'Geranium' and 'Grand Soleil d'Or' must have at least six weeks of cold.

Fragrant hyacinths are naturals for small pots.

Fragrant Flowers for Container Bouquets

It's fun to combine fast-growing annual flowers in 15- to 24-inch pots, creating fragrant container bouquets. In devising your combinations, take into consideration color compatibility, growth habit and requirements, the time of day that you want scent and whether the scents might compete with each other.

Put taller plants toward the center of a large planter, or place a stake in the middle for plants that will grow more than 15 inches tall. Surround them with lower-growing plants, plus trailing plants toward the edges. For that luxurious look, include more plants in a container than you would in a similar space directly in the garden. The following selections are widely available and easy to grow.

Fragrant purple heliotrope seems to burst from a nest of rosemary.

Flowering tobacco (*Nicotiana* spp. and cultivars)

From the rosettes of oval leaves rise stalks with trumpet-shaped, 1- to 3-inch flowers emitting an exotic fragrance at night. Flowers close during the day. For containers, look for 2 to 3-foot-tall *N. alata*, which is not as tall and lanky as the other fragrant species. You may need to start it from seed. Many dwarf bedding-type varieties are not fragrant.

Nicotiana.

Heliotrope (*Heliotropium arborescens*)

Hundreds of tiny, vanilla-scented, purple flowers form clusters to 4 inches across. The woody, openly-branched plants grow to 18 inches tall and 12 inches wide. Actually a tropical perennial, this flower is usually sold among bedding plants in spring.

Heliotrope takes center stage.

Sweet alyssum.

Sweet alyssum (*Lobularia maritima*)

A rich honey scent floats like a cloud above rounded clusters of tiny white, pink, magenta or purple flowers on sprawling, low-growing stems. Add this versatile plant to almost any container as a cascading edging plant. Alyssum grows 2 to 12 inches tall and 8 to 12 inches wide.

Petunia (*Petunia* hybrids)

This popular annual often has a strong vanilla scent in the evening, especially white, violet-blue and purple varieties. Both bush and trailing types are available. Fragrance varies among varieties and colors: Be prepared for surprises. A few fragrant selections include 'Primetime Purple', 'White Cascade' and 'Pink Wave.'

Petunias.

Stock (*Matthiola incana*)

This old-fashioned flower produces intensely sweet, clove-scented flowers. Stocks need cool weather; they melt away in high heat. The 15- to 30-inch-tall plants benefit from staking or other support, such as a small wire cage placed inside the container.

Pinks (*Dianthus* spp. including *D. plumaris* and *D. superbus*)

These short-lived perennials produce a spicy carnation-like scent when they bloom in spring. They are easy to grow in large containers filled with a sandy mix amended with lime. They grow 1 to 2 feet tall.

Garden pinks.

MARRYING ROSES AND HERBS

No two groups of plants are more synonymous with fragrance than roses and herbs. For centuries, roses were grown as much for their flowers' medicinal qualities as for beauty and heady scent. Naturally, then, they were planted together with herbs.

Besides this traditional association, the foliage and flowers of certain herbs offer a form and color that makes them a perfect companion underplanting with roses, especially the old-fashioned ones in their sumptuous shades of crimson, pink and white.

So we actually have two weddings here: One combines the fragrant older roses favored for cooking, cosmetics and potpourri in an herb garden setting. The other utilizes softly-textured, low-growing herbs— particularly ones with pastel flowers—either interplanted with roses or as an edging to beds of roses.

Growing Herbs with Roses

The partnership between roses and herbs may be a long-standing one, but like most relationships, some compromises are necessary. For instance, roses generally need fertile, well-watered soil, while herbs tend to do best in leaner, drier soil. Roses are known for their pest problems, often requiring regular spraying; which is not an appealing prospect for edible herbs.

Fortunately, well-prepared soil (enriched with organic matter such as compost) will serve both roses and herbs well. The herbs may not have quite the intensity of essential oils, and the roses may not grow quite so luxuriously, but both will do quite well. If a mulch is used, extra watering for the roses will be needed only in times of severe drought, which will also benefit the herbs.

As for rose pests, the herbs' aromatic foliage will help somewhat as a natural deterrent. Choosing pest-resistant roses is another piece of the puzzle, as is learning to live with a certain amount of disease. Finally, if you do need to use pesticides, choose ones that are "food safe" such as those described on page 177 or the homemade remedies listed on pages 180-181.

Your rewards for these efforts in growing roses with herbs? A garden of splendor for both the eyes and nose!

An orchestra of fine fragrance: A hedge of 'Ballerina' Hybrid Musk rose accompanied by lavender.

BEST HERBS TO GROW WITH ROSES

Artemisia (*Artemisia* cultivars including 'Silver Brocade' and 'Silver Mound')

Artemisia.

Common sage and purple sage (*Salvia officinalis* and *S. o.* 'Purpurea')

Sage.

Hyssop (*Hyssopus officinalis*)

Hyssop in flower.

Catmint (*Nepeta* x *fassennii* cultivars)

Catmint.

Curly parsley (*Petroselinum crispum* var. *crispum*)

Curly parsley.

Lavender (*Lavandula angustifolia* cultivars such as 'Hidcote', 'Munstead', 'Twickel Purple', 'Loddon Pink', 'Jean Davis' and 'Nana Alba')

'Hidcote' lavender.

Chamomile (*Chamaemelum nobile*)

Chamomile.

Dwarf basil (*Ocimum basilicum* cultivars such as 'Green Bouquet' or 'Spicy Globe')

Dwarf basil.

Thyme (*Thymus* spp. and cultivars)

Thyme.

Garden walls help retain the fragrance of roses such as 'Cecile Brunner'.

Most-Fragrant Roses

Many of the most-fragrant roses are antique cultivars from the first 4 groups listed here. You can find better repeat blooming and improved disease resistance in more modern rose cultivars, but the old ones still set the standard for fragrance.

Fragrant Hybrid Roses

- **English roses -** Pale to bright pink, red, yellow or white, 3- to 4-inch single to very double, mostly repeat-blooming flowers; almost all have a strong scent, either "old rose" or myrrh-like; 2 to 10 feet.

- **Floribunda roses -** Beautiful 3-inch blossoms form in loose clusters; plants bloom heavily in early summer and lightly thereafter; mature height is usually less than 4 feet; only a few floribundas have good fragrance (see below).

SCENTED FLORIBUNDA VARIETIES

'Angel Face' - lavender
'Guy de Maupassant' - pink
'Iceberg' - white
'Scentimental' - red striped
'Singin' in the Rain' - apricot

'Scentimental' Floribunda rose.

Aromatic Antique Roses

- **Alba roses -** White or pale pink, 3-inch, semidouble to double, once-blooming flowers; light, sophisticated scent; disease-resistant, gray-green leaves; 4 to 12 feet. Portland roses are similar yet smaller, and often repeat bloom.

Alba rose.

- **Bourbon roses -** Pink, crimson, purple, white or striped, 3-inch, very double, repeat-blooming flowers; strong, fruity fragrance; susceptible to mildew and blackspot; 2 to 7 feet.

'Mme. Isaac Pereire', a Bourbon rose with a heady fragrance.

'Felicia' Hybrid Musk rose.

- **Hybrid Musk roses -** Pink, apricot, yellow or white, 1- to 2-inch, single to double, repeat-blooming flowers; strong, fruity fragrance; 5 to 6 feet.

- **Rugosa roses -** Magenta, pink or white, 3-inch, single to double, repeat-blooming flowers; clove-scented; rough-textured, disease-resistant leaves; 4 to 7 feet.

- **Cabbage roses (also known as Centifolia roses) -** Pink, crimson or mauve, 3-inch, very double, once-blooming flowers; intense and far-reaching fragrance; 2 to 7 feet.

'Fantin-Latour' Centifolia rose.

- **Damask roses -** pink or white, 3-inch, very double, once-blooming flowers; attar of roses fragrance; 5 feet.

- **Gallica roses -** "Apothecary Rose"; bright pink, magenta, crimson or striped, 3-inch, single to double, once-blooming flowers; "old rose" fragrance; rough, dark-green leaves susceptible to mildew in hot, dry weather; spreads by suckers; good for hedges; 4 to 5 feet.

- **Hybrid Tea roses -** Extremely wide color range, elegant vase-shaped buds open into classic florists' type roses. Plants vary in size from 2 to 5 feet, and some are very demanding because of problems with pests, disease and cold injury. The six listed below are among the most fragrant and reliable.

HYBRID TEA VARIETIES

'Dolly Parton' - orange-red
'Double Delight' - white with red bicolor
'Fragrant Cloud' - tangerine orange
'Just Joey' - rich apricot
'Mister Lincoln' - red
'Perfume Beauty' - hot pink

'Mister Lincoln' Hybrid Tea rose.

A SCENTED EVENING GARDEN

As dusk approaches, the garden becomes a place not of chores but of winding down, allowing us to become aware of the garden's more subtle beauties. Pale flowers, especially white ones, become luminous. And the night-fragrant plants send out their delectable bouquets.

How relaxing to follow dim paths, catching a scent here, then another at a turn. The tranquilizing effect is even greater when one can simply rest in a comfortable chair on a patio or deck surrounded by night-scented plants. Let the cool evening breezes bring the various scents to you.

Pruned wisteria.

Sweet autumn clematis is fragrant around the clock, but especially after dark.

Nighttime Fragrance

It is no accident that pale-colored or white flowers have especially strong odors in the evening hours. Both the color and scent serve to guide night-flying moths and other creatures to the blooms for pollination.

Some plants have scent only at night, such as night-scented stock or evening primroses, while others develop a stronger or different scent then. Petunias, particularly, may have a barely detectable sharp scent by day that turns refined and sweet by night. And some plants are generous enough to provide scent both day and night.

Few people would want to devote a garden wholly to nocturnal scent, but to include at least a few brings pleasurable rewards. The greatest number of night-scented plants are those that bloom at the height of summer, but there are plants for both spring and fall as well. Some people never leave air-conditioned homes on hot, humid nights, while others revel in summer evenings outdoors. Plan for those times when the fragrances will be most appreciated, or include a few plants for each season.

In this hectic, never-stop world, a fragrant evening garden reminds us to slow down, breathe deeply and inhale the beauty of the world around us.

Vines for Evening Fragrance

Sweet autumn clematis (*Clematis maximowicziana*, syn. *paniculata*) Sweet vanilla scent, late summer to autumn. Vigorous perennial vine blooms on new wood. May be pruned back hard in winter. Zones 4 to 9.

Everblooming honeysuckle (*Lonicera* x *heckrottii*) Sweet honey scent, summer. Well-behaved perennial, twining vine for porches or pillars. Prune only to control size. Zones 4 to 8.

Moonflower vine.

Moonflower vine (*Ipomoea alba* syn. *Calonyction aculeatum*) Sweet lily scent, summer to autumn. Excellent for screening porches and patios from hot afternoon sun. Annual.

Wisteria (*Wisteria* species and cultivars) Sweet vanilla scent, late spring. Prune back hard in winter to control exuberant growth. Fertilize lightly or not at all. Zones 4 to 9.

Sweet autumn clematis.

'Goldflame' honeysuckle.

Japanese wisteria.

Perennials for Evening Fragrance

Cottage pink (*Dianthus plumarius* cultivars) Clove scent, late spring. Old varieties such as 'Pheasant's Eye' often have the best fragrance, but do not hesitate to try unnamed plants shared by local gardeners. Zones 3 to 9.

Cottage pinks.

Lily-of-the-valley (*Convallaria majalis*) Unique scent, spring. Allow these little plants to grow into a groundcover in shady areas, and gather the nodding bells to enjoy at nose level. Likes acidic soil with plenty of organic matter. Zones 3 to 9.

Lily-of-the-valley.

Hosta (*Hosta plantaginea*) Sweet scent, late summer. All hostas offer a little fragrance, but this one excels with its evening aroma. Large green leaves make it a good foliage plant as well. Zones 3 to 9.

Fragrant hosta.

Annuals and Biennials for Evening Fragrance

Angel's trumpet (*Datura meteloides*) Lemony scent, mid- to late summer. Huge white flowers open at night. This tropical perennial with gray-green leaves is grown as an annual from seeds started in early spring. May reseed heavily in warm climates.

Angel's trumpet.

Dame's rocket (*Hesperis matronalis*) Sweet scent, early summer with a repeat bloom later if cut back. Rose-pink or white flowers. Naturalizes in partial shade. Zones 3 to 8.

Dame's rocket.

Evening primrose (*Oenothera glazioviana*) Sweet scent similar to magnolia or tuberose. Lustrous yellow flowers open quickly at dusk, and plants usually reseed themselves. Zones 3 to 9.

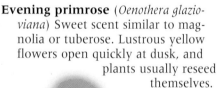

Evening primrose.

Nicotiana sylvestris.

Flowering tobacco (*Nicotiana alata, N. suaveolens, N. sylvestris*) Sweet lily scent, summer to autumn. Adapts to partial shade and often survives as a perennial in Zones 7 and 8. White flowers close during the day. Will rebloom repeatedly if cut back from time to time.

Four o'clock.

Four o'clocks, marvel of Peru (*Mirabilis jalapa*) Lemony scent, summer to autumn. Yellow, pink or bicolored flowers open in late afternoon. Considered a reliable perennial in Zones 7 to 9. Often reseeds.

Petunia (*Petunia* cultivars) Soft, refined, sugar-sweet scent, summer to autumn. Try any white or purple petunias, which tend to have more fragrance than other colors.

Petunia.

NOSE-PLEASING TROPICALS

Tuberose.

Tropical plants provide some of the most exotic and intense evening fragrances. Grow these tropicals in pots and overwinter indoors, as is the case with citrus, or try tender bulbs such as tuberose (*Polianthes tuberosa*), which must be dug and stored through the winter.

Cut back pot-grown ginger lilies (*Hedychium gardnerianum*) in fall and leave in a minimally heated storage room until conditions become warm in late spring.

Ginger lily.

❦ CHAPTER 9 ❦

FLAVOR:
GROWING VEGETABLES,
HERBS AND FRUITS

*Growing your own food gives you better freshness and flavor–and
a sense of pride and accomplishment.*

Anyone who has savored just-picked sweet corn, sliced home-grown tomatoes sprinkled with basil or a juicy strawberry knows that home-grown vegetables, fruits and herbs taste much better than anything store-bought. Freshly-harvested vegetables and fruits are always at their nutritional peak and, of course, you know exactly what pesticides were used in growing them—if you used any at all. Growing your own vegetables and fruits also enhances your health because

Raspberries are a cinch to grow yet costly to buy.

any type of gardening is a good form of exercise.

With careful planning, a kitchen garden also can save you money.

Home-Grown Flavor

There are many different ways to incorporate food plants into your landscape. You can keep a food garden going year-round, or garden only at certain times of the year, perhaps growing lettuce and other salad ingredients in the spring. Some people like to landscape with trees, shrubs, vines and perennials that produce food. Or maybe you just want fresh herbs for flavor and color. And don't forget to give children a chance to have their own little garden plot.

The important thing is to grow food plants that you genuinely like to eat. Keep an open mind about this matter, for you may find that you like freshly-harvested spinach or carrots or blueberries even though you have a ho-hum opinion of their store-bought counterparts.

To keep your edible garden from becoming a burden, it's also wise to grow only as much of any type of food plant as you are likely to harvest and consume. Squash and snap beans are so productive that you will probably need only a few plants. Even juicy raspberries or tender baby lettuce can become worrisome if you plant too much. Every gardener feels guilty when good things go to waste.

Home-grown carrots sometimes are not as pretty as the ones from the store, but their flavor is remarkably sweet, with a crisp, juicy texture.

THE NUTRITIONAL ALL-STARS

The fiber, vitamin and antioxidant phytochemicals in food plants are thought to protect you from over fifty ailments, including cancer and heart disease. In planning your kitchen garden, include at least some plants that are among the best sources of the major nutrients. These include broccoli, carrots, chard, collards, kale, dark leaf lettuce, muskmelons, peppers, tomatoes, sweet potatoes, strawberries and winter squash.

Freshly-harvested broccoli excels in tenderness, and cooks surprisingly quickly.

SEASONS IN THE EDIBLE GARDEN

Most people think of summer corn and tomatoes when they imagine a kitchen garden. But experienced food gardeners don't limit their gardening to the time span between spring and fall frosts.

With good planning, you can keep your garden productive from early spring to the last days of fall. Where winters are mild, you can grow several vegetables all the way through winter.

Starting Seeds

Vegetables vary in their ability to tolerate cold weather and withstand frost or light freezes. Hardy or cool-season crops survive medium to heavy frosts. Seeds of this group are usually planted in spring, as soon as the weather allows and the soil is dry enough to be dug or tilled. You can also plant these vegetables in midsummer for a late fall crop.

Warm-season vegetables are easily injured or killed by frost and do not grow well in cool temperatures, so they are not planted until all danger of frost is past. Both seeds and transplants of warm-season vegetables usually need soil that is 65°F or higher 4 inches below the soil surface at 8 a.m. You can start seeds of many tender crops indoors 6 to 8 weeks before the last frost or buy transplants to get a headstart on the season.

COOL-SEASON VEGETABLES FOR SPRING OR FALL

Arugula, Beets, Broccoli, Cabbage, Carrots, Cauliflower, Celery, Collards, Endive, Kale, Kohlrabi, Lettuce, Mustard, Onions, Parsley, Parsnips, Peas, Potatoes, Radishes, Spinach, Swiss chard, Turnips

A little frost is a great thing for cabbage and cabbage family cousins. They respond to cold by becoming extra sweet and crisp.

Kale comes in a variety of shapes and colors. Most survive winter cold with little or no extra protection.

The Spring Kitchen Garden

Although the spring season varies greatly in different parts of the continent, there is usually a period one to two months before the last spring frost when there are some warm, dry days. However, heavy rains or snow may keep the soil so wet that it is difficult or impossible to plant. Overcome this obstacle by preparing raised planting beds for spring crops in the fall and covering them with mulch. Rake off the mulch in early spring and start planting without re-cultivating the soil.

Although most cool-season vegetables will survive light frosts, sudden or prolonged cold weather can set them back or injure them. To protect against sudden cold periods after planting, consider using tunnels, cloches or other season-stretching devices described on pages 146-147.

Days lengthen rapidly in late spring as temperatures become warmer. These two factors often cause lettuce, spinach and other leafy greens to bolt—the term given to the process of producing flowers and seeds. As soon as these plants bolt and pass their prime, pull them out and replace them with warm-season vegetables.

By mid-spring, the garden's big salad season is in full swing.

Most summer vegetables need plenty of space. Mulch saves water and helps keep plant roots cool and moist.

The Summer Kitchen Garden

Once the last spring frost has passed and the soil is warm and dry enough to work, the big push is on. Intense sunlight, warm temperatures and long days help warm-season crops grow quickly. Monitor them closely for the need to provide water or supplemental fertilizer. Mulching between rows or plants will help preserve soil moisture and suppress weeds at the same time.

Several summer vegetables (tomatoes, peppers, beans) require stakes or trellises to keep them off the ground. Insect pests also become active—there is no better way to control them than to be alert to trouble and intervene at the earliest possible time. See Chapter 13 for help identifying and treating insect infestations in your vegetable garden.

WARM-SEASON VEGETABLES FOR SUMMER

Basil
Beans
Cucumbers

Eggplant
Melons
Okra
Peppers
Pumpkins
Squash
Sweet corn
Sweet potatoes
Tomatoes

To keep weeds at bay, mulch vegetables that stay in the ground for a long time, such as peppers and tomatoes.

SUCCESSION PLANTING

To extend the harvest period for a number of crops, many gardeners make succession sowings or plantings. This keeps the garden at maximum production and prolongs the harvest season. For example, you can usually plant bush snap beans twice, 3 to 4 weeks apart. Do the same with cucumbers, lettuce and squash. Or you might follow spring spinach with a planting of eggplant or peppers. Broccoli, cauliflower or cabbage planted in midsummer after the peas, radishes and lettuce are harvested is another possibility.

As one crop finishes bearing, replace it with something else. In this way, a small garden can produce many abundant harvests.

The Autumn Kitchen Garden

The fall garden combines summer vegetables that continue to produce up to frost—tomatoes and peppers first come to mind. Plant cool-season crops such as leafy greens in late summer for harvest after the weather turns cool.

After a busy summer in the garden, it can be difficult to muster the energy and ambition needed to grow a fall garden, but it is well worth the effort. Most cool-season plants taste fantastic when they mature in cool weather because long, cold nights make them sweeter and give them a crisp, juicy texture. For example, there is a remarkable difference between carrots, broccoli and cabbage harvested in early summer, when the weather is warm, and the same varieties harvested in fall after a few light frosts have sweetened them.

Because fall days gradually become shorter and cooler, many cool-season crops need extra time to grow to maturity. When estimating how long it will take to grow a vegetable in fall, add three weeks to the expected days to maturity listed on the seed packet. Plant early enough.

A few cool-season vegetables will survive winter in the garden if protected with a mulch or plastic tunnel. These include brussel sprouts, kale, parsley and spinach. In mild winter climates, you can often grow broccoli, collards and hardy varieties of lettuce and cabbage through winter.

Fall is a spectacular season for vegetables. Cool nights improve the quality of many cool-season crops.

PLANT AN EDIBLE LANDSCAPE

Fruit-bearing trees, shrubs, vines and perennials can turn your yard into an edible landscape that's as pretty as it is productive. There's no doubt that fruit plants are as lovely in bloom as their strictly ornamental relatives. And there are many shrubs, vines and perennial plants that provide both beauty and food—requiring no more care than popular ornamental plants.

Balancing Aesthetics and Flavor

The range of plants to consider for your edible landscape depends greatly on your adventurousness in eating, your definition of beauty and your willingness to occasionally apply some extra care— especially with pruning. Use all the berries described on pages 128 and 129 to enrich your edible landscape, as well as the plants described here. Edible landscaping also can be interpreted as tucking pretty lettuces between flowers or edging a walkway with frilly parsley.

Ideally, edible ornamental plants have attractive foliage throughout the growing season. They also should have showy flowers, fruit that is enjoyable to harvest and eat, and a neat or interesting growth habit that is useful in the landscape. And they should be easy to grow.

Dwarf fruit trees are fully mature when less than 10 feet tall, so they are easy to fit into small spaces.

Trees

Apple (*Malus* cultivars)

There are apples suited to almost every climate. Many newer cultivars resist common diseases including scab, mildew and fire blight. Obtain a list of locally-adapted varieties from your university extension service. Most apples produce best if more than one variety is grown for cross pollination. Popular varieties are available in three forms: dwarfs (5 to 8 feet tall), semi-dwarfs (12 to 16 feet tall) and standard size (20 to 30 feet tall).

In addition to producing fruit, apples and other fruit trees also enhance the garden with fragrance, color and cooling summer shade.

Cherry (*Prunus* cultivars)

Tart cherries are hardy and easily grown in Zones 4 to 7. The dwarf 'North Star' variety is an especially useful landscape plant. Many tart cherry cultivars are self-fertile, and grow into strong trees that bear for many years. Despite their name, tart cherries are sweet enough for cooking or fresh eating. Sweet cherries grow well in Zone 4 to 6, and may be sensitive to late spring frosts. Grow cultivars that are adapted to your area.

'Montmorency cherry' is beautiful in bloom and can be counted upon for heavy harvests of bright red cherries.

Plum (*Prunus* cultivars)

These fast-growing trees provide pretty spring blooms and heavy crops of fruit in years when they bear. Even when you choose varieties adapted to your climate and plant two compatible cultivars for good cross pollination, you can lose crops every few years to late spring freezes. Plum trees will grow in Zones 3 to 9.

ODD ORNAMENTAL EDIBLES

Besides the choices among the relatively familiar plants listed, don't overlook these lesser known ones.

Trees: Paw paw, American or Oriental persimmon, medlar, jujube, mayhaw, mulberry, quince, chestnut, pecan, edible pine nuts and hazelnut.

Shrubs: Highbush cranberry, edible honeysuckle, Russian olive, cornelian cherry, elderberry, gooseberries, currants, figs and hip-setting roses (but don't use systemic pesticides).

Groundcovers: Strawberries make a good groundcover, as do creeping herbs including thyme and some types of rosemary and mint.

Shrubs

Bush cherry or plum (*Prunus* species)

This group includes several shrubs that produce tart fruits including beach plum, Japanese bush cherry, Nanking cherry, cherry-plum hybrids and sand cherry. The beach plums grow 6 to 10 feet tall while the others grow 4 to 8 feet tall. They are useful as foundation plants, hedges or specimen plants. Bush cherries and plums are easily grown and relatively pest-free. Although some are self-fertile, you get the best fruit production with two or more varieties.

'Hansen's Bush'
Nanking cherry.

Juneberry (*Amelanchier* species)

These include several species of native American shrubs with blueberry-like fruit with a subtle almond flavor. Plants grow from 4 to 10 feet tall and they are hardy in Zones 3 to 8. Plants bear white or pink flowers in spring, and have good autumn color and attractive striped bark for winter show. Use them in foundation plantings, shrub borders or hedges.

Vines

Grape (*Vitis* species)

These woody vines can grow to over 50 feet long, but they can be kept at 20 feet or less with pruning. Hardiness varies among varieties, ranging from Zones 4 to 10. Choose a variety recommended for your area. Yearly pruning is needed and pests may be a problem. Except for muscadines, most varieties are self-pollinating.

'Perlette' grapes.

Kiwi.

Kiwi (*Actinidia* species)

The brown fuzzy fruit, usually found in stores, grow on vines that are only hardy to Zone 9, but there are types with 1-inch, smooth green fruit that are hardy in Zones 5 to 9. The vigorous deciduous vines grow to 20 feet or more in length. The female plants bear small fragrant, white flowers in spring and the fruit ripens from midsummer until frost. 'Issai' is self-fertile, but other varieties need a male plant nearby for pollination.

PRIME PERENNIAL VEGETABLES

Don't let the fine flavor of **asparagus** fool you into thinking it comes from a temperamental plant. Asparagus is tremendously tough and grows like a weed in Zones 3 to 8. You will need a large planting for a good harvest. Because of its ferny foliage, asparagus is ideal for growing as a soft summer hedge.

Asparagus.

Rhubarb can be difficult to grow well south of Zone 7. In northern areas the plants are heavy producers of thick, juicy stalks. Fertilize them with composted manure every spring and divide old plants every few years. Never eat rhubarb leaves, for they contain toxic levels of oxalic acid.

Rhubarb.

GROW A SALAD GARDEN

It's easy to have healthy gourmet salads at your fingertips when you grow your own salad ingredients. Lettuces and many other greens are among the easiest and fastest of any crops the gardener can grow. An added bonus is that they're beautiful—whether you arrange them in blocks or rows in the garden, use them to edge a bed, or plant them in containers.

Salad Crops

Lettuce is a cool season crop, as are many other salad greens and vegetables described on the following pages, including spinach, peas and radishes. Cucumbers and tomatoes help bridge the gap between the two big salad garden seasons—spring and fall.

Because lettuce and other salad crops are eaten raw, it is best to make several small sowings instead of one large one. Plant lettuce a square foot at a time beginning in very early spring, or in late winter under protective rowcovers. To keep your salads interesting, mix lettuce varieties that have different colors and textures. There are dozens of lettuce varieties to choose from, including the representative strains described at right.

In an area that gets sun at least 6 hours each day, plant lettuce seeds only ⅛ inch deep. Lettuce also transplants well after being started indoors, a method particularly effective for summer plantings. Thin seedlings or space transplants 6 to 8 inches apart. For the best growth over the longest period, keep the soil evenly moist, because dry soil leads to slow growth and bitter flavor. Once lettuce bolts into a flower stalk, the lettuce becomes bitter and unusable.

To keep salads interesting, grow an assortment of lettuce varieties that have different colors, flavors and textures.

Lettuce seedlings need plenty of light to keep from growing long and leggy.

GREAT LETTUCES FOR YOUR GARDEN

Type of Lettuce	Variety	Days to Maturity	Color	Comments
Looseleaf These varieties form loose heads that mature very quickly, usually in 45 to 60 days. They are very easy to grow. Leaf color, shape and texture varies with variety.	'Black-Seeded Simpson'	45	Light green	Heirloom; crinkly; best in spring.
	'Green Ice'	45	Medium green	Deeply savoyed; heat tolerant.
	'Red Sails'	45	Bronze-burgundy	Ruffled; heat tolerant; one of the best.
	'Royal Oakleaf'	50	Dark green	Lush, large, tender and sweet; heat tolerant.
	'Salad Bowl'	50	Lime green	Oakleaf form; heat and tipburn tolerant.
Crisphead The classic iceberg type is very crisp, but it is also slow and difficult to grow. The densely packed heads often take 60 to 70 days or more to develop.	'Crispino'	60	Glossy green	Easier to grow than most.
	'Rosy'	70	Red to burgundy	Tolerant of bad conditions; slow to bolt.
	'Summertime'	70	Light green	Sweet flavor; heat tolerant.
Butterhead Also called bibb or Boston, butterheads form loose heads with soft texture. In spring they mature in 55 to 120 days. Some varieties are very winter hardy.	'Arctic King'	120	Pale green	Sow in fall for spring harvest.
	'Brune d'Hiver'	55	Pale green and bronze	Hardy enough to sow in fall for harvest in spring.
	'Buttercrunch'	55	Dark green	Thick, juicy, tender; slow to bolt in spring.
	'Red Riding Hood'	55	Red	Fast grower with good heat tolerance.
	'Tom Thumb'	55	Light green	Produces single serving-sized heads.
Romaine Romaines have upright heads that shed water, so they are great where springs are wet. Heads form late (50 to 75 days), when plants are almost mature.	'Little Gem'	55	Bright green	Dense mini-heads; to 6 inches tall.
	'Romance'	50	Medium green	Smooth, crunchy leaves; disease resistant; also consider 'Medallion'.
	'Rosalita'	60	Purple over bright green	Compact; excellent flavor, 10-inch heads.
	'Rouge d'Hiver'	60	Red over green	Large, broad leaves; good cold tolerance.
	'Winter Density'	54	Dark green	Cold-tolerant variety similar to a tall butterhead.
Batavian Also called French or summer crisp, Batavian varieties form barrel-shaped heads in 48 to 60 days. Texture is similar to crispheads, but this type is much easier to grow.	'Cardinale'	60	Rich green with burgundy edges	Large, open vase shape; frilly edges; disease resistant.
	'Loma'	48	Deep green	Frilly, deeply toothed; short, dense heads; disease resistant; very adaptable.
	'Nevada'	52	Bright green	Frilly, deeply toothed; compact, upright heads; disease resistant; excellent flavor.
	'Sierra'	52	Bright green with red edges	Puckered, wavy; loose, upright heads; heat tolerant; disease resistant.

'Green Ice' lettuce.

'Red Sails' is a reliable looseleaf lettuce.

'Tom Thumb' lettuce.

'Little Gem' lettuce.

'Nevada' lettuce.

More Greens for the Salad Garden

Arugula (*Eruca* spp.) - Also known as rocket or roquette. The peppery flavor of this easily-grown green is best when leaves are small, about 3 to 4 inches long. Make succession sowings every two weeks from early to late spring, thinning to 6 inches apart. Harvest begins in about five weeks. Cut individual leaves or entire plant at soil line, after which they resprout.

Arugula.

Endive/Escarole (*Cichorium endivia*) - A lettuce-like salad green with a nutty and bitter flavor. The broadleaf type is known as escarole and the curly-leaved type as endive. Both are ready to harvest in about 45 days and are best grown in spring or autumn. If desired, blanch by covering the heads with a pot or box 3 days before harvesting.

Mache (*Valerianella* spp.) - Also called corn salad, lamb's lettuce or lamb's tongue. The small, dark, soft, tongue-shaped leaves are very tender and mild-flavored. It grows best in spring or fall, overwintering in mild climates or with protection in colder climates. Harvest leaf by leaf or the entire plant when 3 inches tall.

Mache.

Mesclun.

Mesclun (mixture of several species) - Mesclun is a blend of gourmet baby salad greens that can be mild, pungent or bitter, depending on what mixture you choose. Make small sowings two weeks apart and harvest by cutting the leaves with scissors or a sharp knife. A few weeks later, make a second cutting of tender new leaves.

Spinach.

Spinach (*Spinacia oleracea*) - A dark-colored, uniquely flavored green, popular both fresh or cooked, spinach has oval, smooth to crinkly leaves. It grows best in the cool soil of early spring or when planted in early fall. Plant thinly—about 3 inches apart. Harvest leaf by leaf or cut off the entire plant, usually about 40 days after planting.

Swiss chard (*Beta vulgaris, cicla* group) - Closely related to beets and easily grown, chard produces greens for salads or cooking throughout the growing season. The dark green, crinkly leaves grow to about 18 inches tall with bright white, red, yellow or pink ribs. Harvest by pulling individual leaves.

Swiss chard.

TIP **Gourmet Greens**

Little-known greens to consider for your salad garden include red or green orach, miner's lettuce, minutina, sorrel, purslane, dandelion, red Russian kale, garden cress, nasturtium and leaf amaranth. Many of these have strong flavors, so you probably will not eat a great quantity. Asian greens grown mostly for cooking also can be used in salads; these include mizuna, pak choi, shungiku, tatsoi, Japanese red mustard and Chinese cabbage.

Gourmet salad greens are often nothing more than a mixture of different lettuces pulled from the ground when they are very young.

More Vegetables for the Salad Garden

Lettuces and other greens may be the main ingredient in a tossed salad, but lots of other vegetables add variety, interest and extra taste. Most of the time these are added raw, but sometimes you might use them grilled or lightly steamed. Besides the ones listed below, also consider asparagus, green or wax beans, broccoli, cauliflower and tomatoes. And don't forget to add edible flowers and fresh herbs to your salads!

Carrots - Baby or mini carrots are sweet and pleasurable in salads. These are ready to harvest in 50 to 55 days. Because of their small size they are also easy to grow.

Miniature carrots.

Cucumbers - Cool, mild and refreshing, cucumbers add a pleasant crunch to salads. Plant cucumbers after all danger of frost has passed. Vining plants grow best on a trellis or in a cage. There are also compact bush varieties for small gardens or containers.

Cucumber.

Scallions.

Snow peas.

Peas - Shell, snow, and snap peas are all sweet, crunchy additions to salads. Peas are a cool-season crop, so plant the seeds as soon as the soil can be worked in spring. You can also plant a fall crop, but it will probably be less productive. Train vines up a wire fence, netting or shrubby branches stuck in the ground.

Radishes.

Radishes - Radishes provide almost instant gratification for the gardener in the cool weather of spring and autumn. They are ready to pull in less than four weeks. Their crisp, zesty bite are a familiar addition to salads. Varieties feature different sizes, shapes and colors.

Scallions - Also called green onions, the bulbless bunching onions take up little garden space and are very hardy. The 'Evergreen Hardy White' variety even overwinters in Maine. Sow seed in early spring for summer use, or in midsummer for the fall and following spring. Once established, treat scallions as perennials by dividing the clumps.

Turnips.

Turnips - Forget about strong-flavored winter storage turnips: For salads, you want to slice or shred the sweet, easily-grown Japanese or French varieties such as 'Hakurei' or 'De Milan'. Harvest in five to six weeks after planting, when 1 to 2 inches in diameter. Make successive sowings from early spring to late summer.

TERRIFIC TOMATOES

Nothing seems to fit the kitchen garden more than home-grown tomatoes. Whether your garden is big or small, you should have no trouble raising plenty of rich-tasting tomatoes in a rainbow of colors including red, pink, orange, yellow, striped or even purple.

With so many shapes and colors to explore, growing tomatoes can become a hobby in itself.

Choosing Tomato Plants

When choosing tomatoes for your garden, it's a good idea to grow different types and varieties. Each variety has its own unique look and taste, and you will see big differences in how various varieties actually grow in your garden.

Disease resistance is a huge plus to have on your side. Tomatoes are susceptible to several widespread diseases that live from year to year in the soil. While vigorous hybrids usually produce heavy crops, you may also want to try heirloom varieties in your garden. But don't forsake hybrids entirely: Some of the best-tasting old heirloom varieties produce poorly unless weather conditions are exactly right.

Also consider growth habit. Tomato varieties labeled "determinate" grow to a certain height and then produce a crop that ripens in a short period; this is especially good for canning or preserving. "Indeterminate" types continue to grow and produce all season long. A few varieties have an in-between growth habit that may be called either "vigorous determinate" or "semi-indeterminate." After they bear a heavy crop, pruning and fertilization will often promote a new spurt of growth.

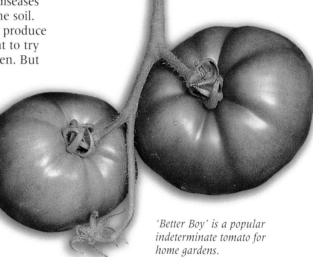

'Better Boy' is a popular indeterminate tomato for home gardens.

Tomato-Growing Tips

- **Buy tomatoes as transplants,** or start seeds indoors six to eight weeks before the last spring frost in your area.

Use insulated cloches such as "Wall-o-Waters" to give tomatoes a head start in spring.

- **Do not set tomato transplants** into the garden until all frost is past *unless* you can provide special protection. Large insulated cloches such as Wall-o-Waters or Aqua-Domes work well with tomatoes.

- **Tomatoes need full sun,** fertile soil and an even supply of moisture. A week before planting, work 1 to 2 pounds of 5-10-10 or similar low-nitrogen fertilizer into the soil. Too much nitrogen will reduce yields.

- **Set plants deeper** in the garden than they were growing in pots. When deeply planted, tomatoes grow additional roots along the buried section of stem.

- **Apply a thick organic mulch** a month after transplanting. Tomatoes thrive in soil that is kept constantly moist and free of weeds.

- **When the first fruit clusters form** and every three weeks afterward, work ½ tablespoon of 5-10-10 or similar fertilizer into the soil 6 inches from the main stem.

- **For best flavor,** harvest tomatoes when they are fully colored but still firm.

- **Never chill ripe tomatoes.** After they are picked, keep tomatoes in a warm place to preserve the flavor compounds that give tomatoes their rich, full-bodied taste.

Staking and Trellising

Except for the very shortest varieties, tomato stems are not strong enough to hold up the vines and fruit on their own. Use one of the support systems below to help your tomato plants stay upright.

Cages. Purchase cages or make your own from concrete reinforcing wire. Cages are often preferred in warm climates where tomatoes grow into large, lush plants. Ideally, tomato cages should be about 2 feet wide and 4 to 6 feet tall. Anchor well by pushing cages deep into the ground or lashing them to sturdy stakes. Install cages soon after transplanting and then mulch over the ground.

Wire cages do a great job of supporting vigorous unpruned tomatoes.

Stakes. Stakes support tomatoes that are pruned to promote earlier harvest of big tomatoes. This method is commonly used in cool climates where tomatoes must be pushed along if they are to ripen well before frost. Prune plants to one or two main stems, and tie them to stakes with strips of soft cloth. In warm climates, pruned tomatoes are more prone to sunscald and cracking.

If you stake your tomatoes, add ties as needed to secure the main stems to the stakes at 8- to 10-inch intervals.

Trellises. Make your own trellis of strings attached to a wire. Or use a wire fence to support your tomatoes. Some pruning is needed to control lateral growth and you will need to tie the main stems to the trellis. Trellising saves space and is a versatile method that allows you to prune or not prune, depending on the size and vigor of your plants.

Five Fine-Tasting Tomatoes

If you are new to tomatoes and confused by all the varieties available as plants and seeds, use this short list as a starting place for choosing a good variety of dependable tomatoes.

'Mortgage Lifter'.

'Mortgage Lifter' (indeterminate heirloom) is more productive and dependable than most old varieties. There are several different strains.

'Celebrity'.

'Celebrity' (vigorous indeterminate hybrid) is a round red tomato that grows in a wide range of climates and soils. Nothing slows it down.

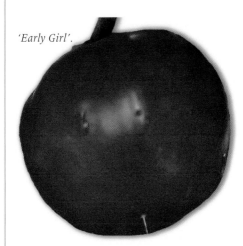

'Early Girl'.

'Early Girl' (indeterminate hybrid) is often the first tomato to ripen. Its dependability and earliness have made it popular for decades.

'Roma'.

'Roma' (determinate hybrid) is ideal for cooking and freezing. The meaty oval fruits have little juice and few seeds.

'Sweet Chelsea' (indeterminate hybrid) produces large cherry tomatoes in pretty clusters. The flavor is very sweet.

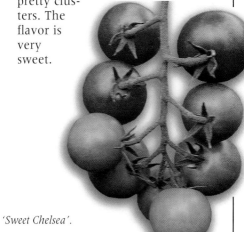

'Sweet Chelsea'.

GROWING GOURMET HERBS

Herbs bring pleasure to the gardener with their interesting forms, fascinating history, folklore and wide range of fragrances. However, it is the flavor of herbs—what they do for foods—that makes them especially loved.

Herbs include annuals (basil, dill), perennials (chives, mint) or hardy biennials (parsley). Growth habit also varies from extremes such as low, ground-hugging thyme to tall, lanky dill. Herbs are grown mainly for their edible leaves, but some produce tasty flowers and seeds too.

Herbal Basics

Herbs are most often planted in their own separate area in the garden, frequently in formal raised beds where they benefit from improved drainage. You can also grow herbs in containers, in your vegetable garden, or tucked into flower beds. As long as herbs get plenty of sun and fertile, well-drained soil, they will likely thrive with little care.

No matter where you grow herbs, use them in all aspects of your cooking. Even though there are certain classic combinations, such as basil and tomatoes, there are no hard-and-fast rules as to what goes with what. Nibble on your herbs, finding the flavors you like best. Then consider which of your favorite foods they might enhance. The right herbs bring fresh flavors to pasta sauces, simple steamed vegetables, salad dressings, breads and many other foods.

Rosemary comes in several different forms, such as this trailing variety. Expect a similar level of diversity with basil, mint and thyme.

A garden of herbs and flowers delights all your senses.

Ten Top Culinary Herbs

Basil (*Ocimum basilicum*)

The most treasured annual herb of summer is a snap to grow as long as the weather is warm. Buy seedlings or start basil from seeds sown indoors four weeks before the last frost. Do not transplant outdoors until the weather has turned summery. Pinch out growing tips to encourage branching; remove flower buds to prolong a plant's life. There are dozens of types and varieties of basil and they are all wonderful.

Basil.

Chives (*Allium schoenoprasum*)

The thin, hollow green leaves of chives offer a delicate onion flavor. Growing in clumps, they produce leaves from early spring to late fall. Established plants bear edible mauve flowers in late spring. Hardy to Zone 3, start chives from seeds or grow from transplants. Divide clumps every two to three years to rejuvenate them.

Chives.

Cilantro (*Coriandrum sativum*)

Cilantro leaves are indispensable in Mexican and Southeast Asian cooking. Resembling flat-leaf parsley, cilantro leaves are best when picked young. A half-hardy annual, cilantro grows best in cool weather and quickly goes to seed. Cilantro does not transplant well, so sow seed directly into the garden monthly from spring until early fall.

Cilantro.

Dill.

Dill (*Anethum graveolens*)

This easy annual is as pretty as it is edible. The ferny plants grow to 3 feet tall, and quickly produce round umbels of yellow flowers. Dill does not transplant well, so sow seed directly into the garden. Make successive plantings every 3 or 4 weeks for a continuous supply of fresh leaves. If allowed to develop mature seeds, dill will often reseed itself.

Mint (*Mentha* spp. and cultivars)

This incredibly vigorous herb comes in a wide range of flavors, some with fruity overtones. A perennial hardy through Zone 4, mint tolerates light shade. Mints can be invasive and are often grown in pots to keep them from taking over the garden. Cut back plants after flowering to stimulate the growth of new stems.

Mint.

Oregano (*Origanum* spp. and cultivars)

Synonymous with Italian food, oregano is a dependable perennial hardy through Zone 5. The bushy, spreading plants grow 1 to 2 feet tall, with small oval leaves and clusters of tiny purple or white edible flowers. Cut plants back almost to the ground in early summer to promote the growth of new stems and leaves.

Oregano.

Parsley (*Petroselinum crispum*)

Parsley comes in two forms, curly and flat. Curly parsley has finely divided and twisted leaves on 12-inch-tall plants. Flat-leaf or Italian parsley has flat, celery-like leaves on 24-inch-tall plants. This type is particularly favored for cooking. Parsley is a biennial hardy through Zone 6, but it is usually grown as an annual. Buy transplants or start parsley from seed, soaking the seed overnight in warm water before planting. Harvest individual stems as needed, picking the outermost ones.

Parsley.

Rosemary.

Rosemary (*Rosmarinus officinalis*)

Rosemary is a woody, evergreen shrub, either upright or cascading, hardy through Zone 8. 'Arp,' 'Salem' and 'Hill's Hardy' survive winter through Zone 6. Grow plants in pots and bring indoors in winter. Rosemary can grow 3 to 6 feet tall, with narrow gray-green and small blue or pink flowers. Grow rosemary from transplants or rooted cuttings.

Sage (*Salvia officinalis*)

Sage has a much more mellow, pleasant flavor when used fresh rather than dried. Sage is a woody perennial hardy through Zone 5. It grows to 24 inches tall. Beautiful stalks of edible purple flowers are borne in late spring. The pebbly, gray-green leaves are evergreen in mild winters. There are also varieties with purple or variegated leaves. Grow sage from transplants. Propagate new plants from old by rooting cuttings (see page 166).

Sage.

Thyme (*Thymus* spp. and cultivars)

Thyme is a versatile perennial, hardy through Zone 5. Start with a rooted cutting or a pot-grown plant of a good culinary cultivar such as 'French' and 'English' or perhaps lemon, caraway and orange balsam. Thyme hugs the ground and grows only 12 inches tall. It also produces tiny pink, lavender or white flowers in midsummer that are edible.

Thyme.

A GARDEN FOR KIDS

Nature's magic transcends chronological age, and those who experience it early seem especially likely to carry the joys of gardening with them throughout life. The memories of giant sunflowers stretching to the sky or the secrets told in a bean teepee last a lifetime. Any mentor—a parent, grand-parent, aunt, uncle or neighbor—that takes the time and effort to teach a child to develop and work a garden, will receive great rewards for their effort.

Children learn many lessons while gardening—from math and reading to various aspects of science like botany, weather and entomology. Patience, responsibility, and the pleasures of physical work are additional benefits. This is most likely to occur when the project is made to be a fun adventure.

The younger they are, the more they like to pick. Share your garden until kids are old enough to have their own garden patch to enjoy.

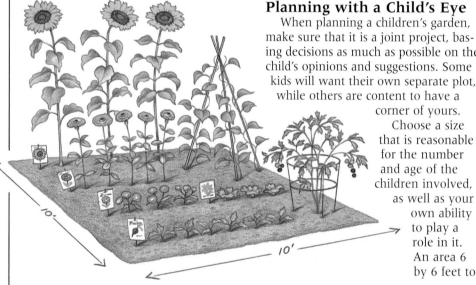

Planning with a Child's Eye

When planning a children's garden, make sure that it is a joint project, bas-ing decisions as much as possible on the child's opinions and suggestions. Some kids will want their own separate plot, while others are content to have a corner of yours.

Choose a size that is reasonable for the number and age of the children involved, as well as your own ability to play a role in it. An area 6 by 6 feet to 15 by 15 feet is a good size to consider. Whether the children do the spading or you provide the tilling depends on cir-cumstances. Let the kids remove rocks, if necessary, and do their own raking and hoeing.

Starting the garden from seed is usually the most exciting, but only with varieties that germinate easily. Use transplants with vegetables or flowers that are difficult to start to give better assurance of success. Kids love to water, so it's a good idea to provide them with a small watering can of their own. When the gardening session is over, get everybody involved in the cleanup.

Children enjoy watering just about anything.

From scarecrows to flags to drawings tacked onto fences or trees, plan ahead to let kids develop their own unique notions of garden art.

Selecting Plants for Kids

To keep the spark of interest burning, plan for special events that keep happening throughout the gardening season. Start out with easy radishes, lettuce and baby carrots. Then build a teepee for scarlet runner beans or purple pole beans. A number of other edible plants that are proven favorites among children are described below. You may be delighted to find that children are willing to eat many raw vegetables that they grow themselves, even if they would never consider consuming the same foods when presented on a dinner plate.

Great Plants for a Kid's Garden

Pole beans - Pole beans grow fast and often stay productive all season long if the beans are continually picked. Scarlet runner beans have bright red flowers and flat, green pods best harvested at 4 to 6 inches long.

Scarlet runner beans.

Popcorn - Few snacks are as healthy as popcorn. To ensure pollination, plant in blocks. Most grow to about 6 feet tall and mature in 95 to 110 days, except for 'Tom Thumb' which grows 3½ feet tall and matures in 85 days. Besides varieties with yellow kernels, there are ones with red or multicolored kernels that make great fall decorations.

Popcorn.

Radishes - Maturing in 24 to 30 days, radishes are easily grown in spring or fall. Of the many varieties, 'Easter Egg' may be the most fun with its mixture of red-, purple- and white-skinned radishes.

Beet, carrot and whopper radishes.

Baby carrots - The round types of baby carrots, such as 'Thumbelina' or 'Parmex' are the quickest and easiest to grow, maturing in 50 to 60 days. But also consider the traditionally shaped "baby" types like 'Kinko', 'Amsdor' or 'Babette'.

'Thumbelina' carrots.

Lettuce - Looseleaf and butterhead lettuces are easily grown spring crops. Harvest leaf by leaf about six weeks after planting, then continue for another month or so.

Cherry tomatoes - Little cherry tomatoes are dependable and prolific, with fruits the perfect size for snacking right in the garden. Besides red ones like 'Supersweet 100' or 'Sweet Chelsea,' consider tangerine-colored 'Sun Gold'.

Cherry tomatoes.

Spaghetti squash - What could be more fun than growing your own spaghetti? This is a type of winter squash that, when cooked, becomes noodle-like. The vining plants need plenty of space and mature 85 to 90 days after planting. Compact varieties mature faster, in about 75 days.

Gourds - Decorative multicolored gourds make great fall decorations and they are as easy to grow as squash. To save space, train the vines up a sturdy trellis.

Sunflowers - Once thought of simply as garden giants with golden flowers and large seedheads, the selection of sunflowers has blossomed into dozens of varieties. Some are only 3 feet tall, or you can opt for gigantic 8-foot-tall varieties including 'Mammoth Russian' or 'Sun Goddess'.

Pumpkins - Although pumpkins take up a lot of space and must have at least 90 days to mature, they can be worth the effort. Miniature pumpkins like 'Munchkin', 'Jack Be Little' and 'Baby Boo' are always a great success with kids.

Giant and miniature pumpkins.

BLOOMING BEAUTIES

Don't forget to include some flowers for their color, beauty and the opportunity to pick bouquets for sharing. Some of the easiest and most pleasurable-to-grow include sunflowers, marigolds and zinnias. Nasturtiums are great too; the seeds are large enough for small hands to handle easily.

Nasturtiums.

BRIGHT AND BOUNTIFUL BERRIES

Many fruit-growing efforts end in disappointment for some gardeners, but not with berries. Berries are the easiest fruits to grow, and they require little space. Plus, compared to tree fruits, berries have few problems with pests or diseases.

Choosing Berries

Choose berries that are known to grow well in your climate. In Zones 3 through 6, you will probably do best with strawberries, raspberries and highbush blueberries. In warmer areas, grow rabbiteye blueberries, blackberries and specially-adapted varieties of raspberries and strawberries. Consult your university extension service for a list of named cultivars recommended for your area.

Sun, soil fertility and soil moisture all influence the size and flavor of berries. In most areas berries grow best in full sun, but where summers are very hot a bit of afternoon shade is often beneficial. If possible, use slow-release organic fertilizers, including processed or composted manure. Many growers have observed that soil fertilized with organic materials result in better-tasting berries.

Not a blueberry will be lost when plants are protected with tunnels covered with polyester bird netting.

Spectacular Strawberries

The favorite fruit of the goddess Venus and thought to have mystical and healing powers, strawberries are an excellent source of vitamin C and potassium. Strawberries are divided into three categories. June-bearers ripen a single concentrated crop in mid- to late spring, while everbearers produce fruits sporadically from spring to fall. Day-neutral types are a type of everbearing strawberry that have the potential to set fruit continuously all summer when growing conditions are very good.

Strawberries share bed space with thyme.

Strawberries ripen so close to ground level that small people often make the best pickers.

- **In Zones 4 to 6**, plant all types of strawberries in early spring. Space plants 18 inches apart in wide rows spaced 4 feet apart, or set plants in raised beds so they are at least 15 inches apart in all directions.

- **Remove flowers** the first year and train runners to form a dense row 18 inches wide. Add a light straw mulch after the ground has frozen in the fall. As growth starts the next spring, move straw to between the rows. Plants begin bearing in about six weeks. When bearing is finished, mow off the leaves, fertilize and keep the plants weeded. A new planting is needed about every five years.

- **In Zones 7 to 9**, grow strawberries as short-lived perennials. Every other year, dig up your healthiest plants in early fall and replant them in a freshly-prepared space.

- **In spring**, use a roll-out weed barrier between rows and mulch between plants with pine needles. There is no need to pick off flowers because plants re-set in the fall will typically grow extensive roots during the winter and produce well the following spring.

- **Mow the foliage** from spring-bearers in early summer to limit diseases, and provide water as needed during summer droughts to keep the plants alive.

Bountiful Blues

In addition to bearing delicious fruits, blueberries are excellent landscape plants. They feature dainty white flowers in spring, fiery red autumn foliage and reddish stems in winter.

Varieties

The right type of blueberry will grow almost anywhere. Northern highbush types are best for Zones 4 to 7 and grow 4 to 6 feet tall. Lowbush blueberries are a species *(Vaccinium angustifolium)* rather than a hybrid and grow 10 to 24 inches tall, mainly in New England. Rabbiteye varieties are best for the warmer areas, growing 6 to 10 feet tall in Zones 7 to 9.

'Collins' Northern highbush blueberry.

'Tifblue' rabbityeye blueberry.

Growing Conditions

Blueberries thrive in moist, humus-rich soil with an acidic pH of 5.0 to 5.5. When setting out plants (preferably in early spring when they are just beginning to break dormancy), make sure that the topmost roots are no deeper than ½ inch below soil level. After planting, apply a 4-inch layer of organic mulch around the plants. Many varieties do not require cross-pollination, but growing two or more varieties increases yields and prolongs the picking season. For the best-flavored blueberries, wait a day or two after they turn blue before picking them.

Pruning

Blueberries benefit from light pruning when they are dormant. Prune primarily to thin out old branches or twigs that droop toward the center or base of the bush. Prune lowbush blueberries by cutting them back to 2 inches every three or four years.

Rambling Brambles

Raspberries and blackberries are bramble fruits. Cultivated varieties are much more productive than wild strains and usually taste better. Some modern varieties have thornless canes, which makes them easy to use in the landscape. Others are huge, rambling plants that are best grown in large thickets.

Because bramble fruits vary in their tolerance of cold and heat, plant cultivars known to grow well in your area. Raspberries and blackberries are typically sold as bare-root plants that must be re-planted soon after they are taken from nursery fields in late winter or early spring, just as they are beginning to develop fat leaf buds on dormant canes.

'Autumn Bliss' red raspberry.

'Chester' thornless blackberry.

'Bristol' blackcap raspberries.

> **TIP Bountiful Berries**
>
> All bramble fruits produce their heaviest crops on new canes that grew the year before. Cut out canes as they finish fruiting and lop off the tops of new canes when they reach chest height. This forces lateral branching, which increases the following year's crop.

§ CHAPTER 10 §

SPECIAL FEATURES:
ACCENTING YOUR LANDSCAPE

Accent your landscape's style or enhance its beauty with water, lighting and high-visibility beds.

Just as you accessorize your clothing or your kitchen, you can improve your outdoor spaces by adding the right finishing touches. If you need color, the solution might be as simple as building a raised bed and planting it with annual flowers. For unbeat-able contrast in texture, create a small water garden and stock it with fish and plants. After dark, you can use soft lights to play with unusual shapes and sil-houettes in your landscape and make it safer at the same time.

Landscape Accents

Depending on your landscape's size and style, you might also use statuary, specimen trees, shrubs or a number of other items as focal points that naturally attract attention. Land-scape accents with practical purposes include a comfortable outdoor bench, a picnic table in the shade, or an art-fully arranged group of container plants. If you love to watch wildlife, a birdbath surrounded by flowers that attract butterflies will bring you many hours of enjoyment. Indeed, it cannot be overemphasized that the

A rope hammock is always an inviting land-scape accent.

fun factor is the most important aspect of landscape accents and other special features.

A stone trough receives a gentle stream of water. Its sound and appearance add a soothing touch to the garden, and will attract birds and other wildlife as well.

ON SOUNDS AND MUSIC

Not all special landscape features are visual. The sounds of wind rustling through the trees, the gentle tinkling of bells or wind chimes, or music from an outdoor speaker all add sensual depth to a garden and can help draw attention away from distracting noises from traffic or neigh-bors. You also can use sound to emphasize a special place, as when you install a small fountain in a water garden or suspend a small wind chime from a limb of your favorite shade tree.

You can easily install weather-resistant speakers under the eaves of your house so you can enjoy music on your deck or patio. Or use a portable stereo as a source of garden music to make weeding go faster or help you hum as you mulch. Look for models built to withstand the hazards of outdoor living.

LOCATING SPECIAL FEATURES

Strategic placement of accents and special features is one of the more powerful ways to structure your landscape. Flower beds or water gardens naturally draw attention, so it is wise to locate them where they become logical destinations or focal points within the landscape. The same is true of statuary or other garden ornaments, which can introduce an element of mystery or surprise when you give special thought to their placement.

Choosing Sites

Consider these four important factors when choosing sites for special features:

1. Style

Flags or banners dramatize every breeze and bring color to the landscape.

Any accent you choose should blend well with your landscape's style. Formal fountains or statues work wonders in a highly structured landscape, but may seem garish in more relaxed settings. Whimsical accents such as flags or windsocks create a festive atmosphere that make a garden more fun. They may be particularly delightful when placed close so that children can touch and enjoy them.

2. Scale

Sometimes small features bring the greatest delight.

Keep features in proper scale to the setting in which they are used. Small landscapes call for small features, whether those features are furniture, statuary or sculpted trees. Massive features will make everything else within a small yard seem dwarf, while tiny features are easily lost within a large landscape.

3. Comfort

Because shady spots are the most comfortable places to sit and relax, they are the best areas for seating or perhaps a cozy hammock. As you develop your relaxation spot, pay close attention to ways you might be able to frame or otherwise enhance your views with specially-selected plants or other garden accents.

Make time to relax and enjoy your garden. A rope hammock is hard to resist when it's time to take a break from work or play.

4. Mood

Color is a potent tool for developing your garden's mood. White and soft pastels tend to invoke a quiet, soothing mood; bright reds and oranges feel more vibrant and exciting. Working with color gives you great flexibility, for you can change color with the seasons or from year to year.

These bright geraniums sizzle amid the cooler green of the surrounding hedge.

Choosing Garden Accents

Getting mail has a special reward in this yard, where a bed of daffodils welcomes you home. Even bills aren't so bad in a setting like this.

Beds

Locate curved island-type beds within an open swath of lawn or beneath a grouping of small trees. Either way, tailored groups of plants with distinctive colors or textures always generate attention and compliments. Annual flowers often give the longest and most intense display of color, especially when planted in large masses. When you want to focus attention on a place where digging an in-ground bed is impractical, use raised beds (see page 134) to grow your favorite flowers, herbs or vegetables.

Statuary

The large statues often seen in big display gardens seldom work well in home landscapes. Instead, choose smaller statues and place them where they look most natural. Small concrete figures of people or animals that blend with their surroundings are a constant source of delight, while larger items can easily overwhelm limited spaces. Small statues also can be moved from place to place—another asset that lets you alter scenes as the seasons change.

A small snail made of cast concrete lurks among the hostas.

Water Features

Every year more gardeners discover the fun of water gardening—the only type of landscape features that can bring you face to face with flowers, frogs and fish at the same time. Still water provides a mirror-like reflective surface, and many of the best blooming aquatic plants grow best in still water. If you want the sound and movement of a fountain, keep it small and simple. See pages 136-139 for detailed information on creating a small water garden.

A single ornate container is an instant focal point when planted with pink geraniums and variegated Vinca major.

"Mossing Up" Concrete

New concrete figures often look stark when placed among lush green plants. To speed up the weathering process, lightly scratch the surface of a concrete figure with a metal brush and put it in a shady, out-of-the-way place. Slather the statue with a slurry made from a quart of buttermilk and one pint each of composted manure and pulverized woodland moss. For about two weeks the statue will smell bad, but the odor will disappear as moss begins to grow in the crevices.

Features such as water gardens, raised beds and comfortable seating transform a courtyard into a unique space intended exclusively for human enjoyment.

Containers

A single large pedestal container planted with a sculpted shrub or showy flowers draws attention like a magnet, or you can use groups of smaller containers to get the same special effect. When composing a grouping of pot-grown plants, place some containers on blocks or bricks to give them extra height. Containers give you the opportunity to work with the colors and textures of both plants and pots, and you can quickly switch them around when you want to move plants in their prime to high-visibility areas.

Yard Art

There is no limit to what you can create when you give your artistic talents free reign in the garden. Simple mirrors framed with plants or shiny reflecting balls bring a new texture to the garden. Or create your own works of art using clay, metal, glass, straw or a number of other materials. If most of your backyard is devoted to vegetables or fruits, a personable scarecrow will keep you company as you plant, weed and harvest. Rustic archways made of driftwood, vines trained over unusual metal frames, or seasonal holiday decorations for shrubs and trees all qualify as yard art.

Maybe you don't know art but you know what you like. Ever seen a scarecrow that doubles as a birdhouse?

Trellises and other functional garden objects can be works of art.

CREATING RAISED BEDS

Raised planting beds are a great way to grow plants if your soil is rocky or drains too poorly to be cultivated. Use a raised bed to grow annual front yard flowers, or frame up beds beneath trees for groundcovers or shade gardens. If you have difficulty bending or squatting to tend your plants, raising the soil level in beds greatly eases the strain on your back and makes it possible to grow vegetables and herbs without pain.

Many plants benefit from the excellent drainage of raised beds—particularly lilies, roses and herbs. Amend your soil with organic matter and use it to fill your raised bed, or fill with a soil mix purchased in bulk or in bags. Either way, your raised bed will probably warm up quickly in the spring and may not need to be dug and cultivated each time you add new plants. As long as beds are kept small (less than 4 feet wide) you will not need to walk in them, keeping the soil from being compacted.

No bending is needed to tend these raised beds filled with herbs. The beds' height also provides plants with fantastic drainage.

Bricking in the base of this oak created a raised bed and a bit of extra seating.

Build a raised bed quickly and easily by using boards held in place with wood stakes.

Framing a Raised Bed

Raised beds generally have some kind of frame around them to hold the soil in place. Almost anything that holds soil will work—including wood, stone, brick or boards made from recycled plastic.

For a bed in the front of your home, choose a framing material that coordinates with the architectural features of your house. Landscape timbers look good near homes with exteriors made of wood or siding, but brick or stone may be needed if these materials are already prominent in your house. In the backyard, simple bed frames made

Cosmos, marigolds and lilies thrive in a lovely bed framed in stone.

of 2 by 12 boards often work quite well. Weathered railroad ties offer another possibility.

How to Build Simple Raised Beds

Only a half day of work is needed to make a rectangular bed ideal for growing colorful annuals or your favorite vegetables. The bed described below is framed with 2 by 12 boards. If you want a permanent bed made of landscape timbers, construct the frame used to contain a water garden, shown on page 137.

1 Prepare the site. In low, poorly drained areas, mark the location of the bed and cultivate the soil to a depth of 4 or 5 inches. Turn the soil over and break up large clods. This helps drainage and allows plant roots to penetrate deeper. Work in lime if the soil is naturally acidic.

2 Build a frame. To build a 4- by 8-foot rectangular bed, buy three 8 by 2 by 12 boards and ask the lumberyard to cut one in half. Assemble the boards by positioning an 8-foot board and a 4-foot board perpendicularly at one corner. Attach the two boards by screwing in two L-shaped brackets spaced 6 inches apart. Do the same for the remaining corners.

An alternative method of connecting corners is to use raised bed connectors made from recycled plastic. These adjust to different angles, so they are ideal for framing up a circular raised bed around the base of a tree. When used in the vegetable garden, beds held together with plastic connectors can be disassembled at the end of the season; they are an ideal choice if you use untreated boards to frame vegetable beds and want to store the boards in a dry place through winter.

Corner connectors made from recycled plastic.

Give your carpentry skills a workout building custom-designed raised beds framed in wood. Use a weather-resistant wood such as redwood or cedar.

TIP   Refreshing Old Soil

After a couple of seasons of use, rejuvenate the soil in your raised beds: Add a 2-inch-deep layer of compost or rotted manure. To amend the soil without actually digging it, poke numerous holes in the old soil with a digging fork before spreading on the compost.

3 Add soil amendments. Fill the bed with a well-mixed blend of good topsoil, compost and aged manure. Use 50 percent topsoil, 25 percent compost and 25 percent aged manure. To fill a 4- by 8- by 1-foot raised bed with bagged topsoil and amendments you will need the following:

- **16 cubic feet topsoil** (10 bags if packaged as 1.5 cubic feet)

- **8 cubic feet compost** (7 bags if packaged as 1.5 cubic feet)

- **8 cubic feet aged manure** (6 bags if packaged as 1.5 cubic feet)

- **1 pound 10-10-10 fertilizer** or balanced slow-release fertilizer

HANDLE TREATED WOOD SAFELY

Boards or landscape timbers treated with CCA (chromated copper arsenate) will not harm ornamental plants, but the chemicals may leach into the soil where vegetables and herbs are grown and, in turn, be taken up by the plants. This is not an appetizing thought to most people, but not exactly relevant if you are only growing inedible flowers or shrubs. Always be careful when handling treated wood, for some of the CCA is present on the outside where it is easily touched. Wear a mask, gloves and long sleeves to protect your skin from contact with the chemicals. Dispose of sawdust and wood scraps in the garbage. Do not burn CCA-treated wood, because arsenic contained in the wood goes up in smoke and can be damaging if inhaled.

In vegetable gardens where the soil is cultivated often, raised beds often require no frames at all.

BUILD AN EASY WATER GARDEN

Water gardens are popular, and with good reason. Even a small water garden becomes an irresistible focal point in the landscape. You can stock a water garden with flowering plants, foliage plants and a few little fish to control mosquitoes. Regardless of what you may have heard about pumps, filters and other electric gear, anyone can create natural ponds that require no cords, and no upkeep beyond occasional cleaning.

Even a simple plastic-formed pool can transform your garden's ambiance with the sound of water.

Building a Water Garden

The first thing you need is a way to contain water. Rigid plastic forms are tempting, but they must be installed in a hole with a level bottom that fits them like a glove. Flexible rubber liners are much easier to handle, and can be used to make either a pond set down in the ground or an above-ground pond like the one described on page 137.

Digging an in-ground pond is simple, though you may be surprised at how long it takes to dig a large hole with a level top edge.

To build an above-ground water garden using landscape timbers, digging is limited to leveling the soil upon which the frame will rest, and perhaps excavating a few inches of soil if you want or need a very deep pond. Where winters are cold or summers are very hot, make at least part of your water garden at least 16 inches deep. At this depth, the water at the very bottom of the pond will not freeze solid in winter (in most climates) nor become too warm in summer, so fish and hardy plants stand a good chance of surviving both types of weather extremes.

Bringing in Fish

Hardy little goldfish, called comets, are the easiest fish to keep in a small water garden. If you buy them at a pet shop in early summer and release them into settled water, expect about a 60 percent survival rate. Goldfish that survive their first week outdoors are likely to live for several years as long as the water at the bottom of the pond does not freeze hard in the winter. Be careful not to overstock your pond or to overfeed your fish. The 4- by 8-foot pond shown at right can comfortably support 3 to 6 goldfish (depending on their size), which can be fed once a day in warm weather. In cold weather, they will get sufficient nutrients from plants and water. Goldfish often reproduce in outdoor ponds that include plenty of submerged plants.

Koi are a more active species and need more room than comets. Use koi only in large ponds where they have plenty of room to swim. Koi need pond water at least two feet deep, with a surface area greater than 24 square feet.

The wide availability of flexible plastic liners makes it simple for anyone to build a water garden or fish pond to suit any site.

Comet goldfish.

Building a Water Garden

This project requires only a few hours of work, though you may want to complete it in stages.

Tools, Materials & Timing

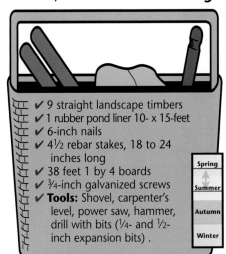

- ✔ 9 straight landscape timbers
- ✔ 1 rubber pond liner 10- x 15-feet
- ✔ 6-inch nails
- ✔ 4½ rebar stakes, 18 to 24 inches long
- ✔ 38 feet 1 by 4 boards
- ✔ ¾-inch galvanized screws
- ✔ **Tools:** Shovel, carpenter's level, power saw, hammer, drill with bits (¼- and ½-inch expansion bits) .

Spring
↑
Summer

Autumn

Winter

1 Cut three landscape timbers in half. Excavate as needed to make a 4 by 8 foot level foundation. Place two long landscape timbers and two short ones on the foundation to check for size and grade. If desired, excavate soil from inside the frame to increase the pond's depth.

2 Set other landscape timbers in place, stacking them so that corner joints overlap in an offset pattern, as shown. Check level again, and adjust the foundation or arrangement of pieces as needed (slight warps in the timbers will be pulled out during construction).

3 Drill ½-inch holes through each corner, and pound in rebar stakes until they protrude only 6 inches from the top. Remove the top tier of timbers. Drill guide holes for two nails in the second-tier timbers on each side, and nail the second tier to the foundation level. Put the top tier of timbers back in place, and nail them to the second tier. Pound in rebar stakes until they are even with the top.

4 Spread liner in the pond, folding corners as needed to make them as flat as possible. Slowly fill the pond with water to within 8 inches of the top, allowing the weight of the water to stretch the liner as the pond fills. Do not trim the excess from the edges of the liner yet.

5 Make a top frame from the 1 by 4 lumber. Pull gently on the edges of the liner and tack the top frame in place with a few small nails. Use screws to permanently fasten the top frame in place. Trim off sharp corners from the frame. Use a utility knife with a sharp new blade to trim off the excess liner from under the outer edges of the top frame.

6 Fill your pond with water almost to the top and let it sit for three weeks before adding plants or fish. A number of easy aquatic plants are described on the following pages.

PLANTS FOR A NATURAL POND

Algae are tiny plants that give pond water a green, cloudy appearance. If you want a healthy natural pond in which one life form helps another by providing food or habitat, a bit of algae is a good thing. But too much algae ruins a pond's mirror effect, and makes the water so murky that you cannot see your fish. As your pond develops into a unique ecosystem, plant foliage on the pond's surface will block light to the water, which will in turn limit the proliferation of algae. Excessive algae is naturally discouraged if at least 60 percent of the water's surface is covered with plants.

All the aquatic plants that produce colorful blooms grow best in full sun, or in a half day of sun in very warm climates. Numerous native plants will grow in partial shade, especially along the shallow edges or in containers set on bricks to raise them to just under the water's surface.

Types of Aquatic Plants

Plants that grow in water are classified into the four groups listed here. Using different types of plants will help keep your water garden biologically balanced, and makes it look great too. Most hardy aquatic plants become dormant in winter and re-emerge in spring. In very cold climates, you may need to drain your water garden in fall and restock it with new plants and fish in late spring.

Container Planting for Ponds

ROOTED FLOATERS   EMERGENT   SUBMERGED PLANTS   FREE FLOATERS

Emergent Plants

This class includes most upright plants found in boggy places, such as cattails and water iris. Their roots are constantly under water, but their leaves and stems grow above the surface. Grow emergent plants in pots set below the surface. Place them to provide vertical interest in your water garden. These species are dependable and hardy, and there are a number of native species.

Iris (*Iris* species)

Flat upright leaves are topped with elegant flowers in spring which may be blue, purple, white or yellow. Some species and hybrids are hardy to Zone 4. All grow best with their roots covered with 2 to 4 inches of water.

Water iris.

Dwarf cattail (*Typha minima*)

Thin grassy leaves stand straight up, and usually produce velvety brown cattails (or catkins) in summer. Cold winters increase catkin production. Dwarf cattail grows best in 12 to 14 inches of water, and plants are hardy to Zone 3. Divide clumps in spring, planting them to individual submerged containers.

Dwarf cattail.

Arrowheads (*Sagittaria* spp.)

Sometimes called water plantain, arrowheads have fibrous roots, leaves shaped like arrowheads and flowers that develop on upright spikes. Several native species are hardy to Zone 4, and typically produce white flowers in summer. Persistent but not aggressive, arrowheads are ideal for shallow edges.

Arrowhead.

Rooted Floaters

These plants have roots anchored in mucky soil, but their leaves float at or slightly above the surface. Popular blooming plants including water lilies and lotus fit into this group. Grow them in broad pots filled halfway with clay and humus in 10 to 18 inches of water.

Dwarf lotus (*Nelumbo* spp. and cultivars)

Flat green leaves rise above the water's surface on stout stems, and produce exotic blooms in summer after warm weather has prevailed for several weeks. Dwarf forms are mostly native to China, and will survive winter at the bottom of ponds that do not freeze solid. Plant dormant roots in containers in spring.

Dwarf lotus.

Dwarf water lilies (*Nymphaea* spp. and cultivars)

Flat leaves with single notches float at the surface. Showy flowers appear in summer, and many selections repeat bloom. Dwarf cultivars grow well in water only a few inches deeper than their containers. Hardy to Zone 3, provided the water does not freeze solid.

Dwarf water lily.

Free Floaters

No pots are needed to grow these plants, which form colonies that station themselves at the surface. Roots filter nutrients available in the water. These plants are often very vigorous and spread rapidly.

Floating heart (*Nymphoides peltata*)

Small yellow flowers rise above heart-shaped green leaves. As roots find muddy earth on the bottom of the pond, colonies become large and vigorous. Hardy to Zone 6.

Water clover (*Marsilea mutica*)

Thrives in partial shade where other water plants struggle. Pretty four-leafed clovers float at the surface. This plant is not reliably winter hardy in cold climates, but grows vigorously from spring to fall.

Water clover.

Submerged Plants

Most plant parts remain below water because the limp stems require water for support. Roots often anchor themselves in pebbles or silt, but the plants can grow with free-floating roots. Submerged plants work as natural water filters, taking up excess nutrients directly from the water, and make excellent cover for breeding fish.

Elodea (*Elodea canadensis*)

Very hardy, sometimes invasive, but a real asset to ponds that tend to go green with algae. Also a fine host plant for breeding fish. Native to North America. Prune or thin out excess plants in fall and early summer.

Parrot's feather (*Myriophyllum aquatica*)

Ferny blue-green foliage rises a few inches above the surface, while roots and submerged stems spread through the water. Tolerates partial shade. Hardy to Zone 6.

Parrot's feather.

LIGHTING YOUR GARDEN

After the sun goes down, outdoor lights can make your yard safer while transforming the landscape into a mystical new world. Strategically-placed lights work wonders, illuminating your landscape's best features while keeping the bad ones in the dark.

Elegant brass lamp-posts lend a historical note to an asphalt driveway.

A walkway gets extra light from a fixture that is attractive as a small sculpture in the daytime.

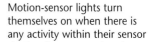
In Motion

Motion-sensor lights turn themselves on when there is any activity within their sensor range—whether from you, a burglar or a band of raccoons. These lights are great as security and garage entry lights, but can be bothersome in places you might enjoy more with steady, subdued lighting.

To add lighting in other parts of your yard, the first step is to go outside at night and think about what you see or don't see. Identify problem areas where darkness creates unsafe conditions, as well as promising places that are lost in shadows. Think about what you want your outdoor lighting to do, and set priorities. Perhaps you are most interested in creating a softly lit conversation area or making sure visitors reach your front door safely. Don't be surprised to discover that pursuing a practical goal—like using light to deter burglars—also creates a better place to barbecue.

Make a few sketches on paper, using simple bubbles to show where you most would like to have puddles of light. Then go back outside and spend a few evenings using shop lights and extension cords, battery-operated lanterns, and high-intensity flashlights to experiment with ways to bring your landscape to light.

Outdoor Lighting

Most homes already have two types of outdoor lights: incandescent bulbs enclosed in glass fixtures near exterior doors, and perhaps high-intensity floodlights that shine from the house's eaves. If either of these is unsatisfactory, switch to new fixtures quickly and easily by following the instructions that come with new light fixtures. Porch lights in particular can be greatly improved by switching to a new fixture.

A post-mounted light illuminates an outdoor dining area in a courtyard garden.

Tips for Placing Lights

- **If your main goal** is to use lighting to beautify your yard, try to place at least one light high up in the branches of a tree that drops its leaves in winter. Mounted up in a tree and pointed downward, a durable bullet light will bathe the ground below in soft light while casting interesting shadows through the tree's limbs. Artificial moonlight from several soft lights placed high in trees results in a soft glow that is never harsh or glaring.

- **Use small spotlights** to uplight special features such as statuary, attractive stonework or large evergreen trees. Whenever it is used, uplighting creates drama. If your yard includes a water feature, uplighting a nearby tree or shrub will make it reflect on the water's surface.

A small bullet light hides in pine mulch during the day, uplights nearby trees and shrubs at night.

- **When using low-area lights** to illuminate walkways, hide the fixtures from view with plants, but don't block the fixture's light. Shrubs with large, glossy leaves are especially useful for this purpose. Locate lamps as close as possible to steps to help ensure safe footing.

- **Adjust the position of floodlights** so that they never shine in your eyes. Point them up or down instead, or place them so their light will be filtered through trees.

- **For occasional entertaining,** use strings of miniature white lights installed in nearby trees or shrubs. More colorful types of string lights, such as Japanese lanterns or illuminated chili peppers, invoke a more festive mood.

A spotlighted sculpture adds drama and intimacy to the nighttime garden.

Installing Lights

If you are inexperienced with electricity yet determined to do this project yourself, choose a low-voltage system that uses 12-volt wire and lamps. These are inexpensive to purchase and install, and do not require special grounding hardware. With 12-volt systems, the wire connects to a transformer which in turn plugs into regular 120-volt household current. These systems are widely available in kits that include step-by-step installation instructions.

Complicated systems for large areas require the expertise of an electrician, especially if some fixtures will be located in or near water. Most people also enlist professional help to install an indoor control switch for their outdoor lighting systems. For extensive lighting projects, you also may need special permits from your city or town.

Regardless of their size, electrical lighting systems are connected with wire that is buried in shallow trenches or simply laid on the ground and covered with mulch. As with all home improvement projects that require digging, make sure you will not accidentally nick your phone or water lines before you start digging trenches.

Before installing any wiring that cannot be left unplugged until the last moment, turn the power off to the circuit you are using at the switchbox. If you have any doubt that the wires you are about to touch are not dead, check them with a volt meter first.

Choose a lighting system that allows quick and easy access when you need to replace a bulb.

SOLAR LIGHTS

If you need a light in a place where burying electrical wire is impractical, consider landscape lights powered by the sun. The batteries in solar lights are constantly recharged by sunlight gathered in small collector panels. Motion-sensor solar lights are ideal for remote activity areas such as your vegetable garden composting corner.

◊ CHAPTER 11 ◊

WINTER CARE:
PROTECTING AND
MAINTAINING PLANTS

*Make use of the special opportunities that come in winter, from
growing hardy plants to reshaping those that are weary.*

Winter offers its own special pleasures—especially if you know your garden is prepared for whatever extremes the season may bring. In mild winter climates where many plants prosper through the coldest months, gardeners are doubly busy because winter offers comfortable temperatures to attend to projects that involve heavy work. In colder areas where hard freezes rule through winter, you can use special techniques to coax a few hardy vegetables through the winter months. In all climates, certain perennials, shrubs and trees benefit from ongoing winter protection. Gardeners in warm climates must watch their tropicals, while those of us who look upon a dormant landscape until spring have plenty of mulching, covering and pruning to do while our plants are at rest.

How Plants Prepare for Winter

As fall progresses, plant cells gradually lose moisture so that when freezing temperatures finally hit, there is little moisture left in the cells to freeze. In hardy annuals and evergreens, concentrated sugars act as natural antifreeze and replace moisture.

Cold damage to hardy plants occurs when night temperatures plummet very rapidly and plants have not had a chance to lose cell moisture. Trapped water freezes into crystals, which expand within the cells and rupture cell membranes. This destroys the plant's leaves and they wither and die. Tender new growth often dies too.

One of the simplest ways to prepare plants for winter is to stop fertilizing them in late summer. Tender new growth is more easily damaged than mature woody tissues. If needed apply a water-soluble fertilizer in August or September. This will provide immediately available nutrients but not long-term nutrition.

Watering in Winter

Winter watering is important for evergreens that continue to lose water through their leaves during the winter. Even in winter, sun and wind cause leaves to dry out rapidly. Roots will replace the lost moisture if there is water in the soil and the soil is not completely frozen. The best water management strategy for evergreens is to have the soil evenly moist through fall and as wet as possible (short of standing water) prior to the soil freezing. If natural rainfall or melting snow is limited, water during temporary warm spells when the soil thaws.

In all climates, you may need to occasionally water plants that grow beneath your house's eaves. Even though the weather may be wet, the soil under the eaves may remain dry; plants growing there may be damaged from the combination of dry roots below ground and desiccating winds above the surface.

A light covering of ice or snow helps insulate plants from cold drying winds.

Winter Injury

Assuming that you grow plants that are winter-hardy in your region and that they are growing in well-drained soil, herbaceous plants (plants that die to the ground in the winter then re-emerge from underground roots and crowns) generally come through winter unscathed. Deciduous woody plants with above-ground trunks, branches, and stems and evergreen plants are different matters. These plants are subject to several forms of winter damage; we'll show you how to prevent it.

A garden at rest in winter evokes a look back at last season and anticipation of next year's successes.

Don't attempt to "help" your plants by removing accumulated ice. They are better off taking care of themselves.

TYPES OF WINTER INJURY

- Rotting—crowns and roots
- Sun scald—bark
- Winter kill—dormant flower buds
- Winter burn and dieback—evergreen foliage
- Breakage due to snow on branches
- Frost heave

PREVENTING WINTER DAMAGE

Root and Crown Rot— Perennials

Gardeners lose many hardy perennial plants every winter due to root or crown rot caused by excess soil moisture. Clay soil and low areas are especially prone to holding too much water. To avoid this, incorporate plenty of organic matter at planting time to improve drainage, or grow your hardy perennials in raised beds. It is also important to avoid smothering the crowns of perennials with too much winter mulch. Plants that hold onto a small tuft of green leaves through winter usually benefit from exposure to winter sun. They may become subject to disease if smothered beneath a damp mulch.

Lightening Snow Load

A blanket of snow is a wonderful insulator, but too much snow or heavy ice can cause exactly the kind of natural pruning you do not want. Avoid planting brittle shrubs under the eaves of your house or other places where ice and snow tend to accumulate. When heavy ice bends a plant, do not attempt to help it until after the ice melts. Frozen branches splinter and break very easily.

To give the crowns of peonies and other shallow perennials a bit of breathing room under snow or ice, mulch them lightly with a loose pile of evergreen branches. Covering the ground with evergreen branches may also benefit spring-flowering bulbs after they are planted in the fall.

Sunscald— Trees

Young, smooth-skinned trees, such as fruit trees and Japanese maples, sometimes develop sunscald, which appears as ragged cracks in the trunk. Sunscald is the result of rapid temperature changes during the winter and usually develops on the west or south side of the tree. On sunny days, a tree trunk may be warmed 18°F above air temperature. When the sun goes down, the temperature plummets and the trunk suddenly freezes, splitting wood and tearing bark. In spring, pests and diseases are able to enter the trunk through these openings in the bark.

- **Avoid sunscald**
  Wrap young trees with at least 2 feet of stretchy waterproof paper (sold as tree wrap) when temperatures get near freezing. This moderates daily temperature extremes. Do not wrap trees too early because it inhibits the photosynthesis process and can rob plants of needed nutrients. Remove tree wrap in early to mid-spring.

- **Minimize sunscald**
  Plant smooth-skinned trees where they receive minimal afternoon sun in winter—such as the northeast corner of a building. Position a new plant so that the side with the most branches faces southwest so the trunk has some added protection.

This tree isn't yet stressed by its load of snow, but if heavy, wet, snows threaten to break tree branches, use a broom to brush the snow off.

Wrap the trunks of young trees with burlap or tree wrap to prevent sunscald—cracking of the bark due to repeated freezing and thawing.

Winter protection can take the form of boxes, cold frames, inverted bushel baskets, pots or other coverings.

Protecting Evergreens

Evergreen shrubs usually need no winter protection in Zones 6 to 9, where they typically thrive in bright winter sun. In these areas, planting evergreens in the fall is a common practice because the plants then have more than six months to prepare themselves for stressful summer weather.

Screens

Where winters are cold or unusually windy (Zone 5 northward), screen evergreens with burlap to shelter them from damaging weather. Drive wood or metal stakes into the ground around the plants, then wrap burlap around the stakes. Attach the burlap with a heavy staple gun or wire.

Sprays

Anti-transpirant sprays also protect young evergreens from moisture loss due to wind, sun and frozen ground. Plants that have been in the ground for a full growing season should be able to hold their own and will not need anti-transpirant sprays.

A burlap screen, set up on the prevailing windward side of the garden, will protect evergreen hedges from drying winter blasts.

Protecting Dormant Flower Buds

Plants

Plants that develop stem buds in fall that produce new growth in spring benefit from extra insulation to protect at least some of those buds. These buds may be difficult to see, as they do not fully swell until early spring. In addition to the rose family, popular plants that set growing buds in fall include hydrangea, some clematis and figs.

Roses

To protect roses, make a mixture of one-half good garden soil and one-half compost or aged manure. Cover the base of the canes to a height of 12 inches. Do not take the soil from around the base of the plant because this can injure the roots.

Shrubs

Encircle larger shrubs with a wire cage wrapped with burlap that cuts the wind. To protect even more, stuff the inside of the cage with loose straw or shredded leaves.

Limit Frost Heave

Unprotected ground that alternately freezes and thaws also expands and contracts. This soil movement breaks roots and can make small plants pop out of the ground. Shallow-rooted plants such as chrysanthemum, Shasta daisy, fall-planted pansies and other small flowers are especially susceptible to frost heave.

To limit frost heave, mulch the soil with a 4- to 6-inch layer of organic material in autumn after the soil has frozen slightly. Instead of keeping the soil warm, the mulch helps keep the soil frozen all winter and prevents wide temperature fluctuations at the base of the plants.

You may be able to use mulch to keep hardy vegetables such as carrots and parsnips in good shape in the ground through winter. Mulch the soil with 6 to 12 inches of loose organic matter, such as straw, before the ground freezes. This will prevent it from freezing deeply, if at all.

Use mulch to insulate shallow-rooted annuals and perennials from heaving, which is caused by repeated freezing and thawing of the soil.

WORKING WINTER UNDER COVER

No matter where you live, you may be able to grow a surprising number of plants through the winter; and you won't need a proper greenhouse. Many different types of covers can be used to form little greenhouses over plants—some of them costing little or nothing. Cold frames, cloches, tunnels, blankets and other "season stretching" devices can turn anyone's dream of winter gardening into reality. They also may make it possible to grow plants that normally would not make it through winter on their own in your

Frost improves the flavor of spinach and other hardy vegetables, but be sure to wait until they thaw completely to touch them. Frozen plants are brittle and easily injured.

climate, or that would be much worse for the wear.

Light is the biggest limiting factor to growing many plants in winter. In addition to short days, light intensity is reduced in winter, when the sun is at its farthest point (and lowest angle) from the earth. Most plants grow very little in winter's low light, but if they are protected from harsh winds and frigid temperatures they often grow into tough, stocky specimens that show amazing vigor when days become longer and warmer in early spring.

Cold Frames

One of the most versatile ways to hold plants through winter is to use a cold frame. A cold frame is basically a box with a translucent top that lets in light and collects solar warmth.

Materials

Make a cold frame from wood, concrete blocks or bales of hay. Material options for the top include sheets of corrugated fiberglass, old window frames or heavyweight clear plastic attached to a wood or wire frame.

Placement

Place your cold frame so that it faces south or west and gets full winter sun. Vent cold frames on warm days or they will heat up so much inside that the plants will dry out or bake.

Winter Survivors

Some of the best plants to keep in a cold frame through winter include hardy annuals grown in roomy containers—for example pansies and dianthus, and short-lived perennials propagated from stem or root cuttings in early fall (sweet William, Shasta daisy, hollyhock).

Hardy flowers that do not die back completely in winter, such as sweet William, need a little sunshine through the coldest months. Be careful not to smother their crowns with a heavy blanket of mulch.

Spring Usage

You can also grow hardy biennials like parsley, forget-me-not *(Myosotis)* and foxglove in your cold frame.

Set them out in early spring, several weeks before your last frost. If you like, try pruning back marginally hardy perennials such as chrysanthemum, santolina, lavender, rosemary and sage. Hold them through winter in a cold frame. In spring, put your cold frame to work as a hardening-off chamber for seedlings started indoors under lights.

Use a temporary cold frame made from bales of hay to insulate hardy plants from winter winds and extreme cold, as is done here with bulbs being forced to bloom in pots.

SPRING COLD SNAPS

What do you do when a sudden drop in temperature threatens tender new growth just as plants break dormancy in spring? The best bet is to keep insulating materials on hand to cover plants in danger. Bushel baskets, hay bales, old blankets or sturdy cardboard boxes held in place with bricks can be placed over plants and removed when mild weather returns.

Tunnels

Plastic-covered tunnels are a dream come true for vegetable gardeners. These tunnels make it possible to grow hardy vegetables through the winter, and keep them in good picking condition. To explore the vast potential of tunnels, see the detailed discussion on pages 148 and 149.

Mulching with such materials as leaves or plastic is a good wintertime practice.

Cloches

Cloches are small covers set over individual plants. Cloches work as miniature greenhouses. Old-fashioned cloches were made of heavy glass and looked like

Cloches used during the winter should either be heavy enough to stay in place when cold winds blow, or anchored to the ground by lashing them to stakes.

bells. Modern cloches can be home-made (most often from plastic milk jugs) or you can buy cloches through garden supply catalogs.

Fall

One of the best uses for cloches is to pop them over hardy annual flowers set out in the fall. A bed of pansies, snap-dragons or annual dianthus, in mid-winter zones, may sail through winter when protected with cloches, They will then bloom very early in the spring. Install a deep mulch around cloched plants to provide extra insulation and to keep the cloches from blowing away in strong winds.

Spring

Cloches also come in handy in early spring, when you want to set out young plants before the last frost has passed. Many hardy vegetable seedlings (such as cabbage, broc-coli and parsley), and flowers like cosmos and alyssum, will easily survive late spring freezes when they are securely cloched.

In a pinch, even plastic shower curtains or spun rowcovers can protect tender plants when cold or winds threaten.

Blankets and Boxes

Use old blankets, mattress protec-tors, sturdy boxes or bushel baskets to insulate hardy plants from frigid winds or ice for short periods of time. This approach is especially beneficial in Zones 6 and 7 where winter seems to come and go in mighty gusts. When a winter storm is predicted, simply cover young roses, fall-planted perennials or hardy vegetables.

Leave the covers in place until the stressful weather has passed. Even though these types of covers do not keep the ground from freezing, simply easing the stress caused by cold winds and ice can make a big difference in your plants' survival.

If you find yourself frantically dash-ing about on the eve of a winter storm, it's a good idea to keep a list of plants that need extra protection so you won't accidentally forget to cover or bring in a beloved plant. You might also keep a wheelbarrow in your garage loaded with blankets and boxes so you can quickly distribute them.

Cloches made from plastic milk jugs help give tomatoes and other tender plants a head start in spring.

Cover the tops of plants with burlap to protect them from snow damage.

USE A WINTER TUNNEL

If you dream of home-grown vegetables in December or delight in growing seldom-seen flowers, try gardening through winter beneath a plastic tunnel. Season-extending tunnels work by improving growing conditions through the cold season. They warm the soil and shelter plants from cold winter wind. On a clear winter day, the air temperature in a plastic tunnel can be 20 to 30 degrees warmer than the air temperature outside the tunnel.

Experimentation is the only way to know if tunnels will work in your garden and Zone. Give them a try—they've worked as far north as Maine!

Materials and Placement

For maximum winter production, position your tunnel so it will not have to take prevailing winter winds broadside. Wind is a plastic tunnel's worst enemy, and the more the plastic must flex in the wind, the weaker it becomes. Also use the heaviest clear plastic you can find. Greenhouse-grade plastic is 6 mils thick, but you may need to special order through a garden shop or buy it through a mail-order company.

Hardware and home supply stores often sell plastic sheeting that is 4 mils thick, which usually needs to be replaced after about two months. Buy sheets at least 8 feet wide so you will have plenty of extra plastic to tuck under along the sides of your tunnel.

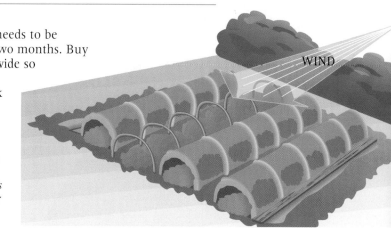

WIND

Orient your tunnels to take prevailing winter winds head-on, not sideways. This will prolong the life of your plastic covers and keep the insides warmer.

Creating Tunnels

Tailor your tunnel to fit over an existing bed, or create special beds in the fall to be covered with tunnels in early winter. All tunnels include bowed support hoops or arches of concrete reinforcing wire that supports the plastic so that it does not come into direct contact with plant leaves. If the plastic freezes to brittle leaves, they will often blacken from damage to the cells. A tunnel that arches over a bed about 36 inches wide and is 15 to 18 inches high in the center of the bow is a good size to work with.

Supports

Choose support for your tunnel based on the type of winter weather expected in your area. Where heavy snow is common, use wire support hoops made from 9- or 10-gauge galvanized steel wire or PVC pipe, and cover the hoops with concrete reinforcing wire or chicken wire before you put on the plastic. In areas where snowfall is scant, simply stretch plastic over hoops placed 2 to 3 feet apart to provide sufficient support. To cover a 36-inch-wide bed, cut the support hoops about 76 inches long. This length allows for pushing each end 12 inches into the ground.

Cover

After the support hoops and reinforcing wire are in place, stretch the plastic over the frame and secure the sides with 4-foot-long sections of heavy boards or landscape timbers. Roll up the excess plastic around the boards until the edges are snug with the base of the tunnel. To get to your plants, unroll as many boards as needed to open the side of the tunnel. Be careful when opening your tunnel on a windy day.

4-5'

2'

15"

6"

A plastic-covered arch made from concrete reinforcing wire protects salad crops from cold and is sturdy enough to stand firm under snow and ice.

TUNNEL TIPS

To avoid overheating on warm, bright days, keep the ends of your tunnel open. On warm days, open the sides of the tunnel halfway and secure the plastic with clothespins. Use the opportunity to weed, feed or water your plants. Be sure to close the tunnel before sunset to conserve the heat that builds up in the soil. Should ventilation be a persistent problem, cut downward facing V-shaped vents in the plastic about 14 inches from the ground, and reinforce the cut edges with duct tape.

Ventilation is crucial when using tunnels in the spring. This tunnel retains warmth and buffers wind, but does not heat up on sunny days.

To protect summer vegetables from fall's first frost, cover them overnight with old blankets or rowcovers.

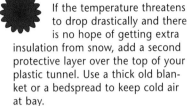

Super-hardy kale.

Undercover Winter Crops

Plastic tunnels keep many hardy leafy vegetables in good condition through winter, including arugula, collards, kale, hardy lettuce, mache, parsley, radicchio, spinach and sometimes Swiss chard. Root crops including beets, carrots, leeks, parsnips and turnips also work well under tunnels. All these vegetables should be growing vigorously in fall before they are covered with a tunnel in early winter. As days shorten and light levels drop, growth will slow considerably. New growth will pick up when light levels increase in late winter.

Flowers Under Cover

Several lovely, hardy annuals are ideal candidates for planting in fall and growing under tunnels through the winter. Two—larkspur and Shirley poppies—are rarely sold as spring bedding plants because they are so difficult to transplant. They make great partners under tunnels. In addition to these, you may want to try growing snapdragons, chamomile, sweet alyssum and annual candytuft under tunnels.

Annual larkspur.

PERFECT PARTNERS FOR WINTER

Annual larkspur (*Consolida ambigua*) and Shirley poppy (*Papaver rhoeas*) are perfectly matched in terms of hardiness, bloom time and color range. Sow seeds in the fall, directly in the garden where the mature plants will grow. Barely cover the seeds with soil. Small rosettes of leaves will emerge in about four weeks. Place a tunnel over the bed before heavy snowfall or about two months after planting. Thin plants to 12 inches apart in late winter when plants show new growth. Both of these flowers bloom in late spring. After the flowers fade and the seed pods dry to brown, gather seeds for planting the following fall.

Shirley poppy.

NATURAL PRUNING: TREES

Every woody plant possesses a predetermined shape or growth habit. Elm trees are upright and vase-shaped, weeping cherries cascade, dogwoods tend to grow horizontally and redbuds develop a spreading, flat-topped or rounded crown. Natural pruning is the name we give to selectively removing branches in accordance with a plant's natural pattern of growth. No matter what the tree or the shape you want, though, late winter is a great time to prune.

Pruning Phases

There are generally two phases of pruning trees.

New Growth

The first phase comes when plants are young and you prune them to encourage the proper shape. Buds are pinched to promote branching, branches are redirected and the main framework of the young tree is selected if it wasn't done at the nursery. This is how weeping and spiral-shaped trees are formed.

Attentively prune fruit trees when they are young so they have a strong form when they reach mature size. These are mature standard-size 'Kieffer' pears.

Pruning Mature Plants

Mature trees are pruned to enhance their health, beauty and productivity. Growth might be removed if it crowds surrounding trees or if it threatens structures. Sometimes low limbs are removed from mature trees to allow more light to pass through to plants growing in their shade. The notion of "topping back" trees to control their size is often a death sentence to old trees. It stimulates the development of weak, twiggy growth and is not nearly as attractive as trees that are thinned and trimmed in keeping with their natural shapes.

Trees with weeping forms like this weeping willow show a lovely winter silhouette. When pruning is needed, remove whole branches rather than trimming back stem tips.

TOOLS FOR TREE PRUNING

Several tools make tree pruning easy. Use scissors-type *pruners* (1) on small stems and twigs. Long-handled *loppers* (2) give you good leverage on larger branches. Never force a lopper to cut through a branch that is too large or you will damage the plant.

A *folding pruning saw* (3) with a narrow, curved blade makes it a cinch to work between closely spaced branches. A longer, *arched pruning saw* (4) with larger teeth easily saws big limbs. A *pole saw* (5) is essentially a handsaw on a stick, extending your reach so you can cut higher branches without leaving the ground.

Pruning tools.

When to Prune

There are many different opinions about which times of the year are best to prune. Timing depends on the plant species, the length of the growing season, bloom time and if new buds are formed on old or new wood.

In general, prune most woody plants in late winter when days are getting longer and warmer but before buds have swelled or new growth emerges. Pruning during the dormant season is easier than pruning when a plant is in leaf because you can clearly see the framework and make better choices about which branches to keep and which to remove.

Pick a cloudy, gray day when the wood is not frozen but the sun isn't warming plants, causing sap to flow. Don't worry if sap does bleed from your pruning cuts. The tree will not be permanently harmed.

TIP Pruning: Safety First

Hire an arborist if you find it necessary to use a ladder or climb a tree to prune. Do not use a pole saw anywhere near overhead power lines. Wear goggles to avoid getting sawdust in your eyes as you look up.

Tree Pruning Step-by-Step

An apple tree before pruning, with weak shoots growing across each other. If left untamed, they will rub, break, or promote poor fruiting habit.

The same apple tree after judicious pruning, opened up to encourage maximum fruiting.

1 Remove dead, dying, diseased and damaged branches.

2 Remove suckers or watersprouts emerging from the tree's base.

3 Remove crossing branches.

4 Remove low branches if you want head clearance or if the bark is handsome and you want to see it.

5 Thin dense growth to allow more light and air into the center of the tree.

6 Stand back and look at the tree for balance. If one side is denser than the other, thin branches accordingly.

Pruning Large Branches

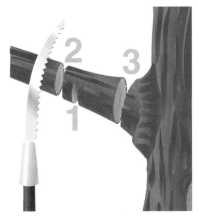

When removing large tree branches, make three cuts to keep the limb from splintering and injuring the trunk:

1 Make the first cut 12 to 24 inches from the branch attachment, sawing until the blade begins to stick or bind: This takes pressure off the branch, preventing binding, for the next cuts.

2 Make the second cut on top of the branch 1 inch out from the first cut.

3 Remove the stub with your third cut, sawing it off just above the branch collar.

Knowing the different types of bud structures helps you make the right pruning decisions. (See page 153.)

Making Pruning Cuts in Trees

Because trees grow in one place for many years, it is not surprising they have special self-defense mechanisms that help protect them from injuries and diseases. When a tree is damaged or cut into with pruning tools, the tree responds chemically by "walling off" the area that has been injured. A barrier forms which prevents disease organisms from entering and causing further damage to the tree.

In nature, tree limbs tend to break off in predictable places—the joints or crotches where small limbs join larger ones. At each of these joints, there is usually a small raised ring of bark, called the branch ring collar, that contains high concentrations of the chemicals trees use to wall off injuries. If you make all pruning cuts just above the branch ring collar, the tree will form its own internal bandage under the cut.

If you prune a limb properly, a branch ring collar will grow naturally, and protect the cut area.

Prune crossing branches or they'll rub against each other and cause damage. Pruning also opens up the remaining branches to more sunlight, which will help them grow strong.

PRUNING SHRUBS AND VINES

B efore you prune any shrub or vine, determine exactly what it is you want to accomplish by pruning. Pruning should always be done for one of the following four reasons: to enhance a plant's inherent form, to increase its flowering, to control its size or to rejuvenate a neglected shrub that has become terribly overgrown. As with trees, winter is a good time to do this pruning on many types of shrubs and vines, but different seasons do suit other plants.

Enjoy how your boxwood hedge glistens in the snows of winter, but don't prune it until spring (to stimulate new growth) or summer (to shape it).

Pruning Flowering Shrubs

With most shrubs, late winter is the best time to thin out crowded growth because you can clearly see the woody framework. But it is important that you not remove wood that is on the verge of producing flowers. As a general rule, plants that bloom in spring are pruned in summer, while those that bloom in summer are pruned in winter. The lists provided show the best times to prune the most popular flowering shrubs.

Lilacs need little pruning unless they become badly overgrown or are somehow seriously injured. Rejuvenating them by pruning them back reduces flowering for a year or two, but the plants resume strong blooming after new wood matures.

PLANTS TO PRUNE IN WINTER

Vines
Akebia (*Akebia quinata*)
Bittersweet (*Celastrus* spp.)
Clematis (some varieties)
Climbing hydrangea (*Hydrangea anomala* subsp. *petiolaris*)
Dutchman's pipe (*Aristolochia durior*)
Honeysuckle (*Lonicera* spp.)
Hops (*Humulus lupulus*)
Porcelain berry vine (*Ampelopsis brevipedunculata*)

Redtwig dogwood (*Cornus sanguinea*)
Silver lace vine (*Polygonum aubertii*)
Wisteria (*Wisteria* spp.)

Shrubs
Althaea (*Hibiscus syriacus*)
Beautyberry (*Callicarpa* spp.)
Blue mist spiraea (*Caryopteris* x *clandonensis*)
Butterfly bush (*Buddleia davidii*)
Crape myrtle (*Lagerstroemia* spp.)
Glossy abelia (*Abelia* x *grandiflora*)
Summer blooming spiraea such as billiard spiraea (*S.* x *billiardii*), bumald spiraea (*S.* x *bumalda*) and Japanese spiraea (*S. japonica*)

One-year-old stems of redtwig dogwood bring welcome color to the winter season. Wait until winter's end is near to prune this plant back close to the ground.

PLANTS TO PRUNE IN SUMMER

Vines
Clematis (spring blooming)

Shrubs
Alternate-leaf butterfly bush (*Buddleia alternifolia*)
Beautybush (*Kolkwitzia amabilis*)
Azalea and rhododendron (*Rhododendron* spp.)
Daphne (*Daphne* spp.)

Deutzia (*Deutzia* spp.)
Japanese pieris (*Pieris japonica*)
Lilacs (*Syringa* spp.)
Mock orange (*Philadelphus* spp.)
Smoke tree (*Cotinus coggygria*)
Spring blooming varieties of spiraea such as bridal wreath (*S. prunifolia*), thunberg spiraea (*S. thunbergii*) and Vanhoutte spiraea (*S. vanhouttei*)
Weigela (*Weigela florida*)

Purposeful Pruning

Understanding how plants grow will make you a better pruner. Make pruning cuts just above a bud or shoot, because pruning helps bring buds to life.

If the bud at the end of a shoot or stem (the terminal bud) is removed, the remaining topmost bud takes over and becomes the leading terminal bud. Buds along the sides of a stem are responsible for the lateral growth that makes plants bush out. Dormant latent buds that lie underneath the bark of some plants becoming active if the more mature buds are removed.

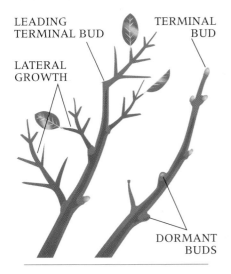

LEADING TERMINAL BUD

TERMINAL BUD

LATERAL GROWTH

DORMANT BUDS

Pruning to Enhance Form

Thin the Branches

When pruning a plant to maintain its natural form, thin branches rather than shorten them at the tips. First, cut off dead or damaged stems at ground level. Stand back and move around the plant. Shape the plant to its natural form by taking out any stems that make the plant unbalanced. Use this method to prune forsythias, azaleas, viburnums and other flowering shrubs.

Pruning Hedges

Prune hedge plants by heading them back—a method that results in a profusion of new stems that will need pruning again about eight weeks later. Prune hedges in late spring and again in late summer. Avoid fall pruning, which encourages tender growth that may die when exposed to cold weather.

Grapes require aggressive pruning in late winter, just as the buds begin to swell.

Pruning to Increase Flowering

Roses: How to Prune

Climbing roses that bloom once, in late spring, should be pruned after they bloom because flower buds are formed on one-year-old canes. Prune repeat-blooming climbing roses to remove dead or diseased wood in spring and again in midsummer. To thin, cut entire canes back to the ground.

Roses: When to Prune

Rose bushes are pruned according to the variety you are growing and where you live. Gardeners in northern climates are wise to prune plants in early spring when buds are just swelling. Gardeners in milder climates prune their almost-evergreen roses from December through February.

Get to know a climbing rose's natural bloom cycle before deciding how and when to prune it. Most climbers bloom from buds that developed during the previous summer.

Rejuvenate an Old Shrub

If you have and old shrub that has become overgrown or spindly, cutting it back severely may produce a vigorous new plant. Use a pruning saw to remove all the dead stems at the clump's base. Then select the strongest, healthiest remaining stems and cut them back to about 24 inches. Sprinkle a slow-release fertilizer around the base of the plant after pruning, then water as needed during the growing season to encourage new growth. You will not see any flowers the first year or two after pruning lilacs and viburnums this way, for these shrubs flower on the growth from the previous season. The winter following rejuvenation, thin out new shoots that are growing towards the interior of the plant and fertilize.

Pruning to Control Size

If you find that a certain shrub or vine needs constant pruning to keep it in bounds, consider replacing it with something that naturally grows smaller. Exuberant vines like wisteria benefit from aggressive pruning. Do major shaping in late winter, before buds swell. Lighter pruning to control size should be handled during several mini pruning sessions during the growing season.

Follow the natural shape of the plant when pruning forsythias and other flowering shrubs. Remove entire branches at ground level instead of lopping off stem tips.

Cut back very old boxwoods and other long-lived shrubs that simply get too big. It may take them a year or two to regain their fullness.

◀ CHAPTER 12 ▶

PROPAGATION:
SEEDS, DIVISIONS AND CUTTINGS

Growing new plants from seeds, or from pieces taken from old plants, is a fun, inexpensive way to fill your garden.

To grow a bountiful supply of almost-free plants, you need nothing more than some basic knowledge of how plants reproduce and an interest in participating in the process. You don't need fancy tools or expensive supplies. The most complicated equipment you might need would be hanging fluorescent lights and a spare table for seed starting, but even these are easily and inexpensively obtained.

Why propagate your own plants? Purchasing garden plants can get expensive, especially if you have a big yard and garden. Growing plants from seeds, divisions or cuttings can save you a lot of money and enables you to propagate rare or unusual plants. Simple propagation skills will help you fulfill many personal gardening goals, whether you want 20 pink celosias or a clone of your neighbor's rosemary. You also may need to propagate to keep your plants healthy. When a perennial stops flowering well or starts to die out in the middle, it's time to renew it through some form of propagation.

Starting your own annuals from seed greatly expands your selection of varieties and colors.

Reproductive Programming

Plants are genetically programmed to perpetuate themselves by reproducing. To take advantage of this become familiar with the different ways plants reproduce, then harness those natural processes for your garden's benefit.

Sex, Seeds and Regeneration

Many plants reproduce sexually by making seed that reaches the soil, germinates and grows into a new plant. This is the most common form of reproduction for flowering plants. You can propagate plants from seed by gathering seed or by purchasing seed from commercial sources. Directly sow seed where you want it to grow in the garden, or start it in flats and then transplant the seedlings to the garden. See pages 158-161 for details on starting plants from seed and saving seeds.

Other plants reproduce vegetatively (also called asexually) by forming new plants directly from the mother plant. Strawberries put out runners and form new baby plants at the end of each runner. It's easy to separate the offsets to fill a new bed. Bulbs produce offsets that can be separated and replanted. Daylily, coneflowers and hosta clumps enlarge in size and can be dug, divided into more plants and spread throughout the garden or shared with friends. Many shrubs such as forsythia, and vines like English ivy, root naturally to form new plants when their stems bend and touch the soil; these are good candidates for multiplying by softwood stem cuttings.

Tomatoes and most other annual plants specialize in sexual reproduction. Fertilized flowers enclose sexual organs which gradually produce ripe seeds.

Taking cuttings of English ivy will give you a bounty of new plants that will root readily.

REPRODUCTION AND PROPAGATION

How Plants Reproduce

Some flowers produce copious amounts of seed that can be yours for the taking. These are sulfur cosmos (Cosmos sulphureus).

Seeds

Most flowering plants produce seeds. The process is called sexual reproduction because flowers have male and female parts which must be united before a seed can develop. Annual flowers and wildflowers are heavy seed producers, as are annual weeds and many trees.

The production of flowers and seeds is under hormonal control, and special environmental factors trigger those hormones to flow. Biennial plants need a period of winter cold before they can flower, spinach waits for long days and short nights, and many tropical plants flower best when days are quite short. Many plants respond to stress by putting all their energy into flowering—a desperate effort to reproduce before they die.

Root buds

Bramble fruits including raspberries and blackberries, rugosa roses and many invasive species, such as obedient plant (*Physostegia*), produce special spreading roots with buds a few inches below the ground. After moving out a short distance from the parent plant, the buds come to life and form new plants. The plant is said to be "suckering"—a crafty reproductive cycle that enables the new plant to take sustenance from the old plant until ready to live on its own. Suckering plants may also reproduce other ways. Formidable weeds like bindweed and bermudagrass reproduce themselves this way and shed plenty of seeds as well.

Plants that go through a period of dormancy as storage roots also reproduce by producing root buds. Some examples include iris, dahlia, sweet potatoes, potatoes and other plants that grow from tubers or fat rhizomes.

Offsets and Supplemental Roots

Strawberries are a clear example of how a "mother" plant produces offspring that settle nearby and grow to maturity. Lamb's-ear and other mat-forming perennials reproduce themselves this way. Vigorous annuals including crabgrass and tomatoes are quite willing to grow supplemental roots along their lowest stems. You will often see herb stems planting themselves in nearby soil.

Ajuga divides into multiple crowns that you can easily cut apart and replant when you want more plants to set out in a new location.

Clumps

Many perennial plants are equipped with numerous buds (at or below the surface) that become active when the previous season's growth deteriorates. The result is a clump-forming growth habit. This means of reproduction is often found in the most vigorous herbaceous perennials including hosta, daisy and chrysanthemum. Bulbs and corms also divide off little bulblets or corms. This process takes place unseen, under the ground.

Easy Propagation Methods

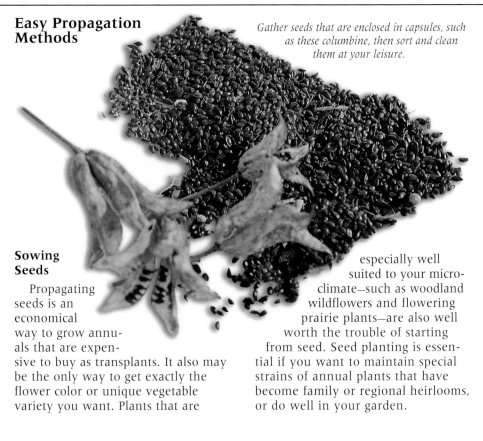

Gather seeds that are enclosed in capsules, such as these columbine, then sort and clean them at your leisure.

Sowing Seeds

Propagating seeds is an economical way to grow annuals that are expensive to buy as transplants. It also may be the only way to get exactly the flower color or unique vegetable variety you want. Plants that are especially well suited to your microclimate—such as woodland wildflowers and flowering prairie plants—are also well worth the trouble of starting from seed. Seed planting is essential if you want to maintain special strains of annual plants that have become family or regional heirlooms, or do well in your garden.

Cuttings

Stem cuttings are the way to go for many perennials and woody plants that don't naturally divide themselves into ready-to-grow divisions. Rooting stem cuttings is an easy and clean process. Often you get new plants faster than you would if you started with seeds.

Because it is a vegetative propagation method, new plants grown from stem cuttings will be of the same genetic makeup as their parents.

You'll find a list of top plants for propagating this way—as well as specific instructions—on pages 166-167. Don't be afraid to try rooting stem cuttings from any plant, but also be prepared for a certain percentage of failures. No matter what you do, some cuttings will wither and rot rather than develop roots.

Digging and Dividing

Divide many perennials and bulbs regularly to alleviate overcrowding and to promote health and heavy flowering. Clump-forming plants and plants that expand by runners, underground rhizomes or offshoots, are great candidates for this method of propagation.

Division is often the best method for propagating named cultivars of high-quality perennials that you want to remain unchanged from one generation to the next. Plants that are outstanding in terms of blooms, growth habit, disease resistance, fragrance or flavor are well worth the trouble of digging and dividing as needed. When properly done (see pages 162-165), you can expect a high percentage of plants to survive when using the division method.

A pair of daylily crowns, groomed and ready for replanting.

Chrysanthemum cuttings set to root in spring quickly develop roots. The plants will be ready to bloom by fall.

STARTING SEEDS INDOORS

Basic Requirements for Starting Seeds

All seeds have similar basic requirements for soil, moisture, warmth and light.

Soil

Large seeds usually do a good job of germinating in garden soil, but seeds sown in flats or containers need a light, loose soil that does not host the fungi that cause seedlings to rot. To prevent these "damping off" problems, use a sterile, soilless potting mixture. Peat-based mixes designed specifically for starting seeds or a mixture of vermiculite, perlite and milled sphagnum moss works well.

Any container that drains easily and holds 2 or 3 inches of growing medium will work for growing seedlings. Styrofoam cups with drainage holes punched in the bottom, reusable plastic flats, pots, cellpacks and peat pots all work well. Peat pots are especially good for species that resent being transplanted because you can peel the pot back to soil level, remove the bottom of the pot, break open the sides and then transplant pot and all to the garden with minimal disturbance of plant roots. When reusing plastic containers, scrub them with a mild bleach solution and rinse well.

Dampen the planting medium well before planting seeds. Use a pencil or small stick to make holes for seeds.

Moisture

Moisten the germinating medium thoroughly before sowing your seed. Seeding depth should be about three times the diameter of the seeds. Keep the moisture in the medium the consistency of a wrung-out sponge. Cover your containers with plastic wrap or a plastic bag to keep the soil moist while the seeds are germinating. Remove the cover as soon as seeds sprout to avoid disease problems. Cut back on watering then too.

When seedlings are two inches tall, let the top half-inch of the growing medium dry out between waterings.

Warmth

Many seeds need extra warmth to germinate. In general, seeds germinate best if the soil temperature is around 75°F. However, some cool-natured plants (like lettuce and snapdragon) prefer cooler germination temperatures around 65°F.

Place containers planted with seeds in a warm place, keeping in mind that light bulbs placed near flats generate heat. You can also buy moisture-proof soil-heating cables at garden centers or by mail order. Place the cable beneath containers to provide steady and even warmth. After the seeds germinate, normal room temperatures between 65 and 75°F are adequate.

Light

Seedlings need lots of light to flourish. Light-starved seedlings are leggy and pale, stretching toward the closest light source.

The best way to provide adequate light is with fluorescent tubes. Use a pair of 4- to 6-foot-long fluorescent shop tubes in a fixture that hangs from chains. Chains and cup hooks will allow you to raise or lower the height of the lights based on the height of your seedlings. Position the light so it is 2 to 4 inches above the plants. One shop light fixture provides enough light for two full-size flats.

Cover propagation flats with plastic sheets supported by sticks, pencils or even plastic drinking straws.

A tabletop light fixture that can be adjusted for height makes it simple to provide sufficient light for young seedlings.

Caring for Seedlings

When too many seeds germinate in containers, you can either thin them or gingerly transplant them to flats or individual pots. When growing seedlings that resent transplanting, thin them by snipping off unwanted seedlings at soil level with small, sharp scissors. Two-inch wide cellpacks can accommodate only one seedling per cell, but you can often leave two in a 4-inch wide pot. If you are growing a mixture of different colors of flowers, for example snapdragons or stocks, do not thin out the smallest seedlings. Frequently flowers of differing colors grow at different speeds, so it's impor- tant to keep a balanced collection of small, medium and large seedlings.

If you'd rather transplant than thin, do so early, just as the first true leaves emerge. If you wait

If you want to grow a large number of seedlings, flats are often easier to keep watered than individual containers. When you are ready to transplant the seedlings, cut the soil into squares and remove the plants with a spatula, as shown here with old-fashioned fragrant nicotiana.

longer, the roots will be so tangled that they will break as you pull them apart.

Working with Seedlings

Tools, Materials & Timing

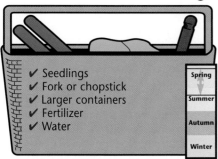

- ✔ Seedlings
- ✔ Fork or chopstick
- ✔ Larger containers
- ✔ Fertilizer
- ✔ Water

Spring
Summer
Autumn
Winter

1 Lay the clump of seedlings on its side and use a fork, chopstick or your fingers to carefully work seedlings free. Transplant them to a larger container filled with moist potting soil immediately. Handle young seedlings only by their seedling leaves and avoid touching the true leaves, stem and roots.

2 By the time seedlings show their first true leaves they are ready for a little fertilizer. (Seedling leaves are usually shaped like rounded ovals, while true leaves are shaped like those of the mature plant.) Water-soluble, all-purpose fertilizers or fish emulsion works fine when mixed at half the recommended strength and applied once a week. Move up to full strength a week or two before setting out your plants in the garden.

3 One to two weeks before trans- planting seedlings outdoors, harden them off by setting contain- ers outside in a lightly shaded spot that is sheltered from strong winds. Set plants out for a few hours at first, gradually

A diluted fish emulsion will feed these young zinnia seedlings.

increasing the amount of time they spend outdoors and the amount of sun they receive. Transplant to the garden on a cloudy, still day, if possible. Water well and provide temporary shade if the weather becomes very warm and sunny.

To separate seedlings, gently pull the plants apart without touching the main stems. Replant them right away in slightly larger containers filled with damp potting soil.

Harden off rooted cuttings before transplanting to the garden. To do this, place the containers outdoors for one to two weeks.

SAVING YOUR OWN SEEDS

It's easy to become your own seed supplier! How? Just gather seed to plant in future seasons. In some cases, saving seed is the only way to propagate a cherished plant handed down from gardener to gardener. It is also a rewarding way to develop a special variety that is particularly well suited to your garden's climate and growing conditions.

Any plant that produces flowers will probably produce seeds. Annual flowers and vegetables produce large quantities of viable seeds, so they are the easiest types of plants for the first-time seed saver. After mastering annuals, move on to saving seed from perennials and biennials as well as hardy vines, trees and shrubs.

After gathering seeds you want to save, dry them for several days before storing them in a cool, dry place.

How Seeds Happen

Down in the middle of a flower is an organ called an ovary. Seeds develop within the ovary after pollen grains land in special receptor sites, which take different forms in different types of plants. In most flowers, stamens hold pollen up so that it can shower down into the ovary. However, nature is full of unique approaches to fertilization. In corn, pollen from the tassels must reach the silks several feet below. Squash develops distinct male and female flowers, and insects move pollen from male stamens to female ovaries.

After a flower is pollinated and ovules are fertilized, the petals fade away as the plant channels its energy to the developing seeds. Over a period of weeks, the seeds mature and develop hard coats. Finally the ovary dries up, splits open and releases the seed. It is then disbursed by wind, water, animals and gardeners.

HYBRID AND OPEN-POLLINATED VARIETIES

Many vegetables and annual flowers are hybrids. A **hybrid**, often referred to as the F1 generation, is a plant developed by crossing two unlike parents. The parents are usually chosen because of special characteristics including disease resistance, color or improved productivity. Hybrid plants tend to be very vigorous and productive, which is why we like to grow them.

However, because of their unstable genetic background, seeds gathered from hybrids grow into plants that often resemble their grandparents more than the plant that produced them. You are more likely to get the plants you hope for when you save seed only from non-hybrids, called **open-pollinated** varieties.

Some mail-order seed companies specialize in open-pollinated varieties. And some vegetables and flowers are so productive and pretty without hybridization that most varieties are open-pollinated. Popular open-pollinated plants include beans, peas, lettuce, radishes, herbs and most old-fashioned flowers.

Hybrid varieties are not the best candidates for saving seed. Plants grown from seeds taken from these hybrid tomatoes may not have the same shape, color, flavor or vigor as their parents; rather, they may take after any one of their grandparents.

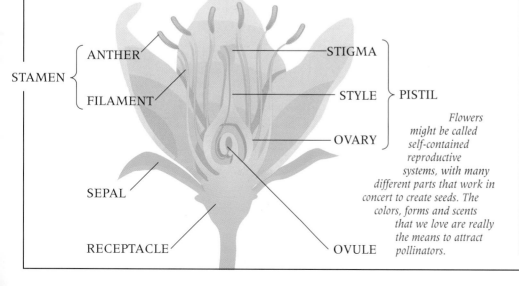

STAMEN
ANTHER
FILAMENT
PETAL
STIGMA
STYLE ⎱ PISTIL
OVARY
SEPAL
RECEPTACLE
OVULE

Flowers might be called self-contained reproductive systems, with many different parts that work in concert to create seeds. The colors, forms and scents that we love are really the means to attract pollinators.

TIP The Seed Saver's Exchange

If you are especially interested in growing old-time vegetables and flowers, you might be interested in joining Seed Saver's Exchange, an organization dedicated to saving heirloom food crops from extinction. SSE members maintain thousands of heirloom varieties by saving and sharing seeds. For more information, send a self-addressed, stamped envelope to:

Seed Saver's Exchange
3076 N. Winn Rd.
Decorah, IA 52101

Harvesting Seeds

Collect zinnia seeds by tying a paper bag over the drying flower heads.

- **Flower Seeds.** To save seeds from flowers, wait until the flowers fade and dry to tan or brown. When the seeds are ripe, the flower head often becomes somewhat fluffy and loose. On a dry day, pop off a sample flower and crush it in your hand. Look for hard, dry seeds or nutlets, which are heavier than the bits of dried flower. You will usually find the seeds in the middle of the dried-up flower heads.

Always look for seeds in the center of ripened flowers, as seen here with marigolds. With experience, you can judge the ripeness of seeds by looking at their size and color.

- **Vegetable Seeds.** These seeds are much more obvious, but they may be suspended in juicy material (tomatoes) or stuck inside pods (beans,

EASY PLANTS FOR SAVING SEEDS

Flowers		Vegetables
Bachelor's button	Poppy	Arugula
Black-eyed Susan	Sunflower	Beans
Cleome	Sweet pea	Lettuce
Cosmos	Sweet William	Kale
Daisies	Zinnia	Okra
Hollyhock		Peas
Marigold		Pepper
Morning glory		Tomato

Sweet William.

Airtight containers (here, film canisters) will protect dried seeds from moisture.

peas and cabbage family crops). To free tomato seeds, squeeze them into a glass of water, stir and then dip out some of the seeds and dry them on paper towels. You can save most other vegetable seeds by opening the pods and laying out the seeds to dry on a sheet of newspaper.

- **Drying Seeds.** After collecting any type of seed, let the seeds dry thoroughly before you store them. Spread out the seeds on paper or lay them in a shallow box; stir through the seeds every few days. After one to two weeks of drying, remove plant debris and place seeds in storage containers. Glass jars make good storage containers since they keep out humidity. Place small amounts of seeds in paper envelopes, and place several envelopes inside a single jar.

Brightly-colored flower petals help attract pollinators (such as insects or birds), but some flowers need no help from insects. Their pollen gets where it needs to go with a little help from the wind, as is the case with corn, tomatoes, peppers and peas.

If collected seeds are fairly dry to begin with, finish the job by placing them on leftover sheets of newspaper.

- **Selecting Seeds.** When you get ready to plant your collected seeds, look through the seeds and select the biggest, plumpest seeds you have. These are likely to produce the biggest, most productive plants.

DIVIDING PERENNIALS

Division is a fast, reliable way to propagate perennials that form clumps of stems and multiple roots. Dividing by division is a simple matter of digging plants, separating them into smaller plants with a few attached roots and replanting them as quickly as possible. If desired, you also can plant small divisions in containers, then transplant them to the garden weeks or months later.

Many vigorous perennials benefit from being divided after they have been growing in the garden for a few years. Dividing and replanting promotes healthy growth and renewed flowering of numerous perennials, bulbs and tubers.

Superior cultivars of many perennial flowers are best propagated vegetatively because they may not breed true from seed.

DIVIDING IN SUMMER

When you divide actively growing plants, cut back the foliage by at least one-half to reduce moisture loss from the leaves. Keep as much soil packed around the roots as possible and avoid cutting roots into very small pieces. Water divided plants often, and never allow the soil to dry out.

If you want more of a particular plant but the plant doesn't need to be divided yet, you can "shovel divide." Insert the back of your shovel against the main clump but near the perimeter of the plant. Dig out a piece of the mother plant and transplant with soil still packed around its roots. Refill the hole around the mother plant and trim away any broken plant parts.

When to Divide

Fall and spring are the best times to dig and divide perennials. During these seasons, cool soil temperatures promote new root development, plants are not stressed by hot sun, and natural rainfall will reduce the amount of watering you have to do. Spring is generally the best time to divide perennials in northern climates, while fall is usually preferred in Zones 6 to 9. Another guideline is that if you want to see flowers on plants that bloom in early spring (like daisies or dianthus), divide them in the fall. You can divide later-blooming plants in spring without risking the loss of summer flowers.

TIP Tips for Dividing Perennials

• **Divide perennials** on a calm, overcast day when the wind and sun won't dry roots as you work.

• **Keep divided plants** from drying out by moistening them with a hose and covering with moist newspaper.

• **Perennials bloom** best on young, active growth from the plant's perimeter, so discard old, woody centers that don't produce blooms.

• **Mulch perennials** divided in fall to keep them from frost heaving.

As each division from these garden phlox are cut from the clump, they must be planted in pots right away, before they begin to dry out.

PERENNIALS THAT BENEFIT FROM DIVISION

Ajuga	Daylily
Artemisia	Dianthus
Aster	Foxglove
Astilbe	Helianthus
Bee balm	Hosta
Chrysanthemum	Iris
Coreopsis	Lamb's-ear
Delphinium	Phlox
Daisy	Yarrow

Note: These generally need dividing at least once every three years.

Digging and Dividing

Tools, Materials & Timing

✔ Digging fork
✔ Garden hose attached
  to water source
✔ Garden gloves
✔ Pruning saw or axe

Spring
Summer
Autumn
Winter

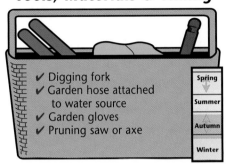

1 The first step is to dig up the old plant. Push a digging fork into the soil in a circle around the outside of the old clump, pulling back on the fork to work the clump loose. After the clump is loose, lift the mass of roots out of the ground.

2 Wash soil away from the clump with the garden hose if it helps you see the plant's crown, buds and roots. You need not wash the roots of most plants. In fact, keeping some soil packed around the roots reduces trauma to the plants.

Pull apart masses of spreading plants such as ajuga, bee balm and daisies with your bare hands. Plants with fleshy roots such as astilbe, daylilies and hosta must be pried or cut apart with a sharp non-serrated knife. To divide thick clumps of ornamental grasses, you may need a pruning saw or an axe.

Before you make cuts, look at the crown to see where natural divisions occur and use those as your guide. First, make cuts to lop off plant parts that are old and woody. Then look for natural divisions in the roots and new growing buds on the crown. A good rule of thumb is to leave three to five buds or growing shoots per division along with a good root system.

3 Replant your healthiest divisions and toss the old ones in the compost heap. Toss divisions with sparse roots as well. Spread the roots out in the planting hole and replant the divisions at the same depth they were growing previously. Water well to keep the plants evenly moist until they are established.

BEFORE YOU DIG

Replant divisions in the same place, or use divided plants to fill new garden areas. Either way, it's important to have prepared soil ready to receive divided plants on the day they are dug. When replanting in the same area, place your dug plants in the shade and cover them with a blanket. Use this opportunity to renovate the bed: work compost or other rich organic matter into the soil. Then divide the plants and replant the divisions. When planting a new bed, prepare the soil ahead of time so that it's ready to plant on dividing day.

DIVIDING BULBS, CORMS AND TUBERS

Bulbs, corms and tubers are natural propagators. These underground storage organs practically clone themselves. If you go to the small trouble of digging them up, they will hand you their offspring, which are exactly like the parent plant. So new plants are yours for the replanting ... absolutely free!

Dividing Spring-Flowering Bulbs

Spring-flowering bulbs such as daffodils, glory-of-the-snow, grape hyacinth, tulips and squill can be dug and divided in summer, after the plants have flowered and the foliage has turned from green to yellow or brown. At this point, the bulbs have finished storing up the nutrients they need. Replant the bulbs immediately, or hold them indoors in an open box and replant them in fall.

- **Dig up the bulbs.** Using a digging fork with flat tines, dig several inches away from the foliage to avoid spearing bulbs. You will need to dig deeply, for most spring-flowering bulbs are at least 6 to 8 inches below the surface. Crowded bulbs will come up in a heavy mass; to shatter it, soundly dump it on the ground.

Daffodil bulb.

- **Separate and select.** Brush away soil and separate the bulbs with your hands. Pick out the largest, plumpest bulbs, which will bloom first and best. Medium-sized bulbs may not bloom until they've been in the ground for another year, but they are ideal for planting in a naturalized area. Discard the smallest bulbs unless you want to put them in a nursery bed for a year or two.

- **Label varieties.** If you are planning to divide several different types of bulbs, place a weather-proof label in front of each clump while they are blooming. Use an indelible pen to note the type of bulb, cultivar name (if known), and the color. Keep the label with the bulbs as you dig them out of the ground so you don't get piles of bulbs mixed up.

After a few years, daffodil blooms can become sparse. Time to divide!

REVITALIZING DAFFODILS

Beautiful daffodils seldom need to be divided, for they often become bigger and better as the bulbs become crowded. If you want to divide daffodils to increase your supply of plants, dig them in autumn, at bulb planting time. Separate and sort them as you would spring-flowering bulbs, but waste no time getting them back into the ground.

You'll know that your daffodils need to be divided when you get lots of green growth, but few flowers. After the leaves brown, dig and separate the bulbs and replant them 2-3 inches apart in newly enriched soil. Plant any leftovers in a new bed.

Dividing Corms

Crocus, gladiolus and crocosmia grow from a special type of storage root called a corm. Each season, the plants produce a new corm which remains attached to the old corm. The plants may produce little corms along the sides of the new corm, called cormels. The cormels seldom flower well, and may produce so much foliage that the bed appears weedy.

Gladiolus corm.

- **Digging corms.** To propagate any flower that grows from a corm, dig the plants when they are dormant (summer for crocus, fall for most other corms). Many plants that grow from corms are not very winter hardy, including gladiolus. These are usually stored through winter like dahlias (see below). Before replanting them, break off and discard the old, shriveled corms and the little cormels. This should leave you with one fat new corm ready for replanting.

- **Planting corms.** As with spring-flowering bulbs, you can hold your harvested cormels for several weeks before replanting if needed. Protect them from extreme cold and heat.

When dividing plants with thin, fibrous roots such as dianthus, don't shake or wash the soil from the plant's roots. Lifting clumps from beneath helps keep soil packed around the roots, and that eases transplanting trauma.

Dahlias grow from fleshy tubers that can easily divide to make new plants. In climates where the ground freezes, dahlia tubers must be dug and stored indoors through winter.

Dividing Dahlias

Because dahlias cannot survive in frozen ground in most regions, you must dig and store them over winter indoors. But it's best to wait until spring to actually divide them. Here's how:

Begonia tuber.

In spring, plant dahlias about the time you set out tomatoes. Stake them when you plant.

- **Dig.** Dig roots in fall just after the leaves and stems turn black from the first killing frost. Wash off the tubers, and then let them air dry for several days. Use an indelible marker to write the name or color of each variety right on the tuber.

- **Store.** Store the air-dried tubers in a box lined with a plastic trash bag. Lay the tubers in a single layer across the bottom, and then add 4 inches of peat moss and vermiculite.

- **Storage Tips.** Leave the bag open to allow air circulation. Store the box in a cool area that doesn't freeze (40 to 50°F is ideal). Check the tubers a few times during storage to make sure they don't shrivel. If needed, dribble a little water into the box to maintain sufficient moisture.

- **Divide.** Prior to planting in the spring, divide each tuber with a sharp knife so the new sections include roots, part of the crown and at least one growth bud. Let the cuts heal for two days in a warm place before replanting to avoid rot.

- **Plant.** Plant the new divisions in the garden when the soil is warm, or start them in pots indoors for later planting.

ROOTING STEM CUTTINGS

You can grow numerous plants from stem cuttings. In nurseries, shrubs are almost always propagated from stem cuttings. At home, you can root cuttings taken from annuals and perennials as well. Here are some secrets.

Taking Cuttings—When

Take stem cuttings when plants are growing but not blooming. Mid- to late-summer is a good time because plants have many stems to cut from and are often in need of pruning to restore a handsome shape. But some plants (especially shrubs) root better if cuttings are taken as new shoots expand in the spring. If some of your cuttings don't root well the first time, try taking cuttings earlier in the season the following year.

PLANTS TO PROPAGATE FROM STEM CUTTINGS

Bee balm	Geranium	Rosemary
Butterfly bush	Heliotrope	Rose
Campanula	Hydrangea	Russian sage
Chrysanthemum	Lantana	Sage
Crape myrtle	Mint	Salvia
Euonymus	Oregano	Sedum
Forsythia	Petunia	Viburnum

To gauge the new root growth of ivy and other cuttings, place them in clear glass containers.

ROOTING POWDER

Most cuttings taken from woody plants root better if they are dipped in a rooting powder. Synthetic rooting powders purchased at garden centers and through mail-order sources are hormones but some may be man-made. Indolebutyric acid (IBA) is a commonly available synthetic rooting hormone that promotes root formation and quality. Some rooting powders also contain a fungicide to reduce the chance of fungal diseases.

Lightly moisten the base of your cuttings then dip them in rooting powder placed in a small container. The powder will stick to the cutting's end. Tap the cutting to remove excess powder, and plant it. Discard the unused powder.

ROOTING STEM CUTTINGS IN WATER

Some annual plants including coleus, begonias, basil and even tomato will root easily within a few weeks after you place a 4-to 6-inch-long stem cutting in plain water. Here's how:

Place cuttings in a jar with room temperature tap water. Insert each stem so the bottom is at least 2 inches below the surface but the leaves are dry. Keep in a warm, brightly lit place.

Replace the old water every few days with fresh water that has come to room temperature. You'll see roots in one to two weeks. Pot up your new plants in containers using a standard well-drained growing mix. If started your new plants indoors, gradually acclimate them to outdoor conditions by placing pots in an area sheltered from harsh sun and wind for a few days before moving them to their permanent home. You also can propagate chrysanthemums this way if you take cuttings in very early spring.

To stimulate root growth in fresh cuttings, dip the cut end in a rooting powder before placing cuttings in a growing medium.

Taking Cuttings—How

Tools, Materials & Timing

- ✔ Sharp knife or pruning shears
- ✔ Small pots
- ✔ Sphagnum moss and perlite, or other sterile growing mix
- ✔ Pencil or small stick
- ✔ Plastic drinking straws or chopsticks
- ✔ Clear plastic
- ✔ Tape or string

Spring
Summer
Autumn
Winter

1 Use a sharp knife or pruning shears to take tip cuttings 2 to 4 inches long. Select stems that are fat and stocky instead of stems that are long and thin. Cut below a leaf bud or node, and remove the leaves along the stem. Leave only two or three leaves at the very tip. If there are flowers, cut them off.

2 Keep cuttings cool and moist at all times. In fact, some gardeners find that scented geraniums and other perennials actually root better if you take the moistened rooting container with you to the cuttings session, and stick the cuttings in it within seconds after the stems are cut.

3 Insert the stem halfway into a small pot filled with a growing mix that stays moist but not soggy, such as a 1:1 mix of milled sphagnum moss and perlite, or any sterile seed-starting mixture. If the stem is too soft to penetrate the soil mix, poke a hole in the medium with a pencil, insert the stem and tuck your growing mix around the stem.

4 Poke two plastic drinking straws or chopsticks in each pot to support a piece of clear plastic laid loosely over the top. The plastic will help keep the cuttings in a very humid environment, which will reduce stress to the rootless cuttings. To increase humidity even more, tuck the ends of the plastic in around the outside of the container and secure it with tape or string. Watch your plants. If they start to rot, vent the plastic by poking several holes in it with the tip of a sharp knife.

5 Place the pots with cuttings in an outdoor area sheltered from direct sun and wind. Cuttings can root indoors but disease problems tend to increase because indoor air does not circulate like it does outdoors. Keep the growing medium moist but not soggy.

6 Most cuttings root easily and should be ready for potting into larger containers in two to four weeks. Test their readiness by pulling gently on the cutting. If they resist, they are probably well rooted. New leaves are another sign that new roots are taking hold.

7 After your cuttings have rooted, transplant them to a larger pot or a nursery bed until they are large enough to be transferred to the garden. With hardy shrubs, you can often wait until the following spring.

8 Even under ideal conditions, every stem cutting will not develop roots. Some will fail, and the failure rate may be quite high if you are working with plants that have woody stems. But one successful viburnum is still quite an accomplishment, as is a yard full of brightly-blooming chrysanthemums, or a deck spilling over with fragrant herbs.

Cuttings of coleus and spider plant will root readily in water until you are ready to pot them.

CHAPTER 13

PESTS:
CONTROLLING DISEASES, INSECTS AND WEEDS

To grow a healthy garden, safeguard helpful creatures and protect your plants from the challenges that talented pests pose.

No matter where you live or what you grow, a gardener never works alone. You are always in the constant company of other living things—plants, birds, frogs, insects, fungi, bacteria and perhaps a curious dog or cat. Taken together, these are all parts of the garden's ecology. When times are good, each part interacts with the other to form a complicated balance that results in a healthy garden and a satisfied gardener. When times are bad, we rant and rave at grasshoppers or wonder what we ever did to deserve powdery mildew.

As the garden's manager, you have tremendous power to keep pests from ruining your gardening fun. You can solve some pest problems easily, while others require lots of thinking and experimenting before you find an answer. The more you know to start with, the faster those answers will come.

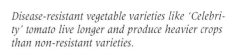

First Step—Understanding Host Plants

It's natural to feel alarmed when a pest damages a favorite plant, but it's important to realize that the insect or disease that hurts one type of plant is usually unable to spread to different species. Diseases and insects often require the presence of specific host plants if they are to survive. If you pluck off a tomato hornworm and place it on a sweet corn leaf, it will give up feeding after a few bites because its digestive system simply can't handle corn.

You can prevent numerous important pest problems by growing a highly diversified garden that includes many different host plants. To displease pests that are prevalent in your area, choose the worst possible host plants.

Tomato hornworm can feed only on tomatoes and closely-related plants such as pepper and flowering tobacco (Nicotiana).

Disease-resistant vegetable varieties like 'Celebrity' tomato live longer and produce heavier crops than non-resistant varieties.

Vegetables

Diseases cannot infect plants that are highly resistant to them, so choosing resistant varieties is a crucial key to preventing diseases in the vegetable garden. By choosing resistant varieties, you can totally eliminate otherwise imminent problems such as fusarium wilt of tomato (in the South and East), pea enation virus (in the Northwest), and cucumber powdery mildew (in the North). Some varieties are even resistant to insects.

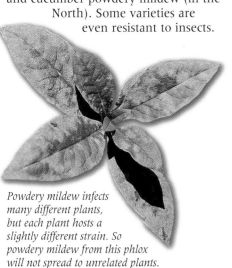

Powdery mildew infects many different plants, but each plant hosts a slightly different strain. So powdery mildew from this phlox will not spread to unrelated plants.

A prevalent disease of tomato, fusarium wilt causes plants to turn yellow and die just as the fruits begin to ripen. To prevent wilt, rotate your location or grow resistant varieties if you have seen this disease in your garden.

Flowers

In the flower garden, you may need to switch to a different species of plant to avoid pest problems, or you might get relief by changing the plant's location. This approach is especially worthwhile with perennial flowers and shrubs, which may struggle in one site and thrive in another that is only slightly different. Site factors including soil, sun and moisture have tremendous influence over the growth of plants as well as the activities of insects, diseases and weeds.

Like many annual flowers, vinca is a host plant for a soil-borne disease that causes the plants' roots to rot. Rotating vinca with other flowers usually keeps the soil from becoming seriously infected.

PREVENTING & IDENTIFYING PROBLEMS

You don't have to live at the mercy of garden diseases, insects and weeds. A few simple preventative measures will go a long way toward controlling disease outbreaks, insect invasions and weed problems.

But alas, sooner or later you will encounter problems. There's just no getting around it. Then it's time to identify the problem and think of it as another gardening challenge—one where you will come out the victor.

Know Your Garden

On this and the following pages, you will get to know a number of common pests in addition to many important allies. Use this information as a starting point, and then turn to your garden for more lessons on how to best manage your garden pests. With each passing season, you will gain new knowledge about the complex web of life in your own backyard.

Rotation Wisdom

Trees and other plants that are naturally long-lived have elaborate ways of defending themselves from all sorts of injuries, but the same is not true of short-lived annual plants. Perhaps because these plants are supposed to live, die and rot away in a brief period of time, there is an abundance of pests and diseases out there ready to hasten their demise and expedite their disappearance.

Most of these pests need time to become established, particularly insects and diseases that spend part of their life cycle in the soil. The presence of a suitable host plant one season gives them a start, but it may take them two or three seasons to really get going. This is where rotations come in. If you have a disease that thrives on tomato roots secretly flourishing in your soil, and you don't plant tomatoes there more often than once every three years, the disease may never get out of hand. Likewise, rotating annual flowers (marigolds one year, petunias the next for instance) keeps soil-borne diseases in a state of constant frustration.

Cleanliness Counts

SPORES SPREAD BY WIND OR WATER

SPORES ON LEAVES

INFECTED BUSH

GERMINATING SPORE

MILDEW ON LEAFLETS

MILDEW ON BUDS AND LEAVES

Most garden diseases are caused by parasitic fungi which release thousands of spores. Keep the garden tidy by pinching off diseased leaves or raking up those that fall to the ground. This stops the disease life cycle dead in its tracks. Old plants may be riddled with insects as well. Insects that burrow into the soil before pupating into adults may perish altogether when thrown into the wild natural world of your compost heap.

Edible marigolds.

TIP The Home Advantage

To learn as much as you can about problems gardeners face in your area, make a call to your local university extension service office and see if they have written information on common insects and diseases. Also, ask if your county has a Master Gardener program. If so, you can ask a trained volunteer to help identify your pest problems, or maybe even enroll in the program yourself.

WHAT'S THE PROBLEM?

- **Seedlings disappear.** Look for deer footprints as well as evidence that rabbits have stopped by. If animals are eliminated, the problem is either cutworms or slugs. Protect remaining plants from cutworms by encircling them with collars (like bottomless paper cups pushed into the ground). See how to trap slugs on page 181.

Watch for telltale garden slug trails.

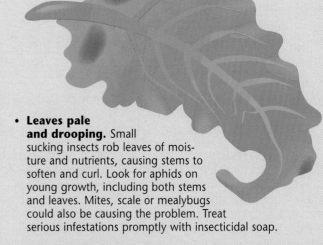

Aphid damage.

- **Large holes in leaves.** This could be the work of grasshoppers, slugs, caterpillars or night-flying beetles. Plants don't mind a few holes in their leaves, but you'll need to find the cause of ongoing damage. Check plants at different times of day (and night) to find the culprit.

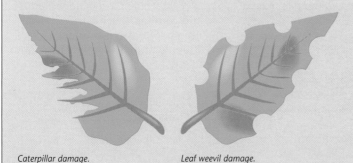

Caterpillar damage.   *Leaf weevil damage.*

- **Leaves pale and drooping.** Small sucking insects rob leaves of moisture and nutrients, causing stems to soften and curl. Look for aphids on young growth, including both stems and leaves. Mites, scale or mealybugs could also be causing the problem. Treat serious infestations promptly with insecticidal soap.

- **Leaves rolled into cylinders.** A wide variety of caterpillars use plants for habitat rather than food. To create a nice shelter for themselves, they pull leaves into a roll and secure them with webbing. The easiest solution is to simply pick off affected leaves and dispose of them.

Spider mite damage.   *Leafroller damage.*

- **Small holes in leaves.** In the vegetable garden, plants with "buckshot" leaves are probably being eaten by flea beetles. Some flea beetles feed on flowers too, as do many small bugs and beetles. Try a neem-based botanical insecticide if the damage is too heavy to tolerate.

Flea beetle damage.

- **Plants collapse and die.** This is evidence that a disease or insect has invaded the plant's roots or the base of its stem. Either way, the plant is doomed since it is cut off from its moisture and nutrient supply. To reduce future problems, fill the spot with a plant unrelated to the one that died.

- **Leaves crinkled with strange color, shape and texture.** Viruses cause plants to grow in wacky ways. In addition to changes in the leaves, look for altered flowering patterns. Infected plants seldom produce well, and are best removed from the garden and disposed of in the garbage.

Leafminer damage.

Cutworms damage plant roots.

WASTE YOUR WEEDS

The single motion that a gardener repeats more often than any other is the pulling of weeds. It's dull, repetitive work that must be done. Left uncontrolled, weeds can quickly overwhelm cultivated plants and pirate away everything they need, including moisture, light and nutrients from the soil.

Getting to know your weeds is the first step toward controlling them. Certain perennial weeds grow so aggressively that it's almost impossible to garden in their midst. These include wild Bermudagrass and Johnsongrass in warm climates, quackgrass, Canada thistle and bindweed in the north and west. If these weeds are firmly established in a place where you want to grow a garden, you must first get them under control. It will not be easy and you will need to use every one of the methods described here.

Weeds on a Mission

Most gardeners have less formidable weeds as garden companions, but it's important to understand that every garden weed is a plant with a mission. In the natural scheme of things, the job of the garden weed is to heal over soil that we leave open and scarred, so that natural succession can proceed. Weeds are nature's bandage plants, and for this they are due at least a passing nod of respect.

In any garden, summer is the season of big weeds. Mulching and regular pulling help reduce weed problems, but a few invaders will always find a way to invade your garden.

Managing Weeds with Mulches

Weeds cannot germinate when they are deprived of light, which is the idea behind using mulches to control them. Just about any mulch will keep plant roots cool and moist, but a few are superior for suppressing weeds.

Besides looking good, wood mulches discourage weeds and retain soil moisture.

- **Mulches for flowers.** In high-visibility flowerbeds in your front yard, use attractive mulches such as bark nuggets or pine needles, provided the material is at least 2 inches thick after it has packed down. A few weeds will sprout and grow through the mulch, but they are easily pulled out with a gentle tug.

- **Mulches for vegetables.** In your vegetable garden, fabric-type, roll-out weed barriers held in place with a thin layer of weathered hay or straw prevent most weeds from emerging. If you're careful with it, you can take up the fabric at the end of the season and reuse it for several years. Or use newspapers and cardboard beneath a straw mulch. Simply turn under your "double mulch" when it has done its job.

Plants that run along the ground, such as cucumbers, need serious weed protection. Here straw mulch tops a layer of plastic roll-out weed barrier.

CRABGRASS: BUILT FOR SPEED

The most common weed in summer gardens is crabgrass— a fast-growing weed that can change its shape depending on its situation. In open ground, crabgrass spreads out its stems in a spiral pattern. In closer quarters it becomes slender and upright. A good mulch will prevent crabgrass from sprouting, but you will still need to pull out crabgrass that pops up close to your garden plants. Chemical crabgrass preventers give seasonal control when applied according to label directions in late spring.

What begins as a little slip of crabgrass can quickly grow to overtake neighboring plants, including this ageratum.

Weeding Tools and Techniques

The only trick to weeding is to pull weeds when the soil is damp and hoe them down when the soil is dry. If the top of a weed breaks off when you try to pull it, the roots and crown left behind will probably regrow into a new plant. As long as weeds have not yet developed mature seeds, you can let them dry in the sun for a day and then use them as mulch; or dispose of them in your compost heap.

Here are the four most essential tools for weeding:

Fishtail weeder.

Table fork.

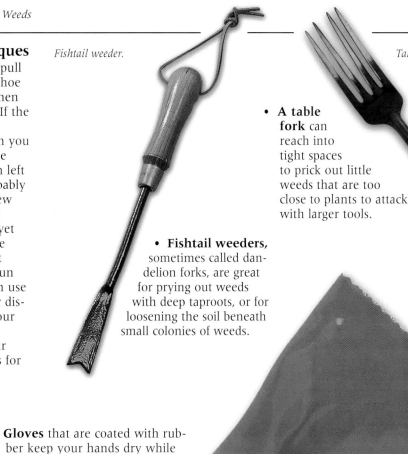

- **A table fork** can reach into tight spaces to prick out little weeds that are too close to plants to attack with larger tools.

- **Fishtail weeders,** sometimes called dandelion forks, are great for prying out weeds with deep taproots, or for loosening the soil beneath small colonies of weeds.

- **Gloves** that are coated with rubber keep your hands dry while you weed, and insulate your fingers from cold soil.

- **Hoes** come in different shapes and sizes. Try different ones until you find a hoe that fits your height and does a good job of slicing off weeds just below the soil line.

Hoe.

Rubber-coated gloves.

Handling Herbicides

To gain control of weeds that are dangerous to touch, use a contact herbicide that kills the weed plants when it is sprayed or painted on the leaves. Appropriate subjects include poison ivy, stinging nettle and knapweed. (Knapweed can cause cancerous tumors if you let its sap get into open wounds on your hands, so wear gloves.)

When handling herbicides, make sure wind cannot carry droplets of herbicide spray to nearby plants that you like.

Use a portable sprayer to apply pesticides or herbicides. Always use a clean sprayer, or keep a separate one for each type of application.

TIP **Cover and Smother Crops**

When areas of the vegetable garden remain vacant for several weeks, keep weeds from sprouting by planting the space with a smother crop. A smother crop is similar to a cover crop, but the primary purpose of a smother crop is to prevent the emergence of weeds. Vigorous leafy greens like mustard or turnips make good smother crops. Also try tough legumes including field peas, soybeans, vetches or fava beans.

A HAVEN FOR BENEFICIAL BUGS

For every pest that causes damage in the garden, there are natural enemies in the insect world. These natural predators and parasites can be a gardener's best friend. A teeming population of beneficial bugs reduces or eliminates the need for time-consuming spraying or hand picking without compromising the garden's beauty or productivity.

Here are strategies and techniques for getting some of this "free pest-control" help in the garden.

Crab spiders are but one of many species of beneficial insects that inhabit a garden.

Attracting "Good Bugs"

Adding plants that attract beneficial insects to your garden is an easy way to invite these allies to share your garden space. Beneficial insects include spiders, wasps, lacewings, lady beetles and thousands or other lesser-known species. The best of these have two things in common: they are adapted to the local area and one of their purposes in life is to kill unwanted pests.

You can buy and release beneficial insects in your garden, but it's often easier to tailor your garden to attract beneficials that occur naturally in your area. The formula for keeping them in your garden consists of three things; food, habitat, and conservation of life.

Food

Look around your garden on a warm morning and you will see numerous tiny wasps and flies visiting open flowers. Bees may be gathering pollen, but most of the smaller insects are sipping nectar—one of their primary sources of food. Good nectar plants include most wildflowers, cover crops, herbs and many ornamentals with small tubular blossoms.

Habitat

Many important beneficial insects survive winter as adults hidden away beneath mulches, in the shelter of evergreen bushes, or in the soil. When the insect world gets into full swing in spring and summer, insects often need places to rest and recuperate from their busy days. A mound or hedge of long-lived plants in or near the garden can easily fill this need.

Conservation

Pesticides that kill a wide variety of insects will also kill most beneficial ones, so it's important to choose and use pesticides with great care. If a pest gets out of control, your first response should be to remove them by hand. If this does not work you should then try biological controls such as *Bacillus thuringiensis* (abbreviated as Bt) or neem, a botanical insecticide. Whenever you use potent pesticides, protect beneficials from harm by placing rowcovers over the treated plants.

Even though disease and storms have damaged this tree, it offers shelter, food, and habitat to woodpeckers and other predators of pests.

Flowers that provide large amounts of pollen attract bees, which in turn visit vegetables and fruits and help fertilize blossoms.

BRING ON THE BIRDS

Chickadees, bluebirds, warblers, some native sparrows and many other birds will actively patrol your garden for pests if you invite them in. Although these birds also eat seeds and fruits, in summer they especially crave extra protein to nourish growing nestlings, which is available from insects. To make birds feel welcome, place perches throughout your garden. These can be tomato cages or other wire structures that stand about 5 feet high—the perfect height for watchful birds in search of a creeping, crawling meal.

Sparrow.

Plant a Beneficial Haven

Use a small area of your garden as a temporary sanctuary for beneficial insects. Fill it with plants that provide food and habitat. Your beneficial insects will use it as a home base.

Here are two seasonal ideas to try in the small space of a 3-by 3-foot mound.

- **In spring.** Plant mint and tansy together in a large plastic pot, and bury it halfway in the soil (the pot will restrain these plants' invasive tendencies). Surround it with white and pink cosmos and bachelor buttons and add an edging of signet marigolds.

- **In late summer.** Pull out the withered plants a few at a time, and sow dill, buckwheat and oats in their place. When cooler weather prevails, add kale and a sprinkling of red clover to the plant community. Leave the haven alone after cold weather turns most of the plants to mush, for they will continue to host beneficial insects by providing winter shelter.

Meet Some Mainstream Beneficials

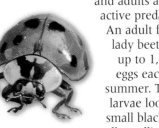

Lady beetles (also called lady bugs) feed on aphids and many other small insects. Both the larvae and adults are active predators. An adult female lady beetle lays up to 1,000 eggs each summer. The larvae look like small black and yellow alligators.

Lady beetle.

Spiders move about the garden, killing and consuming thousands of insects that cross their paths. Mulches give them a safe place to hide and hunt. Some become permanent residents in bushes and trees.

Green lacewing.

Lacewing adults and larvae patrol the garden for aphids, thrips, mites and whiteflies. They may also eat the eggs of serious vegetable pests including Colorado potato beetles and cabbage loopers.

Braconid wasps are the worst nightmare of leaf-eating caterpillars. These tiny wasps lay their eggs inside their prey, weakening them until they die. Over 1,000 native braconid species attack pests including tomato hornworms, armyworms, flea beetles and root maggots.

Braconid parasites on tomato hornworm.

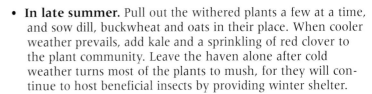

THE NIGHT PATROL

After dark, toads become hopping, croaking bug zappers. They will eat anything that moves including slugs, cutworms, Japanese beetles and even earwigs. Toads breed close to water, but they spend most of their active time close to food. To keep toads in your garden, simply give them cool shady places to catch some shuteye during the day. Toads will burrow under soft mulches or you can place large stones or old boards over small pits dug in shady soil. Any place that stays cool and moist will serve as a comfy toad condo.

An insect-hungry toad.

Spider.

MANAGING GARDEN PESTS

Occupying the top niche in the food chain comes with certain aggravations and responsibilities, especially if you are a gardener. We must understand and interact with more primitive species such as garden insects.

Plan an Attack

The greatest weakness of most garden pests is their predictability. They appear in the garden on regular schedules, they tend to feed only on certain plants, and they disappear like magic when their life cycle is complete. When you can identify the main pests in your garden and predict their activities, controlling them is usually a straightforward matter.

You will usually learn that a pest is present when you see the damage it has caused. Keep a calendar handy to mark down the date. In subsequent seasons, you can use this information to know when to start looking for that pest's seasonal debut.

Besides keeping track of time, you can use special scouting methods to find garden pests before they begin to cause serious damage.

- **Find insects.** To find insects that hop or fly, simply swish a small butterfly net through plant leaves and examine your catch.

If you want to know what types of insects are in your garden, gather a quick sample using a butterfly net.

Sticky traps and coatings catch insects, and also help you monitor infestations.

- **Sticky traps.** Sticky traps are another good monitoring device. Paint a thick piece of cardboard the color of the plant or flower the pest finds attractive. Then coat it with a sticky substance such as Tanglefoot or Stick-em. Place the traps near the plants that are at risk, and you will know right away when the pest becomes active.

Yellow Sticky Cards

The yellow cards hanging above the plants in the greenhouse and vegetable garden are used to trap flying insects such as whiteflies, fungus gnats, and thrips. Attracted to the bright yellow color, the pests get caught in the glue. The cards do not have any pesticides and are disposable.

Yellow sticky cards trap insects that are attracted to the bright color. They're good against white flies, thrips and fungus gnats, and you can use them inside or out.

- **Find eggs.** Go on egg hunts to find pests that appear in large hatches— such as Mexican bean beetles, Colorado potato beetles or imported cabbageworms. These larvae are easier to control if you can treat plants as soon as the eggs hatch. You need not scramble about on your hands and knees waiting for the hatch to occur. When you find an egg cluster (usually attached to the underside of a leaf), place it in a jar outdoors in a shady place. When those eggs hatch, you can assume that the ones in your garden have hatched as well.

To detect pests before they cause damage, check both sides of plant leaves on random plants. Some insects such as Colorado potato beetles lay eggs exclusively on leaf undersides.

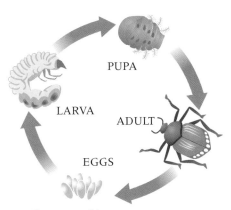

Understanding Metamorphosis

All insects begin their lives as eggs, but after that they may undergo radical changes as they grow to adulthood. Insects that undergo "gradual" metamorphosis slowly gain size and change colors until they become adults. Grasshoppers and most true bugs (such as squash bugs) develop this way.

The vast majority of insects—including all beetles, moths and flies—go through "complete" metamorphosis that includes four different growth phases: egg, larva, pupa and adult.

Most destructive insects eat plants as larvae and again as adults, though their food preferences may change with their life cycles. For example, cucumber beetle larvae eat cucumber roots, while the adults eat flowers and suck juices from plant stems. Tomato hornworms devour tomato leaves, then pupate into large hummingbird moths that sip flower nectar.

Gentle Intervention

It's natural to feel alarmed when an insect launches a lunch attack on a plant you have been nurturing for weeks. But before you declare a chemical war on the enemy, see if you can capture it in your hand. Hand-picking pests and dropping them in a jar of soapy water stops the damage immediately and never causes harm to neighboring beneficial insects, birds or other innocent bystanders. If you're squeamish about bugs, wear a latex glove while plucking up pests.

Many gardeners rely on home-made concoctions to confuse pests in search of host plants and deter their feeding. Several popular recipes are given on pages 180-181. Another smart strategy is to cover plants with floating row-covers as described on page 178.

Whether harm has been caused by disease or insects, pinching off damaged leaves is a good preventive measure.

Any pest that does not hop away fast enough can be captured and drowned in a jar of soapy water.

YOUR EARTH-SAFE ARSENAL

When you need to get a pest under control quickly, you do not necessarily need the most potent pesticides on earth. In most cases, a biological or botanical pesticide will be just as effective as a more poisonous synthetic one. When thoughtfully used, these gentle controls will not devastate beneficial creatures including birds or frogs. Here are three types of products to keep on hand so they are ready to use when you need them.

Insecticidal soap. The fatty acids in insecticidal soap desiccate soft-bodied aphids and other small insects and may deter feeding by some larger ones. Use this soap to control rose thrips, scale, mealybugs, whiteflies, mites and all types of aphids.

Neem. This rather new pesticide, derived from the Asian neem tree, makes pests

"Natural" insecticides include sulfur, horticultural oil, insecticidal soap and neem-based treatments. Always read the label and use them only as directed, because even these can be harmful if misapplied.

stop feeding and reproducing but does not taint the environment with persistent toxins. Use it to control all types of plant-eating beetles (including Japanese beetles), leafhoppers and caterpillars.

Bacillus thuringiensis. This long name, often abbreviated as Bt, describes a naturally occurring bacterium that gives pests a terminal bellyache after they eat it. Different strains are used to control different pests. Use the most common strain to control caterpillars; there is a special strain that controls Colorado potato beetle larvae and another that keeps mosquitoes from breeding in standing water. All are non-toxic to humans and beneficial insects.

WAYS TO USE ROWCOVERS

Better than any pesticide, a floating rowcover serves as an impenetrable barrier between insects and the plants they seek. It also eliminates feeding rabbits, deer and other animal pests.

What are these wonderful things? Floating rowcovers are wide gossamer sheets of spunbound polyester or polypropylene that keep pests out while allowing water, air and light to penetrate. Although they are not often seen in stores, rowcovers with brand names like "Reemay" and "Kimberly Farms" are widely available in mail-order catalogs.

Rowcovers exclude most types of pests from garden plants. When properly used, they eliminate the need for insecticides. Heavyweight covers like this one also retain warmth.

Purpose of Rowcovers

In addition to keeping pests at bay, rowcovers block out some sunlight. When the material is first out of the package, light penetration is about 80 percent. But as the fabric becomes dirty, less light passes through it. Surprisingly, some sun-loving crops including celery, carrots and members of the cucumber family actually grow better beneath the white filtered light of rowcovers.

Using Rowcovers

- **Spreading the rowcovers.** At least two weeks before pests are expected, spread a sheet of floating rowcover loosely over the crop you want to protect. Allow plenty of slack in the cover so the plants have room to grow without chafing against the fabric. If you like, spread rowcovers over metal or plastic hoops like those you might use to support plastic tunnels (see page 148). Or plant a few corn plants in the row and let them hold the cover aloft over smaller plants.

Secure the edges of the rowcover in place with bricks or boards.

- **Keep it clean.** To keep the fabric as clean as possible, don't bury the edges in soil (the standard practice in commercial fields). Instead, roll up the edges around narrow boards. This also makes it easy to get underneath the covers to weed or check on your plants.

- **Storage and re-use.** When carefully handled, rowcovers should last for about three years. When a sheet is no longer needed in the garden, hang it on a clothesline and spray it gently with water to clean it. When it's dry, fold it and store it in a dry place where mice won't be tempted to turn it into a winter home.

When warm weather comes, use very lightweight rowcovers to exclude pests without retaining heat.

FACTS ABOUT FROST

Rowcovers are sometimes recommended as frost protection. However, the types used as insect barriers offer little warmth on cold nights. Lightweight floating rowcovers do have a slight greenhouse effect in that temperatures beneath the cover may be 10 degrees higher during a hot sunny day. But the difference at night is much smaller—usually less than 5 degrees. To be on the safe side, estimate your rowcover's frost protection margin at only to 3 degrees, and add additional insulation (like an old blanket) when frost damage is likely. Some suppliers sell extra-heavyweight rowcovers that provide reliable protection from frost. But heavyweight rowcovers retain too much heat to use during warm summer weather.

Rowcovers can let sunlight through and retain a few degrees of heat when frost threatens.

Control These Pests with Rowcovers

Insects that have a narrow range of host plants are usually the hardest ones to control in the garden. These insects use their primitive senses to find the plants they need, and can be amazingly persistent. When plants are protected with a rowcover, expect to see these hungry hordes crawling on the top of the cover, looking for a way in. To keep them out, promptly repair any tears or holes that develop, using a stapler or a needle and thread.

Mexican bean beetle eggs and larva.

Mexican Bean Beetle

Pinkish brown Mexican bean beetles arrive in the garden in late spring and lay clusters of yellow eggs on the undersides of bean leaves. Ten days later, these eggs hatch into spiny yellow larvae that rasp holes in leaves as they feed. Cover bush beans with rowcovers when they are 4 inches tall, and remove the covers about a month later, when the plants develop numerous white flowers. Where deer are a problem, leave beans covered until the pods are ready to pick.

Colorado Potato Beetle

These yellow-and-black-striped beetles sneak into the potato patch in spring and lay clusters of bright yellow eggs on leaf undersides. The eggs hatch into red hump-backed larvae with a voracious appetite for potato leaves and flowers. Mulch potatoes when they are 6 inches tall and check for eggs before covering the plants. Remove the rowcovers after about six weeks, when the potato plants are large and vigorous.

Imported Cabbageworm

Any member of the cabbage family is fair game for these velvety green caterpillars. The adults are small white butterflies that appear in early spring and lay scattered eggs on leaf undersides. To stop this scenario, cover spring cabbage, broccoli and cauliflower with rowcovers as soon as you set out the plants. Remove the covers after four to six weeks, when the weather is warm.

Imported cabbageworm.

Spotted Cucumber Beetle

These bright little beetles with yellow and black spots damage cucumbers by feeding on the plants and spreading disease. In bad years, they also pester beans and lettuce. Use neem to get rid of any beetles present before you install protective rowcovers. Remove the rowcovers when the plants flower heavily, so that pollinating insects can help fertilize the flowers.

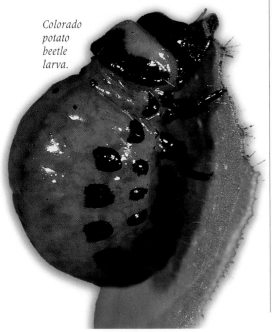

Colorado potato beetle larva.

Spotted cucumber beetle.

PEST CONTROLS FROM YOUR KITCHEN

Sometimes the solution to a pest problem is as close as your kitchen cabinet. As you will see in the recipes that follow, hot peppers are a common ingredient. The reason? All mammals can taste the capsaicin present in hot peppers and they don't like it one bit. When faced with an animal pest, use hot peppers as your first line of defense. Wear rubber gloves when handling hot peppers, for the capsaicin will persist on bare skin for several hours.

For garden-sized jobs, a hand-held pump spray bottle may be all you need. For bigger jobs such as controlling pests on tree fruits, you may want to invest in a pressure sprayer.

Pest Remedies and Warnings

Because most of these recipes are intended to be sprayed onto plants, a word of caution is in order. Never apply a liquid of any kind to leaves in the middle of a hot, sunny day. If you do, the water can heat up very quickly and cause brown burn spots to appear on the leaves.

In addition to these recipes, you might want to experiment with herbal mixtures to deter garden pests. Try making teas with the leaves of mint, tansy and even tomato. These aromatic plants may confuse pests in search of their favorite host plants.

Soap is another substance that many pests find unpalatable, but be careful when using dishwashing detergent or other household soaps. They may contain small amounts of chemicals that can injure plant leaves. Insecticidal soap, mixed according to label directions, does not carry this risk.

Hot Tea

Use this popular brew to deter feeding flea beetles and other garden pests. The hot peppers also will make rabbits and squirrels reluctant to return for a second taste.

HOT TEA

1 whole bulb garlic, broken into cloves
3 hot peppers, chopped, or 1 tablespoon hot pepper flakes
1 quart hot water

Smash the garlic cloves lightly with a hammer or brick. Combine all ingredients in a large glass or plastic jar and allow the mixture to sit in a warm place for a week. Strain through cheesecloth or a coffee filter, and return the strained mixture to the covered jar. To use, pour ½ cup of the hot tea, 1 pint water and 3 drops dishwashing liquid in a pump spray bottle.

No chamomile tea for your garden-chomping Peter Rabbit! Keep him away with hot pepper tea.

Cat Scat Solution

To keep cats from digging in containers and newly-seeded beds, mix 1 cup vinegar and 2 tablespoons chili paste with garlic (sold in Asian markets) with 1 quart water. Sprinkle the mixture over the area cats frequent, and they will never return. This mixture will deter dogs as well.

To make cats avoid soft cultivated soil, apply Cat Scat Solution or another strategy that uses hot peppers.

Triple Punch Cocktail

Both baking soda and horticultural oil make life difficult for rose blackspot, powdery mildew and other fungal diseases that infect plant leaves. This spray will have the greatest impact on these and other diseases if you apply it before the problem becomes widespread. This mixture will also control aphids, mealybugs, whiteflies and most types of scale.

TRIPLE PUNCH COCKTAIL

3 teaspoons baking soda
2 Tablespoons light horticultural oil or vegetable oil
1 Tablespoon insecticidal soap
1 gallon water

Mix all ingredients together in a pressure sprayer. Apply to plants no more often than once a week. If you treat plants repeatedly, watch for signs that oil buildup is harming plant leaves; normal rainfall between applications usually keeps this from being a problem.

Slugs.

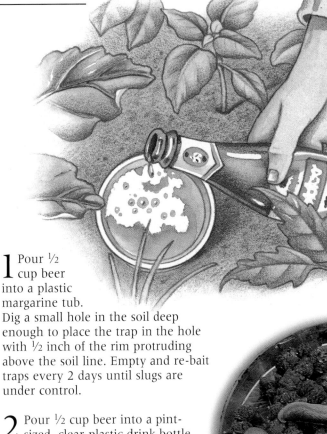

Beer Traps for Slugs

Slimy slugs like beer so much that they are willing to drink it until they fall in and drown. Of the many ways you might bait a beer trap for slugs, these two have stood the test of time and are always effective. When setting out these traps, remember that slugs are active at night. Place the traps where the slugs will find them on their way to your garden plants.

1 Pour ½ cup beer into a plastic margarine tub. Dig a small hole in the soil deep enough to place the trap in the hole with ½ inch of the rim protruding above the soil line. Empty and re-bait traps every 2 days until slugs are under control.

2 Pour ½ cup beer into a pint-sized, clear-plastic drink bottle. Lay the bottle on its side beneath a plant that is being damaged by slugs. Empty and re-bait traps every 3 days until slugs are under control.

Slugs could not resist the bait left for them in a shallow pan. Or try luring them to a drunken death with plain beer.

Orange Rind Snail Traps

If you have snail trouble in the garden, place orange rinds on the ground; this will draw snails. Go out early in the morning and collect the snails by picking up the rinds and swishing off the snails into a bucket of soapy water.

Aphids.

Citrus Spray for Aphids

If you're out of insecticidal soap, try this refreshing spray to get rid of aphids on any plant. This spray also helps if you have a problem with spider mites, whiteflies or other small sucking insects.

CITRUS SPRAY FOR APHIDS

Grated rind of 2 lemons or 2 sour oranges
1 quart water

Combine the grated rinds with the water and allow mixture to sit overnight. Strain through cheesecloth or a coffee filter. Dilute the concentrate with an equal amount of water before spraying it on plants. If the mixture beads up on the leaves, add 2 drops of dishwashing detergent per quart to help it spread and stick a little better.

RESOURCES FOR PLANTS, SEEDS AND SUPPLIES

Vegetable and Flower Seeds

Burpee Seeds
300 Park Ave.
Warminster, PA 18974
800-333-5808

Cook's Garden
P.O. Box 535
Londonderry, VT 05148
800-457-9703

Johnny's Selected Seeds
Foss Hill Rd.
Albion, ME 04910
207-437-9294

Nichols Garden Nursery
1190 North Pacific Hwy.
Albany, OR 97321
541-928-9280

Park Seed
1 Parkton Ave.
Greenwood, SC 29647
800-845-3369

Pinetree Garden Seeds
P.O. Box 300
New Gloucester, ME 04260
207-926-3400

Shepherd's Garden Seeds
30 Irene St.
Torrington, CT 06790
860-482-3638

Perennials and Shrubs

Bluestone Perennials
7213 Middle Ridge Rd.
Madison, OH 44057
800-852-5243

Carroll Gardens
444 E. Main St.
Westminster, MD 21157
800-638-6334

Klehm Nursery
4210 N. Duncan Rd.
Champaign, IL 61821
800-553-3715

Milaeger's Gardens
4838 Douglas Ave.
Racine, WI 53402
800-669-9956

Niche Gardens
111 Dawson Road
Chapel Hill, NC 27516
919-967-0078

Siskiyou Rare Plant Nursery
2825 Cummings Road
Medford, OR 97501
503-772-6846

Andre Viette Nursery
Rt. 1, Box 16
Fishersville, VA 22939
703-942-2118

Wayside Gardens
Hodges, SC 26965
800-845-1124

White Flower Farm
P.O. Box 50
Litchfield, CT 06759
800-503-9624

Woodlanders
1128 Colleton Ave.
Aiken, SC 28901
803-648-7522

Bulbs

The Daffodil Mart
85 Broad St.
Torrington, CT 06790-6668
800-255-2852

Dutch Gardens
P.O. Box 200
Adelphia, NJ 07710
800-818-3861

McClure & Zimmerman
P.O. Box 368
Friesland, WI 53935
414-326-4220

Van Bourgondien
P.O. Box 1000
Babylon, NY 11702
800-622-9997

Roses

Antique Rose Emporium
Rt. 5, Box 143
Brenham, TX 77833
409-836-9051

Jackson & Perkins
P.O. Box 1028
Medford, OR 97501
800-292-4769

Heirloom Old Garden Roses
24062 Riverside Dr. NE
St. Paul, OR 97137

Herb Plants

Sandy Mush Herb Nursery
316 Surrett Cove Rd.
Leicester, NC 28748
704-683-2014

Sunnybrook Farms
9448 Mayfield Rd.
P.O. Box 6
Chesterland, OH 44026
216-729-7232

Fruits

Northwoods Nursery
27635 S. Oglesby Rd.
Canby, OR 97013
503-266-5432

Raintree Nursery
391 Butts Rd.
Morton, WA 98356
360-496-6400

Stark Brothers
P.O. Box 10
Louisiana, MO 63353
800-325-4150

Fertilizers

Gardener's Supply Co.
128 Intervale Road
Burlington, VT 05041
800-234-6630

Gardens Alive!
5100 Schenley Place
Lawrenceburg, IN 47025
812-537-8650

Peaceful Valley Farm Supply
P.O. Box 2209
Grass Valley, CA 95945
916-272-4769

Irrigation Equipment

Gardener's Supply Co.
128 Intervale Road
Burlington, VT 05041
800-234-6630

Worm's Way
3151 S. Highway 446
Bloomington, IN 47401
800-274-9676

Water Gardening Plants and Equipment

Lilypons Water Gardens
P.O. Box 10
Buckeystown, MD 21717
(also locations in Texas and California)
800-723-7667

Perry's Water Gardens
1831 Leatherman Gap Rd.
Franklin, NC 28734
704-369-2056

INDEX OF PLANTS

A

Abelia (*Abelia*), 70, 152
Aconite (*Eranthis*), 23
Aegopodium (bishop's weed), 22
Agastache (hyssop), 13
Agave (*Agave*), 11
Ajuga (*Ajuga*), 51, 156, 162
Akebia (*Akebia*), 152
Allium, 82, 86, 89
Allspice, Carolina (*Calycanthus*), 104
Althaea (*Hibiscus*), 152
Alyssum, sweet (*Lobularia*), 82, 83, 85, 96, 107, 149
Amelanchier (serviceberry), 23, 88, 117
Ampelopsis (porcelain berry vine), 152
Angel's trumpet (*Datura*), 111
Apache plume (*Fallugia*), 13
Apple, 115
Aquilegia (columbine), 77
Arabis (rock cress), 79
Arborvitea (*Thuja*), 70
Arrowhead (*Sagittaria*), 138
Artemisia (*Artemisia*), 12, 13, 82, 103, 108, 162
Arugula, 114, 120, 149, 161
Asclepias (butterfly weed), 95
Asparagus, 117
Aster (*Aster*), 89, 95, 162
Astilbe (*Astilbe*), 23, 162
Aurinia (basket-of-gold), 79
Azalea (*Rhododendron*), 13, 23, 27, 76, 77, 99, 152

B

Baby's breath (*Gypsophila*), 86
Bachelor button (*Centaurea*), 20, 94, 161

Balsam (*Impatiens*), 103
Barberry (*Berberis*), 103
Barrenwort (*Epimedium*), 22
Basil (*Ocimum*), 108, 115, 124, 125
Basket-of-gold (*Aurinia*), 79
Bean, 115, 127, 161, 179
Bean, hyacinth (*Dolichos*), 75
Bean, scarlet runner (*Phaseolus*), 75
Beautyberry (*Callicarpa*), 88, 152
Bee balm (*Monarda*), 13, 88, 162, 166
Beet, 114, 149
Begonia (*Begonia*), 23, 82, 84, 85
Bergenia (*Bergenia*), 13
Bermudagrass (*Cyndon*), 44, 47, 92, 156
Bindweed (*Ipomoea*), 92, 156
Birch (*Betula*), 23, 50
Bishop's weed (*Aegopodium*), 22
Bittersweet (*Celastrus*), 152
Blackberry, 129, 156
Black-eyed Susan (*Rudbeckia*), 92, 95, 161
Black-eyed Susan vine (*Thunbergia*), 75
Bleeding heart (*Dicentra*), 23
Blueberry, 27, 35, 128, 129
Bluegrass, Kentucky (*Poa*), 44, 47
Boltonia (*Boltonia*), 89
Boxwood (*Buxus*), 70, 71, 97, 99
Broccoli, 113, 114, 115, 179
Broom, gold (*Genista*), 21
Buckwheat (*Polygonum*), 92
Buddleia (butterfly bush), 99, 105, 152
Burning bush (*Euonymus*), 71

Butterfly bush (*Buddleia*), 89, 99, 105, 152, 166
Butterfly weed (*Asclepias*), 87, 95
Buxus (Boxwood), 71, 99

C

Cabbage, 12, 114, 115, 179
Cactus, prickly pear (*Opuntia*), 11
Callicarpa (beautyberry), 88, 152
Calycanthus (Carolina allspice), 104
Camellia (*Camellia*), 35
Campanula (*Campanula*), 166
Candytuft (*Iberis*), 93, 96, 149
Cardinal climber (*Ipomoea*), 75
Cardinal flower (*Lobelia*), 13
Carex (sedge), 12
Carnation (*Dianthus*), 103
Carrot, 113, 114, 121, 127, 149
Caryopteris (blue spiraea), 13, 152
Catchfly (*Silene*), 93
Catmint (*Nepeta*), 108
Cattail (*Typha*), 138
Cauliflower, 114, 115, 179
Celastrus (bittersweet), 152
Celery, 114
Celosia (*Celosia*), 86, 87
Centaurea (bachelor button), 20, 94
Centipedegrass (*Eremochloa*), 45
Cercis, (redbud), 68
Chamomile (*Chamomelum*), 108, 149
Chard, Swiss, 113, 114, 120, 149
Cherry, 116
Cherry, cornelian, 116
Chestnut, 116

Chionanthus (fringe tree), 68, 104, 105
Chives, 124, 125
Chokeberry (*Aronia*), 13
Chrysanthemum (*Dendranthema*), 86, 87, 89, 98, 99, 162, 166
Cilantro, 125
Cinquefoil, (*Potentilla*), 13
Citrus, 35
Clematis (*Clematis*), 68, 74, 110, 145, 152
Cleome (*Cleome*), 161
Clethra (summersweet), 13, 105
Clover, crimson (*Trifolium*), 92
Clover, water (*Marsilea*), 139
Cobaea (cup and saucer vine), 75
Coleus (*Solenostemon*), 23, 85, 167
Collard, 113, 114, 149
Columbine (*Aquilegia*), 77, 87, 157
Coneflower, prairie (*Ratibida*), 95
Coneflower, purple (*Echinacea*), 21, 89, 95, 98
Convallaria (lily-of-the-valley), 111
Coral bells (*Heuchera*), 81
Coreopsis (*Coreopsis*), 95, 162
Corn, sweet, 115
Cornus (dogwood), 88, 152
Cosmos (*Cosmos*), 81, 89, 93, 95, 156, 161
Cotinus (smoke tree), 68, 152
Cotoneaster (*Cotoneaster*), 21
Crabapple (*Malus*), 68, 103
Crabgrass, 47, 156
Cranberry, highbush, 116
Cranesbill (*Geranium*), 77

Crape myrtle
(*Lagerstroemia*), 23, 35,
99, 152, 166
Creeper, Virginia
(*Parthenocissus*), 17
Cress, rock (*Arabis*), 79
Crinum (*Crinum*), 103
Crocosmia (*Crocosmia*), 99,
165
Crocus (*Crocus*), 90, 165
Cucumber, 115, 121, 179
Cup-and-saucer vine
(*Cobaea*), 75
Currant, 116

D

Daffodil (*Narcissus*), 23, 90,
97, 98, 106, 133, 164
Dahlia (*Dahlia*), 81, 82, 87,
90, 156, 165
Daisy (*Leucanthemum*), 93,
161, 162
Daisy, mat (*Anacylus*), 13
Daisy, snow (*Tanacetum*),
13
Dame's rocket (*Hesperis*),
103, 111
Daphne (*Daphne*), 104, 152
Daylily (*Hemerocallis*), 13,
21, 74, 81, 98, 103, 157,
162
Delphinium (*Delphinium*),
83, 86, 97, 162
Dendranthema (chrysanthe-
mum), 98, 99
Deutzia (*Deutzia*), 152
Dianthus (*Dianthus*), 81,
88, 96, 111, 162
Dill, 124, 125
Dogwood (*Cornus*), 23, 68,
76, 88, 152
Dolichos (hyacinth bean),
75
Dusty miller (*Artemisia*),
85, 86, 97
Dutchman's pipe
(*Aristolochia*), 152

E

Echinacea (purple cone-
flower), 95, 98
Eggplant, 115

Elderberry, 116
Eleagnus (*Eleagnus*), 105
Elodea (*Elodea*), 139
Endive, 114, 120
Epimedium (barrenwort),
22
Eschscholzia (California
poppy), 94
Eucalyptus (*Eucalyptus*),
103
Euonymus (burning bush),
71, 98, 166
Eupatorium (Joe Pye weed),
13

F

Fallugia (Apache plume),
13
Fennel (*Foeniculum*), 103
Ferns, 13, 20, 23, 35, 36,
51, 76
Fescue (*Festuca*), 44, 47
Fig (*Ficus*), 116, 145
Firethorn (*Pyracantha*), 68
Fivespot (*Nemophila*), 94
Flax, blue (*Linum*), 13, 93,
94
Floating heart (*Nymphaea*),
139
Flowering tobacco
(*Nicotiana*), 103, 107,
111
Forget-me-not (*Myosotis*),
98, 145
Forsythia (*Forsythia*), 70,
155, 166
Four o'clock (*Mirabilis*), 82,
103, 111
Foxglove (*Digitalis*), 17,
162
Fringe tree (*Chionanthus*),
68, 103

G

Gaillardia (Indian blanket),
95
Gardenia (*Gardenia*), 35,
103, 106
Genista (broom), 21
Geranium (cranesbill), 77
Geranium (*Pelargonium*),
83, 85, 103, 106, 166

Geranium, scented
(*Pelargonium*), 102
Gladiolus (*Gladiolus*), 81,
90
Globeflower (*Trollius*), 13
Glory-of-the-snow
(*Chionodoxa*), 164
Goldenrod (*Solidago*), 21,
89, 95
Gomphrena (*Gomphrena*),
87
Gooseberry, 116
Gourd, 127
Grape holly (*Mahonia*), 103
Grape, 117
Grass, buffalo (*Buchloe*), 45
Grass, fountain
(*Pennisetum*), 11
Grass, ribbon (*Phalaris*), 13

H

Hamamelis, 105
Hawthorn (*Crataegus*), 103
Hazelnut, 116
Heath (*Erica*), 21
Heather (*Calluna*), 21
Hedychium (ginger lily), 111
Helianthus (sunflower), 162
Heliopsis (*Heliopsis*), 82
Heliotrope (*Heliotropium*),
103, 107, 166
Hellebore (*Helleborus*), 23
Hemlock (*Tsuga*), 70
Hesperis (dame's rocket),
111
Heuchera, 97
Hibiscus (althaea), 152
Hibiscus, hardy (*Hibiscus*),
13
Holly (*Ilex*), 35, 68, 71
Hollyhock (*Alcea*), 83, 161
Honeysuckle (*Lonicera*),
103, 105, 110, 116, 152
Hops (*Humulus*), 152
Hosta (*Hosta*), 23, 38, 41,
51, 81, 88, 97, 111, 162
Humulus (hops), 152
Hyacinth (*Hyacinthus*), 23,
90, 106
Hyacinth, grape (*Muscari*),
23, 103, 164
Hydrangea (*Hydrangea*), 23,
76, 99, 145, 152, 166

Hyssop (*Agastache*), 13
Hyssop (*Hyssopus*), 108

I

Iberis (candytuft), 93
Ilex (winterberry), 23, 71
Impatiens (*Impatiens*), 23,
36, 81, 83, 84, 85
Indian blanket (*Gaillardia*),
92, 95
Ipomoea (morning glory),
75, 110
Iris (*Iris*), 81, 90, 97, 103,
138, 156
Iris, Japanese (*Iris*), 12, 13
Iris, Siberican (*Iris*), 13
Ivy, English (*Hedera*), 17,
41, 50, 68, 155, 166
Ivy, poison (*Rhus*), 51

J

Jasmine (*Jasminum*), 103
Joe Pye weed (*Eupatorium*),
13
Jujube, 116
Juneberry (*Amelanchier*),
117
Juniper (*Juniperus*), 21, 70,
71, 88, 97
Juniperus (juniper), 71, 88
Jupiter's beard
(*Centranthus*), 13

K

Kale, 113, 114, 149, 161
Kale, ornamental, 12
Kiwi, 117
Kohlrabi, 114

L

Lagerstroemia (crape
myrtle), 99, 152
Lamb's-ear (*Stachys*), 13,
156, 162
Lantana (*Lantana*), 89, 166
Larkspur (*Consolida*), 81,
86, 149

Lathyrus (sweet pea), 75
Lavender (*Lavandula*), 13, 103, 108
Leek, 149
Lettuce, 35, 113, 114, 115, 118, 119, 127, 149, 158, 161
Leucanthemum (daisy), 94
Liatris (*Liatris*), 21
Ligustrum (privet), 71
Lilac (*Syringa*), 71, 98, 103, 104, 152
Lilium (lily), 91
Lily (*Lilium*), 90, 91
Lily, ginger (*Hedychium*), 111
Lily, water (*Nymphaea*), 139
Lily-of-the-valley (*Convallaria*), 103, 111
Linara (toadflax), 94
Linum (flax), 13, 93, 94
Liriope (*Liriope*), 41, 50, 51, 96
Lobelia (*Lobelia*), 82, 85
Lonicera (honeysuckle), 105, 110, 152
Lotus (*Nelumbo*), 138

M

Mache, 120, 149
Magnolia (*Magnolia*), 35, 103, 105
Mahonia, leatherleaf, (*Mahonia*), 103
Mallow, poppy (*Callirhoë*), 13
Maple, Japanese (*Acer*), 23, 68
Marigold (*Tagetes*), 12, 20, 68, 81, 82, 83, 96, 161, 170
Marigold, marsh (*Ranunculus*), 13
Marsilea (water clover), 139
Matthiola (stock), 107
Mayhaw, 116
Meadowsweet (*Filipendula*), 13
Medlar, 116
Melon, 115
Mesclun, 120
Mexican hat (*Ratibida*), 13

Mint, 103, 106, 116, 124, 125, 166
Mock orange, 152
Monarda (bee balm), 13, 88
Moneywort (*Lysimachia*), 13
Moonvine (*Ipomoea*), 75, 101, 110
Morning glory (*Ipomoea*), 75, 81, 161
Moss pink (*Phlox*), 79
Moss, 23, 36
Mulberry, 116
Muskmelon, 113
Myosotis (forget-me-not), 98, 145
Myriophyllum (parrot's feather), 139

N

Nandina (*Nandina*), 70
Narcissus, 90, 98
Narcissus, paperwhite (*Narcissus*), 106
Nasturtium (*Tropaeolum*), 81, 103, 127
Nelumbo (Lotus), 138
Nemophila (fivespot), 94
Nepeta (catmint), 108
Nicotiana (flowering tobacco), 85, 107, 111, 169
Ninebark (*Physocarpus*), 88
Nut, pine, 116
Nymphaea (water lily), 139

O

Oak (*Quercus*), 35
Obedient plant (*Physostegia*), 156
Okra, 115, 161
Old-man's beard (*Chionanthus*), 104
Olive, Russian (*Eleagnus*), 116
Onion, 114
Orange, mock (*Philadelphus*), 104
Oregano, 125, 166
Orris root (*Iris*), 103
Oxydendrum (sourwood), 68

P

Pachysandra (*Pachysandra*), 50
Paeonia (Peony), 98
Pansy (*Viola*), 81, 85, 90, 96, 98
Papaver (poppy), 17, 93, 94
Parrot's feather (*Myriophyllum*), 139
Parsley, 114, 124, 125, 145, 149
Parsley, curly, 108
Parsnip, 114, 149
Parthenocissus (Virginia creeper), 17
Pawpaw, 116
Pea, 114, 115, 121, 161
Pea, sweet (*Lathyrus*), 103, 161, 175
Pecan, 116
Pennisetum (fountain grass), 11
Penstemon (*Penstemon*), 13
Peony (*Paeonia*), 81, 98, 103
Pepper, 31, 113, 115, 161, 169
Perilla (*Perilla*), 82
Periwinkle (*Vinca*), 50
Perovskia (Russian sage), 13
Persimmon, 116
Petunia (*Petunia*), 12, 83, 85, 97, 98, 99, 107, 110, 111, 166, 170
Phalaris (ribbon grass), 13
Phaseolus (scarlet runner bean), 75
Philadelphus (mock orange), 104, 152
Phlox (moss pink), 79
Phlox (*Phlox*), 12, 82, 89, 103, 162
Phlox, blue (*Phlox*), 58, 77
Phlox, creeping (*Phlox*), 51
Physocarpus (ninebark), 88
Physostegia (obedient plant), 156
Pieris (*Pieris*), 152
Pine (*Pinus*), 68, 76
Pink (*Dianthus*), 103, 107, 111
Pistachio (*Pistacia*), 68
Plum, 116
Polianthes (tuberose), 111

Polka dot plant (*Hypoestes*), 85
Polygonatum (Solomon's seal), 77
Polygonum (silver lace vine), 152
Pomegranate (*Punica*), 27
Popcorn, 127
Poppy (*Papaver*), 17, 81, 87, 93, 94, 149, 161
Poppy, California (*Eschscholzia*), 94
Porcelain berry vine (*Ampelopsis*), 152
Portulaca (*Portulaca*), 85
Potato, 114, 156, 179
Potato, sweet, 113, 115, 156
Potentilla (cinquefoil), 13
Primrose (*Primula*), 12, 13
Primrose, evening (*Oenothera*), 103, 110, 111
Privet (*Ligustrum*), 70, 71
Prunus (cherry), 116, 117
Pumpkin, 115, 127
Pyracantha (firethorn), 68

Q

Quackgrass, 92
Queen Anne's lace (*Daucus*), 86
Quince, 116

R

Radicchio, 149
Radish, 114, 115, 121, 127
Ranunculus (marsh marigold), 13
Raspberry, 113, 129, 156
Ratibida (Mexican hat), 13, 95
Redbud (*Cercis*), 23, 68, 76
Rhododendron (*Rhododendron*), 13, 35, 36, 51, 99, 152
Rhubarb, 117
Rhus (sumac), 13
Rodgersia (*Rodgersia*), 13

Rose (*Rosa*), 35, 68, 71, 98, 99, 103, 109, 116, 145, 156, 166
Rosemary, 103, 116, 124, 125, 166
Rudbeckia (*Rudbeckia*), 72, 93, 95
Ryegrass, perennial (*Lolium*), 44, 47

S

Sage (*Salvia*), 68, 82, 98, 103, 125, 166
Sage, Russian (*Perovskia*), 13, 166
Sagittaria (arrowhead), 138
Salix (willow), 12, 13
Salvia (*Salvia*), 72, 83, 85, 87, 98, 166
Santolina (*Santolina*), 13
Scaevola (*Scaevola*), 84
Scallion, 121
Scilla (*Scilla*), 23, 164
Sea thrift (*Armeria*), 20
Sedge (*Carex*), 12
Sedum (*Sedum*), 11, 20, 79, 89, 98, 166
Sempervivum (*Sempervivum*), 79
Serviceberry (*Amelanchier*), 23, 88
Silene (catchfly), 93
Silver lace vine (*Polygonum*), 152
Smoke tree (*Cotinus*), 68, 152
Snapdragon (*Antirrhinum*), 81, 87, 149, 158
Snowbell, Japanese (*Styrax*), 68
Snowdrop (*Galanthus*), 23
Soapwort (*Saponaria*), 13
Solomon's seal (*Polygonatum*), 23, 77
Sourwood (*Oxydendrum*), 68
Speedwell (*Veronica*), 13
Spiderwort (*Tradescantia*), 13
Spinach, 35, 114, 120, 145, 149
Spiraea (*Spiraea*), 152
Spiraea, blue (*Caryopteris*), 13, 152

Squash, 113, 115, 127
St. Augustinegrass (*Stenotaphrum*), 45
Stock (*Matthiola*), 107, 110
Stonecrop (*Sedum*), 51, 79
Strawberry, 113, 116, 128, 165
Strawflower (*Helichrysum*), 87
Styrax (Japanese snowbell), 68
Sulfur flower (*Eriogonum*), 13
Sumac, fragrant (*Rhus*), 13
Summersweet (*Clethra*), 13, 105
Sunflower (*Helianthus*), 81, 83, 86, 89, 127, 161
Sunflower, Mexican (*Tithonia*), 99
Sweet spire (*Itea*), 13, 23
Sweet William (*Dianthus*), 161
Syringa (lilac), 71, 98, 104, 152

T

Thistle, globe (*Echinops*), 82
Thunbergia (black-eyed Susan vine), 75
Thyme (*Thymus*), 12, 13, 20, 101, 108, 116, 125
Tithonia (*Tithonia*), 89, 99
Toadflax (*Linaria*), 94
Tomato, 27, 113, 115, 122, 123, 127, 155, 156, 161, 169
Torenia (*Torenia*), 85
Tuberose (*Polianthes*), 103, 111
Tulip (*Tulipa*), 23, 81, 90, 91, 164
Turnip, 114, 121, 149
Typha (cattail), 138

V

Verbena (*Verbena*), 82, 85
Veronica (speedwell), 13, 86
Viburnum (*Viburnum*), 88, 166
Vinca (*Vinca*), 12, 85

Violet (*Viola*), 103

W

Wallflower (*Cheiranthus*), 5
Weigela (*Weigela*), 152
Willow (*Salix*), 12, 13
Winged spindle (*Euonymus*), 98
Winterberry (*Ilex*), 13, 23
Wintersweet (*Chimonanthus*), 105
Wisteria (*Wisteria*), 67, 103, 110, 152
Witch hazel (*Hamamelis*), 23, 105
Woodruff, sweet (*Galium*), 50

Y

Yarrow (*Achillea*), 13, 21, 82, 162
Yucca (*Dracena*), 85

Z

Zinnia (*Zinnia*), 20, 81, 87, 89, 99, 127, 161
Zoysia (*Zoysia*), 45, 47

GENERAL INDEX

A

Annuals, 81, 85, 107, 111
Aphids, 181

B

Bacillus thuringiensis, 174, 177
Beetle, Colorado potato, 176, 179
Beetle, Mexican bean, 176, 179
Beetle, spotted cucumber, 179
Berries, 128-219
Bird gardens, 88-89
Birds in the garden, 174
Birds, feeding, 89
Bog garden, 12
Borders, 96-99
    Designing, 97-99
Boron, 27
Bulbs, 81, 90-91
    Storing, 165
Butterfly gardens, 88-89

C

Cabbageworm, 176, 179
Calcium, 31
Clay soil, 25, 26
Cloches, 147
Cold frames, 146
Colors, using, 82-83
Compost, 28, 32-33
    Problems, 33
Composting, 32-33
Concrete, 60-63
Containers, fertilizing, 85
Container gardening, 84-85
    102, 106-107
Copper, 27, 31
Cutting gardens, 86-87
Cuttings, 157, 166-167

D

Diseases, preventing, 170
Division, 156, 157, 162-165
    Bulbs, 164-165
    Corms, 165
    Perennials, 162-163
    Tubers, 165
Drainage, improving, 12
Drainage, testing, 13
Drip irrigation, 37

E

Edible gardening, 112-129
Entryways, 56-57
Evening gardens, 110-111

F

Fences, 69, 72-75
    Metal, 74
    Wood, 72-73
Fertilizer, 29-31, 34-35
    Foliar, 34-35, 37
    Instant, 31
    Organic, 30
    Special-purpose, 31
    Synthetic, 31
Fish, 136
Flowers, 80
Formal designs, 82
Fragrance gardening, 100-111
Fragrance, kinds, 103-104
French drain, 12
Frost dates, 9
Frost, 178
Fruit trees, 116
Fruiting shrubs, 117
Fruiting vines, 117

G

Garden accents, 17, 131-133
Garden exposure, 11
Garden journal, 15
Garden planning, 14-15
Garden rooms, 16-17
Greensand, 29
Groundcovers, 50-51
Gypsum, 29

H

Hardening off, 159
Heaving, 145
Herbicides, 173
Herbs, 108, 124-125
Hummingbirds, 88
Hybrids, 160

I

Informal designs, 82
Insects, 176-181
    Beneficial, 174-175
    Eggs, 176
    Metamorphosis, 177
Insecticidal soap, 177-178
Iron, 35

K

Kids' gardens, 126-127

L

Lacewings, 175
Lady beetles, 175
Lawn grass, kinds, 44-46
Lawns, 16, 40-49
    Dethatching, 47
    Edging, 48-49
    Fertilizing, 42
    Mowing, 49
    Planting, 43, 47
    Updating, 46-47
    Watering, 42
Layering plants, 19
Light exposure, 11
Lighting, 56, 140-141
    Installing, 141
    Kinds, 141
Lime, 27, 28
Loam, 25, 26

M

Magnesium, 31
Micronutrients, 31
Minerals, 29
Mirrors, 17
Moisture, 11-13
Mulch, 28, 36, 38-39, 55, 59, 172
    Kinds, 39

N

Neem, 177
Nitrogen, 27, 31, 35
Nutrients, 27, 30-31, 34-35

O

Open-pollinated plants, 160
Organic matter, 25, 28
    Kinds, 28

P

Perennials, 81, 93, 111
Pest controls, 177-181
    For aphids, 181
    For cats, 180
    For fungi, 180
    For insects, 180
    For rabbits and squirrels, 180

For slugs, 181
For snails, 181
Pests, diagnosing, 171
Pests, garden, 168-181
Pests, on flowers, 169
Pests, on vegetables, 169
Phosphate, 29
Phosphorus, 27, 31
Potassium, 27, 29, 31
Propagating plants, 154-167
Pruning tools, 150
Pruning, 150-153

R

Rainfall map, 9
Raised beds, 134-135
Building, 135
Rejuvenating plants, 153
Rooting powder, 166
Roses, 109
Rotation, 170
Rowcovers, 178

S

Salad gardens, 118-122
Sandy soil, 25, 26

Seed Saver's Exchange, 160
Seedlings, 159
Seeds, 155, 156-161
Collecting, 161
Saving, 160
Starting, 158-159
Sexual reproduction, 155
Shade gardens, 22-23
Shade, types, 22
Shrubs, 68, 70-71, 104-105
Pruning, 152-153
Silty soil, 25, 26
Site analysis, 11
Slope, 11, 20-21
Slugs, 181
Small spaces in the garden, 18-19
Snails, 181
Snow load, 144
Sod, 43
Soil
Improving, 28-31
pH, 27
Testing, 26
Types, 25-26
Spiders, 175
Sticky traps, 176
Suckers, 156
Sulfur, 29
Sunscald, 144
Surveys, 67

T

Terracing, 21
Toads, 175
Tomato gardens, 122-123
Tools, weeding, 173
Treated wood, 135
Trees, 68, 104-105
Pruning, 150-151
Tropical plants, 111
Tunnels, plastic, 147-149

U

Understory areas, 76-77

V

Vegetables, 127
Cool-season, 114
Perennial, 117
Warm-season, 115
Vines, 74-75, 110
Pruning, 152

W

Walkways, 16, 18, 53-65

Walls, garden, 66-75
Walls, stone, 78-79
Wasps, braconid, 175
Water gardens, 136-139
Building, 137
Water plants, 138-139
Water, conserving, 36-37, 38
Watering, 36-37
Watering, containers, 85
Weeds, 172-173
Wildflower meadows, 94-95
Wildflowers, 92-95
Wind chimes, 131
Wind, 11
Winter in the garden, 142-153
Winter injury, 143
Winter, preparing plants, 143
Winter, protecting plants, 145-149
Wood, treated, 135

Z

Zinc, 27
Zone map, 8
Zones, hardiness, 8

PHOTO CREDITS

ILLUSTRATION CREDITS